TURNASTONE

Stability and Change
in the Herefordshire Countryside
1800-2000

Edited by Brian S. Smith

Golden Valley Studies Group
& Logaston Press

GOLDEN VALLEY STUDIES GROUP
The Cross House, Turnastone, Hereford HR2 0RD

LOGASTON PRESS
Little Logaston Woonton Almeley
Herefordshire HR3 6QH
logastonpress.co.uk

First published by Logaston Press 2010
Copyright © Golden Valley Studies Group 2010

ISBN 978 1 906663 45 2

Typeset in Garamond by Logaston Press
and printed in Great Britain by
Bell & Bain Ltd., Glasgow

*Front cover photograph: Turnastone country looking west to the Black Mountains,
with the village (left) and water-meadows in the foreground and Whitehouse Woods,
Slough valley and the hill farms of Cothill and Dolward in the middle distance
(Carl Davies)*

Contents

Preface

It is a great pleasure to contribute a brief Preface to this excellent and imaginative history of the parish of Turnastone, and I congratulate all those whose enthusiasm, knowledge and diligent research have come together top tell a remarkable and fascinating story.

My own contact with Turnastone began in a curiously unplanned way. In 1960 my parents had spent some time on holiday in Radnorshire, and strongly recommended, when my wife and I were planning our honeymoon in September 1961, that we should consider the delights of the Welsh Marches. We took their advice, and fell in love with this beautiful, remote and warmly welcoming part of Britain, not least the Golden Valley.

Parish clergy do of course spend all their working lives in tied housing, and we wanted if possible to find somewhere which would be our own, where we could spend our holidays as a family. Agents sent us various suggestions, and the outcome was that in February 1964 we found a very small, very basic cottage at Urishay, on the hill above Peterchurch, where over the years we spent many happy holidays, and which now belongs to our two sons. During four years as a school chaplain, when I had generous time off in the summer, I offered to help Prebendary John de la Tour Davies with Sunday services in the benefice, and so it was that I began my particular link with Turnastone church. Our fondness for the village has never faltered, and it is always a pleasure to return to it.

One of the most notable characters in Turnastone in recent years, who is referred to several times in the text, was Mr Hedley Wilding. His life spanned almost the whole of the 20th century, and he was a very well-known figure at the shop and petrol station, held in great affection and respect. He was born in November 1917, and his birth coincided with the announcement of the appointment of one of my predecessors as Bishop of Hereford, Herbert Hensley Henson, who was to come from the Deanery of Durham. Very soon after Hedley was born, his father returned one day from a visit to Hereford to announce that he had found a middle name for the boy; he should be called Hensley after the new bishop, and I was delighted to discover recently this link between one of Turnastone's most notable sons and the bishopric of Hereford.

I was also pleased to see on a visit to Turnastone that, despite the smallness of the present population the monthly Family Service is very flourishing, with encouraging numbers of children. Many small villages are seemingly inhabited only by the elderly and retired, but the young people of Turnastone suggest that the village can look forward to a new lease of life. The likely need to increase food production also augurs well for the farming industry, and means that the future of this small community will be as interesting as the past which is so well portrayed in this welcome new study.

The Rt Revd John Oliver, Bishop of Hereford (1990-2003)

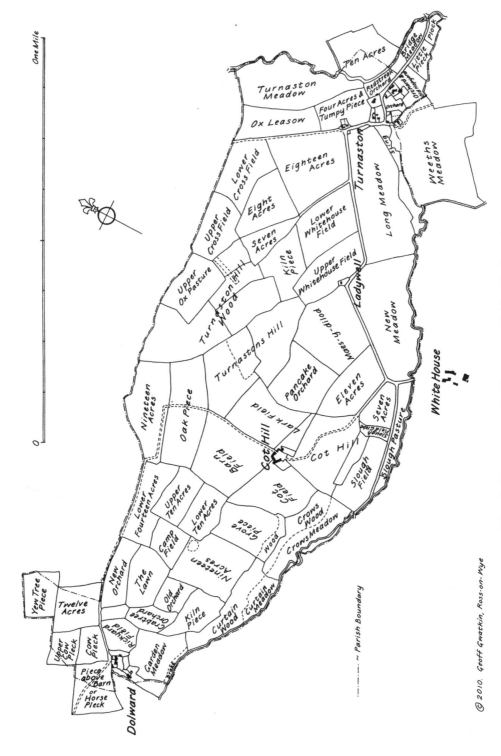

Fig. 1 Turnastone field-names 1842 (G. Gwatkin)

© 2010. Geoff Gwatkin, Ross-on-Wye

Foreword

This book is the outcome of three years' research, concluded in December 2009, by nine members of the Golden Valley Studies Group whose names appear in the chapter headings. The Group was formed in 1999, initially to study the pioneering scheme of an Elizabethan squire, Rowland Vaughan, for 'drowning' the water meadows in the Golden Valley to improve their fertility. By contrast this history of Turnastone has been a broader community project. The researchers have explored the archives, landscape and oral history of the area, sharing information and all drawing upon the remarkable database of 'Who's Who in Turnastone' compiled by Cynthia Comyn, about which further details are given in the Appendix. Other members of the Group have also contributed, including: Carl Davis as photographer, Eva Morgan for her family history of the Watkins and Powell families, Robert Wilding for information about the Wilding family and their century-old family shop.

The research would have been impossible without the additional support and involvement of the people living in Turnastone today, who have allowed us to wander across their land, welcomed us into their homes, readily answered our questions, lent us old photographs and checked our drafts. We are particularly grateful to Robert and Chrissy Fraser of Turnastone Court Farm and its owners, the Countryside Restoration Trust, Robert, Alison and Poppy Lloyd of Cothill and Cliff and Hazel Price of Dolward, John Carter of Yew Tree House and Charles Drury of Ladywell House. Among those who used to live in the parish we have been greatly helped by George and Margaret Disley, David and Jean Jones all of Peterchurch, Mary Layton of Vowchurch, Percy Powell of Llanveynoe and David Watkins of Abbey Dore. Farther afield, Tim Wood of Littleham, Devon has supplied information and photographs of the Wood family of Whitehouse and David Lovelace of Norton Canon opened to us sources in the National Archives and his own research on Turnastone Court. We also wish to record the extensive guidance and expertise offered by the archivists at Herefordshire Record Office and the librarians at Hereford Library. Publication would not have been possible without the patient and always helpful enthusiasm of Andy Johnson of Logaston Press and a generous and much appreciated grant from the Geoffrey Walter Smith Fund of the Woolhope Naturalists' Field Club of Herefordshire.

So much help and advice makes us well aware of our own shortcomings. For many, both researchers and informants, it has been a first experience of historical research, analysis and composition. Some of us are newcomers to the neighbourhood.

We have tracked down sources of evidence locally and far afield, but inevitably will have overlooked some and, as with all contemporary history, we have also met with conflicting memories of the same event. Any failings are our responsibility alone, and we would like to hear of any omissions or mistakes. Our prime object has been to produce a history of the last two centuries in one parish in the Golden Valley of west Herefordshire that might be of interest to our neighbours and hopefully might lead to further topics for research. We have learnt much about our community. We hope that you, our readers, will share the enjoyment of our discoveries.

Brian Smith
Bryn Farm, Vowchurch

Illustrations

We warmly thank the many people who have searched out and allowed us to reproduce their old photographs. These have added enormously to the character of the book and their provenance has been acknowledged somewhat inadequately in the captions. Three such sources require explanation. Geoff Gwatkin of Ross-on-Wye provided from his archive of the tithe maps of Herefordshire parishes in the 1840s the drawing of Turnastone parish with its field-names in 1842, used here in the frontispiece and as a base for the maps of land-use. The photographs accredited to *Watkins* came from the family photo albums of the late Misses Watkins of Turnastone. After their death these were copied by David Lovelace before becoming divided among the family; the originals of some are now in the possession of David Watkins and Mary Layton. No replies have been received to enquiries to Mrs S. Major of Cheshire, the last known owner of two photographs originally from the Dodgson family of Vowchurch of which there are existing copies surviving locally. All the recent photographs which are not accredited have been supplied by Carl Davies, Brian Smith or other members of the Golden Valley Studies Group.

Judy Seymour, a member of the Group, has brought order to making the selection of the large number of photographs considered for publication and Andy Johnson of Logaston Press has edited and arranged them in the book.

1   BEATING THE BOUNDS

Brian Smith

Turnastone is one of the smallest parishes in Herefordshire, close to the English border with Wales. Farther to the west the dark line of the Black Mountains, running from north to south, dominates the horizon. Lower ridges of rolling farmland run parallel to the mountains separated by a succession of fast flowing streams, the Olchon brook immediately beneath the mountains, the infant river Monnow, the Escley brook and, easternmost, the river Dore. All flow southward and merge together on their way to Monmouth and the river Wye and thence eventually into the Severn estuary.

A string of villages punctuates the Dore valley – from north to south these are Dorstone, Peterchurch, Turnastone, Vowchurch, Bacton, Abbey Dore, Ewyas Harold and Pontrilas, where the Dore joins the Monnow. Peterchurch and Ewyas Harold are the two largest settlements. To the west of Turnastone is the upland parish of St Margaret's. 'No man is an island, entire of itself', wrote John Donne four centuries ago. Nor is a village, especially one as small as Turnastone. Therefore, in this story of Turnastone, the landscape, people and events since 1800 are unavoidably interwoven with those of its neighbours.

First and briefly, some basic facts. The parish is eleven miles west of Hereford, rectangular in shape, measuring about one and a half miles (a little over two kilometres) from east to west and three-quarters of a mile (one kilometre) from north to south. The church, small shop and filling station, one of the three farms and six of the ten houses in the parish are concentrated in the south-east corner. The whole parish covers an area of 539 acres (218 hectares) and is bounded on the north, east and south by Vowchurch and on the west by St Margaret's. The eastern boundary at the river Dore is at a height of about 365 feet (110 metres), where the river flows through broad flat meadows between one-quarter and half a mile wide. From these meadows the ground climbs steadily to 700 feet (210 metres) at the western boundary. Only one road passes through the length of the parish but a network of well-marked public footpaths allow all parts of the parish to be easily explored.

In centuries long past, before the days of large-scale maps, it was essential for the payment of taxes, tithes, church rates and rents to know the limits of your parish and of your own lands. It was accordingly customary for the churchwardens and parishioners to walk the parish bounds periodically from landmark to landmark, impressing the route on the younger members by halting at each traditional landmark, sometimes to read an extract from the scriptures and sometimes to give the small boys a symbolic birching. No one now living in Turnastone can remember the parish bounds being beaten in this way, but in 1824 the jurors of the lordship of Snodhill in Peterchurch, which then also embraced Turnastone, walked the boundaries of the manor. The record of their perambulation recalls long vanished landmarks and gives the flavour of the event.[1]

From Snodhill they went clockwise, across the valley and along the ridge which forms the eastern skyline of Stockley Hill before turning down westwards past Poston House to the river Dore:

> ... and by the side of the same river which divideth the Parishes of Vowchurch and Turnaston (leaving the said river on the right) to Vowchurch Bridge from thence by the side of the said River to an old House, lately a Blacksmith's Shop, then short to the right from thence to Weath's Barn leaving the said Barn on the right to Slough's Brook by a floodgate on to the Slough Lane, then turn up the road on the left hand and up to the White House, from thence to the right through the Slough Lane to the Slough House, then turn up to the right by a valley and up to Great Dolworth House leaving the house on the right from thence to little Dolworth from thence along the footpath to Whitwal House, leaving the House on the right to a certain lane called City Lane from thence along the Footpath to Werwillyam ...

By this point they had left both the parish boundary of Turnastone and the farmland of Dolward, partly within St Margaret's parish, to continue their route northward over Urishay Common and back to Snodhill.

To walk the parish boundary today remains a good way of defining the area for research. Although public footpaths do not follow the parish boundaries precisely, it is possible to trace their course in a walk of less than three hours. Just as for the men in 1824, the obvious starting point is Vowchurch Bridge over the river Dore where the road from Vowchurch to Michaelchurch Escley enters the parish from the main road (B4348) between Hereford and Hay-on-Wye.

The boundary with Vowchurch follows the course of the river downstream for a few yards before turning at right angles to head across the lush water meadows. To join the boundary conveniently, walk down the road from the bridge with Vowchurch church at your back for a hundred paces where a broad track strikes off on the left. This is the former railway line at Vowchurch station. The old blacksmith's shop mentioned in 1824 was probably part of the then subdivided half-timbered Old House, immediately downstream of Vowchurch Bridge where the boundary turns sharp right to cross the meadows; early in the century it was described as in the occupation of a labouring man.[2] A few yards down the track take the branch on

Fig. 2 River Dore at Turnastone Court

the right to pass the late 19th-century brick-built cottage called The Birches and a modern wooden pavilion on your right. The boundary zig-zags here but in general runs in the same westerly direction behind the farm buildings of Turnastone Court to come out into the full expanse of the water meadows.[3] Turn right to the white-washed Brook Cottage, which stands at a bend in the road through the village, crossing the hollow of the 'trench royal' which formed the spinal feature of the elaborate network of channels and dykes designed by Rowland Vaughan (1559-1628) to irrigate the water meadows. Passing through the gateway on to the road the route almost immediately re-enters the meadows by a gate on the left, where there is a footpath sign. The broad expanse of the water meadows stretches ahead.

The footpath runs close to the left-hand hedge of this meadow, Long Meadow, the large field beyond the hedge being called Weeths Meadow (variously spelt) in which Weath's Barn stood in 1824. The hedge takes a rather erratic course dating from a time when the Slough brook (pronounced 'Sloo') ran alongside it. The main stream of the brook has long flowed in a different south-easterly direction, possibly one of Rowland Vaughan's diversions, but near the point where the footpath across Long Meadow reaches New Meadow it meets this main stream where the floodgate stood in 1824. Remains of the stonework can still be seen in the brook. Across the upper part of New Meadow a double fence marks the route of the national grid gas pipeline from Milford Haven to the Severn valley above Tewkesbury. A gateway through the fence brings the path out at a waymarked stile on the Vowchurch-Michaelchurch road. Road and brook then run side-by side past the drive to Whitehouse for the short distance to Slough Bridge, where 'Slough House' (1824) stands.

Here the boundary parts from Vowchurch to run alongside St Margaret's parish, which lay within the ancient manor and hundred of Ewyas Lacy centred upon Longtown castle. It continues up a branch of the Slough Brook that flows on the right through the length of Lower House Wood before turning right-handed to Dolward farmstead. There is no path or right of way. The only choice for the walker today is to go for nearly a mile up the gently winding road. (Take care: the road is quite narrow with poor visibility and can be unexpectedly busy.) At Merryhurst Green, an unfenced stretch of land on the right-hand (north) side of the road, a footpath sign marks the way due north across the fields to Dolward farmhouse. The parish boundary is reached again at the crossing of the stream in the field below the farm. Up here at 210 metres (690 feet) high there is a fine view eastward, past the brow of Cothill Farm and over Turnastone and the Dore valley stretching from Peterchurch spire to the wooded hill ridge above Vowchurch Common.

Dolward Farm, with its large pastures, bleak and windswept in winter, filled with lambs in the spring, is at the western extremity of Turnastone and spilling over into St Margaret's, with the line of the Black Mountains looking deceptively near on the horizon. The boundary runs close behind the farmhouse, crossing the middle of the fields immediately ahead to include an irregular parcel of land north of the farm buildings. This curious diversion pre-dates the existing hedges and must therefore go back to a time when this was open pasture or woodland. It then again abuts on to Vowchurch to run almost due east down a little valley in which an ancient tree-filled hedge is partly visible from the public footpath, which takes its own route one or two fields farther north to skirt the uninhabited farmhouse at Shegear.

Follow the track down to Rowland Vaughan's 'trench royal'. Here, close to the prominent house of Poston Court with its fine brick-built manorial dovecote, the route turns right for a field's length along the 'trench royal' with its line of pollarded willows until a stream is reached. Here the boundary and path turn left by the side of the stream to reach the river Dore at a footbridge leading into Poston Mill caravan site. The boundary then goes along the river all the way to Vowchurch Bridge with one short variation where it follows a pre-1842 meander of the river. Footpath and boundary part where the river flows closest to Turnastone's little parish church of St Mary Magdalene, the footpath bearing right across the pasture grazed, depending on the season, by the Hereford cattle or Ryeland sheep of Turnastone Court to the field gate on to the road by the church. From there it is but a short walk along the road back to Vowchurch Bridge.

The largest group of dwellings in the parish, comprising Turnastone Court and six houses, are clustered in the short distance along this road near the church. The population of the whole parish in 2001, including the other more distant farms and houses, was only 28 people, living in 13 dwellings. It was not always so small. Like many parts of rural England away from the sprawl of 19th- and 20th-century towns, its population at the beginning of the 19th century was appreciably larger than now, growing to a peak of 76 inhabitants in 1841. The population then dropped steadily until World War II, since when the decline has been steeper.

Fig. 3 Population and Houses from the census figures 1801-2001

Year	Inhabited houses	Population		Year	Inhabited houses	Population
1801	9	55		1901	11	48
1811	9	45		1911	11	63
1821	12	60		1921	-	61
1831	13	54		1931	12	53
1841	12	76		1951	12	47
1851	14	70		1961	12	47
1861	10	54		1971	-	41
1871	12	51		1981	-	33
1881	11	57		1991	-	21
1891	11	58		2001	[13]	28

(No census was taken in 1941 during World War II)

Throughout there is no consistent trend in the balance of men and women, though in the first half of the 19th century there is a tendency for the men to outnumber the women due to the presence of young unmarried farm workers. In 2001 12 men are recorded and 16 women and in 2009 there were 23 electors and 9 children, the largest number of minors for over thirty years.

The parish registers provide supporting evidence with some subtle differences. In the first half of the 19th century there were between 12 and 19 baptisms each decade, with the exception of 1820-1829 when there were only four. Then between 1860 and 1889 there were 20 to 28 in each decade. The figures subsequently dropped and in the 80 years from the end of the Great War to the end of the 20th century there were only 48 baptisms altogether. The number of burials follows a more stable pattern of one a year from 1830 to 1930, after which the number declined in line with

Fig. 4 Parish Register Statistics 1800-2000

	Baptisms	Marriages	Burials
1800-1809	12		2 (?)
1810-1819	16		7
1820-1829	4		5
1830-1839	19	1 at least	10
1840-1849	16	2	10
1850-1859	14	5	11
1860-1869	24	4	10
1870-1879	28	2	10
1880-1889	20	0	10
1890-1899	12	4	8
1900-1909	14	3	9
1910-1919	16	4	10
1920-1929	6	5	11
1930-1939	4	5	7
1940-1949	4	2	5
1950-1959	10	4	11
1960-1969	10	7	4
1970-1979	5	2	7
1980-1989	3	2	6
1990-1999	6	0	3+

the fall in the population, the parish churchyards being the only burial grounds in the area before the opening of the Hereford cemetery in 1894. Baptisms, however, do not necessarily account for all the number of births. Some parents may not have had their children baptised by the Church of England and though it was the custom to have a baby christened soon after birth the baptism may have occurred months or even years later. The figures for burials may similarly distort the number of deaths, as it was not uncommon in the farming community for a person to be buried in the parish from which they hailed, even if several miles away.

The number of houses in the parish is not revealed in some of the summary census returns but it is quite clear that despite the population changes the number of dwellings has hardly altered since 1821. This apparent contradiction is due to several factors: the shrinking size of families, especially in the 20th century, the division of some cottages into two households and the presence of servants and live-in farm workers.[4]

The houses themselves are described individually in later chapters. Here, whilst taking stock of the size and character of the parish and before considering its early history, it is sufficient to note that they are built in a mixture of styles, the older ones constructed from the locally available sources of abundant timber, quarries, claypits and limekilns. The two earliest are timber-framed like those in the central plain of Herefordshire. The two upland farmhouses of Cothill and Dolward are of the local grey-pink slabby sandstone, as are farm buildings and the church. The remainder are built in brick or modern materials. Although some have been designated as 'listed buildings of architectural or historic interest' none is of outstanding merit. As a whole they form a varied collection of typical houses of the English countryside from the early 17th to late 20th centuries.

2   'THE GILDEN VALE'

Brian Smith

The river Dore has given its name to the Golden Valley in which Turnastone lies. The name was first recorded as 'the Gilden vale' in Christopher Saxton's atlas of England and Wales in 1577 and as the Golden Vale a few years later in William Camden's history, *Britannia,* in 1586. The popularity of both great works ensured that the name stuck.[1] It is, in fact, either a genuine misunderstanding or an Elizabethan pun. The name Dore was attached to the medieval Cistercian abbey lower down the valley and used to be explained as derived from the French *d'or* (of gold). Not so. The derivation is centuries earlier from the ancient Welsh *dwr*, meaning water, applied to the river and perhaps even originally referring to the remnants of the glacial lake that spread across the flat lands of the valley. The abandonment of the medieval lost village of *Walterstone* by the bank of the river in Vowchurch and occasional mild flooding of the water-meadows and road in Turnastone are reminders of this prehistoric lake. The name *dwr,* like the sites of the some of the villages and their earliest recorded place-names, recall the Welsh foundations of this ancient landscape.

Neolithic burial sites, Iron-Age defensive settlements and Romano-British farms have all been found in the Golden Valley. There is an unexplored tump in Camp Field on Dolward Farm and Romano-British settlements on the opposite hillside near Poston House and Holsty Farm. A Roman road ran up the valley from the town at Abergavenny at least as far as Abbey Dore and traces of its extension northward along the riverside have been found both south and north of Turnastone. It would be another five centuries before the incoming Anglo-Saxons were suffi-ciently numerous for the names of estates in the valley to be recorded in English, not Welsh. Even then, and despite the presence of a pre-Norman Conquest castle at Ewyas Harold dating from about 1050, their security was fragile. At the time of the Domesday Book in 1086, when some of these English settlements were first recorded, the whole valley had been a wasteland since the destructive Welsh incur-sion of 1055. Turnastone is not mentioned in the Domesday Book but it has been identified with *Wlvetone*, or 'Wulfa's-estate', which was part of Peterchurch and had passed from its English owner Loefled to William the Conqueror's follower, Hugh Lasne or 'Hugh Donkey'[2]. By about 1130 it was the estate of Ralph of Tornai (his family home in Normandy) and so from this Norman incomer and his son Robert came the name Turnaston(e).[3]

The original centre of this *ton,* or estate, is thought to have been near the Slough bridge where in the early middle ages the little chapel of St Leonard's may have stood. A small plot of former glebe land here could mark its site, safely above the flood meadows, but near the brook and the powerful spring known since the early 20th century as Lady Well, presumably in imitation of other wells named in honour of Mary mother of Jesus.[4] Whatever the likelihood of this conjecture, by the later 1100s a stone church was built beside the river Dore. It is a simple rectangular building comprising an undivided nave and chancel with a small timber turret at the west end holding two bells. The late Norman south doorway and the nave walls survive in the present building, which was modified in following centuries – the windows and north doorway replaced 1280-1300, a south porch added a hundred years later and the barrel roof rebuilt in the early 1500s.

The extent of the parish, almost entirely surrounded by Vowchurch, reflects not just the size of the estate of Wulfa the Englishman and Ralph de Tornai the Frenchman, but an even more ancient Welsh landholding comprising the larger combined area of Peterchurch, Vowchurch and Turnastone, later subdivided among the English and Norman incomers. The English brought in their system of open-field agriculture in which large arable fields were divided into unhedged strips and communally worked in a three-, four- or five-field rotation. Meadows were similarly divided. A relic of these so-called 'common fields' is recorded in a glebe terrier of 1607, a survey of lands belonging to the parish church, and is identifiable on the tithe map of 1842 as a single small strip on Turnastone Court cutting across two enclosed fields on the lower slopes of Turnastone Hill. The repetitive ploughing of the strips left a ridge-and furrow mark on the landscape, still faintly visible on Turnastone Hill and in the Weeths Meadow.[5]

The pre-Conquest English estates were perpetuated as manors and parishes under the Normans and it was the Normans who introduced the castle to England. The principal castles in the valley were at Ewyas Harold and Snodhill in Peterchurch but there are many smaller motte and bailey castles in this border country – nearby at Chanstone and Monnington, both in Vowchurch. At Turnastone the field at the east end of the church, called Tumpy Piece, contains some raised ground that might have been the site of a former motte and bailey castle or the house platform of a medieval manor house. More prosaically it may have merely been the site of a barn or byre. Only archaeological excavation might provide an answer.

The manor adjoining Turnastone on the north is Poston, which by about 1350 was in the hands of a Welshman called John Gwillim. In the Welsh manner, his son was named Henry ap [son of] John, and his son was known as John ap Harry. Thereafter and following the English custom, his descendants retained the second surname of ap Harry, later anglicised to Parry. In 1410 John ap Harry is recorded as the owner of both Poston and Turnastone, as probably were his grandfather and untraced earlier forebears. In Turnastone church there is a fine white marble slab depicting Thomas

Fig. 5 Poston Court with manorial dovecote

Aparri (d.1522), dressed in armour with his feet resting on a dog and his wife Agnes at his side. In the tax assessment for 1543 a dozen men are named in Turnastone and Poston, a remarkably large number even though the tax threshold that year was low. Only one was called ap Harry. Nevertheless, the Parrys continued at Poston Court until the 17th century when their ownership of Poston and Turnastone became split.[6] By that time the extent of the Poston and Turnastone estate was confined to the lower lands between the river Dore and Ladywell, namely the area still forming Turnastone Court. The upland half above Ladywell was by Elizabethan times in the hands of distant relatives, the Parrys of Newcourt in Bacton, who seven generations earlier had a common ancestor with the Parrys of Poston.[7]

Early in the middle ages much of this upland was wooded like the rest of the Golden Valley hills, as also indicated by the dedication of a chapel to St Leonard, often a patron saint of churches built in cleared woodland. Its conversion to sheep pasture may be attributed to the Cistercian monks of Dore Abbey, founded in 1147. In a royal charter of 1232 Henry III confirmed earlier grants made by Norman barons to the abbey of lands, among which are mentioned places all along the broad uplands of Newton, St Margaret's and Michaelchurch Escley immediately to the west and south of Turnastone. They include the common of pasture in the whole of *Eskelyn*, the forest of *Mascoyt* [Maescoed] and 'all the grove in *Kesty* [Cefn-Ceist, about a mile west of Dolward] which is at the spring called *Wythewell*', [Whitewall, pronounced 'Whit-well', halfway between Dolward and Cefn Ceist].[8] From the late 12th century Dore Abbey had been establishing granges worked as sheep farms and Whitewall was one of these, recorded at the dissolution of the abbey in 1537.

In the distribution of monastic property by the Crown after the dissolution it appears that the lands of Whitewall Grange came into the hands of the Parry family and formed the manor of Jenkin ap Richard *alias* Newton. Its extent is described in

9

perambulations of the manorial boundaries in 1667 and 1701, which echo the grant of 1232.[9] When in 1607 John Parry of Poston sold the estate and its newly built manor house of Whitehouse to Rowland Vaughan, it included the lands 'stretching in length from pasture grounds in St Margaret's called Tyre Whitewalle' (Tir Whitewall in Welsh, or Whitewall House in English).[10] These later became that part of Dolward Farm lying in St Margaret's parish and forming part of the Whitehouse estate.

The first written record of 'Dollard', 'Dollworth' or Dolward does not occur until 1643 when the farmhouse was probably newly built. It stands literally on the parish boundary of Turnastone and St Margaret's, at the very centre of its farmland spread across both parishes. The boundary of manor, parish and lordship was also, until the mid 19th century, a boundary between England and Wales, Turnastone being in the diocese of Hereford (England) and St Margaret's in St David's (Wales), reflecting ecclesiastical and political ties going back to before the Norman Conquest. To under-line this Welsh connection, at the time of Dore Abbey's dissolution all the taxpayers in both Turnastone and St Margaret's had Welsh patronymics or derivative names and the name 'Dolward' may also be a Welsh-English hybrid from *dol* (Welsh, meadow or pasture) and *worth* (English) or *worthign* (Herefordshire, an enclosed place or homestead).[11]

The earliest reference to the Whitehouse estate sprawling across the parishes of Vowchurch, Turnastone and St Margaret's was in 1545 on the death of Myles Parry of Newcourt, described as the elder brother of Symond Parry of the Moore in Vowchurch. Some thirty years later in 1577, when the next owner, Griffith Joanes, died, the estate was clearly identified as 'Whitehouse or Moore'.[12] Symond Parry's own will of 1573, referring to his mansion house, suggests that he was the builder of the oldest half-timbered part of Whitehouse still standing today. During the course of its recent restoration this has been dated to about 1560, and it was remodelled or extended in about 1600.[13] The surviving Elizabethan western part of the mansion stands in the parish of St Margaret's, but the eastern wing of 1812-13 that replaced two-fifths of the gabled half-timbered house is in Vowchurch. The Turnastone boundary is a few yards down the drive.

Myles and Symond Parry were widely connected with many of the local gentry, Parry of Moorhampton in Abbey Dore, Vaughan of Bredwardine and Talgarth, Herbert of Raglan and Syssil of Walterstone, from whom William Cecil, Lord Burghley (1520-98), Elizabeth I's great minister, was descended. Their sister, Blanche (1507-89), was Elizabeth I's Chief Gentlewoman of the Privy Chamber for 56 years. The descents and wills of these families, whose members served at court, in government and in county affairs, reveal their complex relationships with each other, but here only a few of these connections need be mentioned. The first name to remember is Griffith Joanes of Llowes, sheriff of Radnorshire in 1567, who is thought to have acquired the Whitehouse estate through marrying Jane, only legiti-mate child of Symond Parry. The second pair of names to remember is Rowland Vaughan of Bredwardine and his wife and cousin Elizabeth Parry, who were both descended from Myles Parry of Newcourt. By inheritance they eventually came into the possession of both the Newcourt and Whitehouse estates. Rowland Vaughan's activities would draw national attention to Turnastone.

Rowland Vaughan, born into a well-connected gentry family of Bredwardine, briefly a courtier and soldier in his youth, Herefordshire magistrate and landowner, was restlessly energetic, inventive, litigious and untrustworthy. He promoted schemes for improving the salmon fisheries in the river Wye and breeding farm stock, planned a 'commonwealth' of skilled artisans to provide employment and relieve poverty in the Golden Valley, established one of the first, perhaps the first, iron forge in the county at Peterchurch, lent money to some neighbours and ran up huge unpaid debts to others, and involved himself in endless lawsuits and occasional brawling. One of his most grandiose and expensive schemes, begun in 1588 when he and his wife were living at Newcourt in Bacton, was to devise a system of ditches, banks and sluices to induce and control the flooding, or systematic 'drowning', of the meadows of the river Dore. By bringing flowing water across the meadows in winter he aimed to limit the effects of frost and bring on the early growth of grass for the sheep and thereby raise lambs for market a month ahead of his rivals. By flooding them again in the summer he aimed to obtain an extra crop of hay. After obtaining possession or control of the lands in Turnastone and Poston of John Parry of Poston he vastly extended the scheme over the meadows between Peterchurch and Vowchurch.

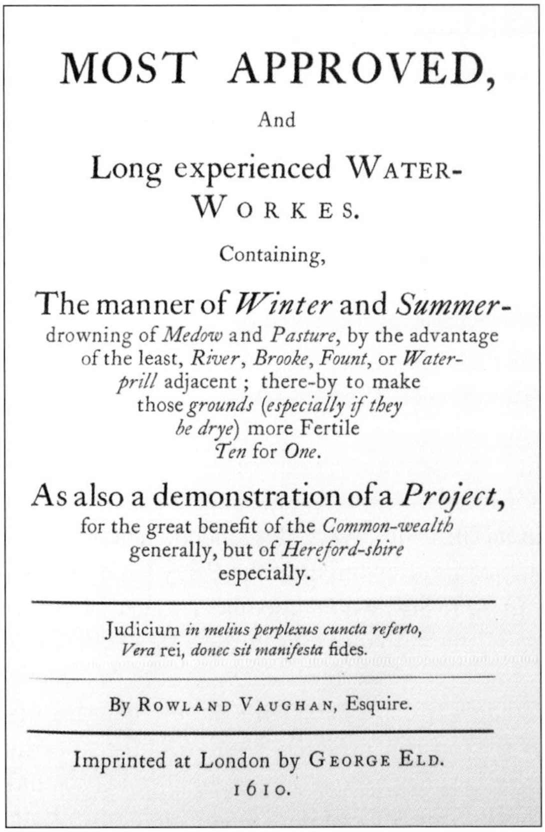

The spinal 'trench royal', as he named it, ran parallel with the river, fed from the Dore and its tributary streams. From the trench royal, which was broad enough to take punts for carrying hay, side trenches were dug to spread the water moving across the meadows, with dykes and sluice gates at intervals to control the water levels, movement and drainage. It has been estimated that the length of the trench royal alone would have taken ten teams each of three men up to three years to dig, and the whole scheme would have been expensive to operate and maintain. Rowland Vaughan's neighbours thought it crazy. At about the same time or a little later there were similar schemes elsewhere, notably in parts of Wiltshire, Hampshire and Surrey, so Rowland Vaughan may not have been the originator of

MOST APPROVED,

And

Long experienced WATER-WORKES.

Containing,

The manner of *Winter* and *Summer*-drowning of *Medow* and *Pasture*, by the advantage of the least, *River*, *Brooke*, *Fount*, or *Water-prill* adjacent ; there-by to make those *grounds* (*especially if they be drye*) more Fertile *Ten* for *One*.

As also a demonstration of a *Project*, for the great benefit of the *Common-wealth* generally, but of *Hereford-shire* especially.

Judicium *in melius perplexus cuncta referto,* Vera rei, donec sit manifesta fides.

By ROWLAND VAUGHAN, Esquire.

Imprinted at London by GEORGE ELD. 1610.

Fig. 6 Rowland Vaughan's book

11

'drowning' meadows. The diversion of natural floods and domestic drainage had long been practised, though a suggestion that in the Golden Valley the Cistercian monks of Dore Abbey may have manipulated the drainage of the abbey's own water-meadows lacks documentary or archaeological proof.[14] However, the innovation spread further in the 18th century and has been hailed as the first major agricultural improvement in England,[15] and where Rowland Vaughan undeniably took an influential lead was in the publication of his book, *Most Approved, And Long experienced Water-workes, Containing, The manner of Winter and Summer-drowning of Medow and Pasture* (London 1610).

Rowland Vaughan's book, which appears to have been started several years before its publication, marks a high point in his life. His wife Elizabeth died the following year and Newcourt passed to her daughter Jane, wife of Stephen Parry of Moorhampton. By 1616 Vaughan's debts to London moneylenders were mounting and he mortgaged Whitehouse, leading him into further disputes and lawsuits with his neighbours and lenders. Among these were the heirs of the Parrys of Poston. Griffith and Jane (née Parry) Joanes had a daughter Blanch who in 1590 married Epiphan Howorth of Hereford, a man of similar social standing. Blanch may have had some residual legal rights in Whitehouse and certainly before 1624 Howorth had bought out the interest belonging to Rowland Vaughan's son Richard. Howorth was among the lenders, respectable and upright men, who (so Rowland Vaughan complained) had broken into and stolen the deeds of Whitehouse. Howorth was then successful in evicting Vaughan and acquiring a lease of the estate for himself despite Vaughan's claim that he had settled all his debts. Soon after Vaughan's death in 1628 the dispute was settled by the Vaughan family conveying the estate to Epiphan Howorth.

Today scattered traces of trenches and dykes can be observed in the meadows, especially when the sun is low or shallow rainwater or snow lies on the ground, as was further confirmed by a geophysical survey carried out in 2004. A lease of Whitehouse required the landlord to erect floodgates in 1796 and the floodgate mentioned near Whitehouse as a landmark in the perambulation of the manorial boundary of Snodhill in 1824, both suggest that the sluices on the Slough Brook and at the sheepwash on the meadows below Whitehouse remained in use.[16] But there is no evidence that Rowland Vaughan's systematic waterworks survived his lifetime or was even fully carried out as described in his book.[17] His more lasting legacy is the enclosure of the medieval open fields, accomplished after he had obtained control of both the Whitehouse estate in 1603 and the Poston and Turnastone estate in 1607 and now still boldly marked by the hedges striding over the Turnastone landscape.[18]

The tangled story of Rowland Vaughan's life is a key to the more recent history of Turnastone. Quite apart from the lively accounts of the behaviour of Elizabethan and Jacobean gentry the period marks the decline of the Parrys of Poston, Turnastone and Whitehouse and their replacement by a new line of landowners at Whitehouse. All this occurred against the background of constitutional changes in government, the rise of the county gentry as magistrates and local administrators and the religious changes caused by the Reformation, including the dissolution of the monasteries, the dispersal of their estates and the introduction of protestant worship in the churches. Some of these changes are expressed in the buildings – the new timber-framed houses of Whitehouse and old Turnastone Court, demolished in the 19th century, the adjacent large timber-framed barn, two surviving 17th-century timber-framed cottages in the village and the stripping of the church. The red-painted decoration of the wallplates to the church roof was allowed to fade, the east altar was replaced by a table, the rood screen and nave altar were removed and in the early 17th century a preaching pulpit was installed. The pulpit could have been installed by Rowland Vaughan, perhaps part of larger repair work, as he claimed in 1610 that 'Wee build our Church which is downe'. He had acquired the advowson of Turnastone with his purchase of Poston from John Parry in 1607 and in his book expressed his desire to appoint a good preacher, who was neither 'a counterfeit Puritane', like his first mistaken choice, nor a Papist like the aged former monk of Dore Abbey who left everyone confused and 'a few of the simpler sort more inclined to Masse then to sound Religion'. His self-seeking attitude makes him a dubious witness and he may not have been writing about Turnastone but he evokes the uncertainties and differences within the still emergent Church of England. Unfortunately the parish registers do not survive before the 1670s and there are no other parish records until more recent times to provide evidence about religious affairs, the care of the poor and repair of the highways.

The Whitehouse estate remained in the ownership of the Howorth family from 1629-30 until the death of Isabella Howorth in 1775. Dolward was the one portion of the estate which Epiphan Howorth (1566-1647) had hived off by leaving it to his daughters Blanche and Frances, with the condition that their brother Humfrey (c.1625-c.1675) had a right to buy it from them within a year on payment of 800 marks (£533). It appears that although for a time Humfrey managed Dolward with Whitehouse he did not exercise his right of purchase for by 1734 Whitewall was in the hands of John Ravenhill of Woolhope. In 1793-4, still called Whitewall Grange, it was owned and mortgaged by John Jones of Ross, a timber merchant. Shortly afterwards it was bought, together with Dolward, by Philip Davis of Leominster, a man of properties in Radnorshire and west Herefordshire, whose wife Rebecca Tudor came from Michaelchurch Escley. [19]

There are no such complications about the ownership of Cot Hill. Throughout, it stayed firmly attached to Whitehouse. Four generations later Herbert Howorth (1695-1745) ran up enormous debts on the security of the estate, failed to carry out the terms of his father's will and eventually left the crippled Whitehouse estate to his three sisters, Magdalen, Isabella and Elizabeth, the last two being spinsters, with the husband of a fourth sister Mary given powers as his executor. Inevitably, rival claimants to the estate appeared, among whom was Frances Haselden (1760-1830), a granddaughter of Magdalen. Uncertain of her rights she sensibly sought the advice of solicitors but with singular misjudgement chose first one and then a second who were flagrantly guilty of misrepresentation and sharp dealing. The second, William Downes, had by 1795 succeeded in obtaining personal control over the estate. It was the first time since 1545 that Whitehouse had changed hands outside the descendents of the Parrys of Newcourt.

Meanwhile, the Poston-Turnastone estate had been sold by the Parrys of Poston. Its subsequent ownership is unclear. James Parry was leasing it in 1645 when its owner was Henry Somerset, 5th Earl and 1st Marquess of Worcester (1576-1646) but when or how this powerful Marcher family came into possession has not been established.[20] Earlier in the 17th century Francis Moysey and Thomas Barnseley (possibly the rector of Turnastone *c.*1599-1607) appear to have owned it, or at least had an interest or mortgage in it, and that same interest was later in the hands of Nicholas Philpott (*c.*1615-1681), his son Nicholas (*c.*1646-1683) and grandson, also Nicholas in 1725.[21] However, the Somerset family retained their connection for in 1699 Henry Somerset, 3rd Marquess of Worcester and 1st Duke of Beaufort (*c.*1629-1700) settled it upon his fifth son Lord Arthur Somerset. The Duke's widow Mary, Dowager Duchess of Beaufort, acquired property in Peterchurch, Vowchurch and Turnastone from Nicholas Philpott and on her death in 1714 these all passed to Lord Arthur Somerset. He lived at Poston Court until his death in 1743, when he was buried at Vowchurch. His two daughters, Anna wife of Uvedale Price of Foxley, the advocate of the 'picturesque' landscape, and Mary, wife of Algernon Greville, son of Fulke Lord Brooke, came into the estates which eventually passed as a dowry to the latter's daughter Mary Greville, who married Shuckburgh Boughton. His son Sir Edward Boughton (d.1794 and buried at Vowchurch) had Poston House built as a shooting lodge on the wooded hill and parkland above Poston Court, designed about 1765 by a leading architect of the day, Sir William Chambers.[22] At about the same period the large stone barn at Turnastone Court was also built. His widow held the estate in 1800.

3 FARMING CONDITIONS FROM 1800

Judy Seymour and Peter Gunn-Wilkinson

The natural environment and farming patterns

The changes in farming patterns in the parish of Turnastone over the last two centuries reflect in part the response to both natural and socio-economic factors. Amongst these factors are the opportunities and constraints provided by the underlying geology, soils, climate and water supply found in the parish and the inevitable demands on their owners to meet the economic pressures on agriculture in the region, and the country as a whole. The transition from mixed arable to predominantly livestock production has defined the pattern of changes experienced by upland fringe farms on the borders of the Black Mountains and on the edges of the Golden Valley. The situation is particularly marked for Dolward and Cothill farms, since their land-use pattern has been influenced by their position on the edge of the more fertile soils of the Golden Valley. In the fields on the banks of the river Dore, the alluvial and glacial deposits combined to form a soil which is more fertile than that of the neighbouring valleys. The floor of the valley has always been generally under grass of good quality, and the owners of Turnastone Court have been able to sustain traditional livestock grazing methods into this century. The arable fields formerly found on the tableland at Dolward and Cothill have now been replaced by grassland.

Two of the three Turnastone farms, Dolward and Cothill, stand on the platform of higher ground (200-240 metres above sea level) marked out by the sandstone and limestone outcrops that resisted the glacial and water erosion which formed the rich alluvial and glacial deposits of the Golden Valley. The upland fringe areas were formed of mudstones and siltstones with red, green and purple sandstones that break down to form medium clay loams supporting cereal production. Phillip Dodd's *Herefordshire Agriculture in the Mid-Nineteenth Century* argued that 'the soils developed on the Old Red Sandstones support a diversity of herbage, which is sufficiently rich in calcium and silica to support sheep grazing pastures in summer and winter'.[1]

One of the main factors influencing the location of Dolward and Cothill farms, on the sandstone outcrops in Turnastone, is the spring-line marked by the junction of the pervious limestone rocks overlying the sandstones and clays. A further spring-line runs between Shegear, Whitewall Coppice and the Ford. This reflects another

Fig. 7 David Jones of Dolward at a ploughing match (Mrs. G. Davies)

underlying fault-line running south-west and north-east across the northern part of the parish. These springs provided a secure supply of water for livestock production and would have been a major factor in determining the productivity of these farms. Even where the soils are heavier clays, the undulations of the ground enable the water to run off and permit cultivation.[2] In some fields extensive drainage works and ditches were necessary to make the land suitable for cultivation.

The underlying sandstones and the superficial drift deposits have also influenced the main land-form differences and farming conditions between the adjacent Black Mountain fringes and the Golden Valley. The lower step of the escarpment of the Black Mountains is heavily mantled with glacial drift, which consists of reddish sandy boulder clay with embedded pebbles. These conditions support predominantly grazing and fodder crops with limited arable production. Below this escarpment, the main distinction is between the medium loams on the sandstone and limestone outcrops underlying Dolward and Cothill farms, and the alluvial deposits of the Dore Valley. The alluvial deposits now form extensive areas of excellent grazing and meadows at Turnastone Court which support higher densities of sheep. The flood plain has been managed to maintain fertility and provide early growth of spring pasture.

For much of the 19th and 20th centuries, both in terms of farming practices and in terms of the proportion of potential arable land, Turnastone parish was more similar to adjacent areas in the Wye Valley than to the smaller upland farms located in the adjoining St Margaret's and Craswall parishes. Those farms extend up to a height of 350 metres and are characterised by poorer soils and more undulating landscapes which are less suited to arable crops and mixed farming production on small fields. The 1936 *Land Utilisation Survey Map* shows clearly that Dolward and Cothill farms, by contrast, have relatively large areas of arable land on their gently sloping terrain. Turnastone Court, with its heavier alluvial clay soils, was also used for arable production where the land was not subject to flooding. [3]

After the war, the government introduced an ambitious programme of farmland 'improvement' through the rationalisation of farm holdings and changes in field boundaries in order to make possible the use of modern agricultural developments and machinery. There was a particular concern to expand ley farming to improve permanent grassland through reseeding. The three farms therefore stand out as being well endowed with good arable soils, on slopes that were relatively easily worked and have benefited from government policies to support mixed farming into the late 20th century. For economic reasons, more recent changes in farming patterns have substantially shifted the emphasis from a mixed arable/livestock-grazing pattern to a predominantly grazing and livestock pattern.

Land-use changes in the late 19th and 20th centuries
Statistics comparing agricultural change in Herefordshire for the period 1870 to 1931 show that over this period the proportion of land under arable declined significantly. The 19th century had witnessed several periods of high cereal prices and shortages, and during the Napoleonic Wars over 60% of Herefordshire farmland was arable. This was reduced to 46% in the early 1840s, a figure that was not subsequently exceeded.[4] The latter part of the 19th century saw a general depression in farming with the fall in cereal prices, especially in arable cultivation.

The conservation plan prepared for Turnastone Court in 2001 contains an analysis of the cropping patterns in the agricultural census returns for the period 1901-1971 for the Golden Valley parishes and Turnastone.[5] The 1901 returns showed that in Turnastone parish almost a quarter of the farmland was still arable, and grassland occupied the rest except for a small area of orchards. Over the period 1901-1971 the Turnastone parish farmland saw a significant increase in grassland, and a corre-

Fig. 8 Cider apple orchard, Michaelchurch c.1880 (HRO)

sponding depletion in arable land to a fifth in 1971. This was below the peak during World War II when arable land increased to almost a third of total farmland (see below).

Grassland farming

Since grassland is such an important component of land use in the Golden Valley a more detailed analysis may be useful for the parish of Turnastone. The pattern of grassland has changed over the period 1901-1971 with the proportion of permanent grass for grazing declining from 70% in 1901 to 60% in 1971. The inter-war years were characterised by a significant increase in rough grazing as 10% of the total grassland reverted to rough pasture with the land becoming increasingly marginal because of low returns. Since the war there has been a significant increase in ley grassland (from 4% in 1938 to 20% in 1971) as farmers responded to government incentives to improve permanent pastures and to develop grassland leys. Turnastone experienced a major increase in rough grazing in the 1950s before declining to 3% in 1971.

Livestock levels

During the inter-war years the decline in arable production was compensated for by a substantial increase in livestock in Turnastone parish. Between 1901 and 1938 the density of cattle per square kilometre of farmland doubled and continued to increase to 93/sq.km in 1971. Sheep increased by even greater proportions, doubling between 1901 and 1938, and almost doubling again between 1938 and 1971 to 515/sq.km. This intensification of livestock production in the post-war period may reflect the pattern of incentives and subsidies developed by the European Union to maximise production and increase productivity.

Fig. 9 Ryeland sheep and Hereford cattle at Turnastone Court

The stocking levels in Turnastone parish in the 1950s were significantly higher for cattle than the adjacent upland areas, and marginally lower for breeding ewes. This difference probably reflects the greater opportunities to grow supplementary feed for the cattle on the richer soils of Turnastone parish and the reduced carrying capacity of the grasslands for breeding ewes, compared to that required for fattening lambs on the upland grazing. The 1936 *Land Use Survey* confirmed that the Turnastone farms had more than twice the area of arable land compared to the adjacent areas in the Black Mountain tablelands.[6] The upland areas have a much greater proportion of land committed to hay and rough grazing. Common land is also more prominent.

The War Agricultural Executive Committee (WAEC) 1940/41
Records for the three Turnastone farms

In looking at agricultural change in the 20th century of special note are the detailed records of government intervention to increase domestic food security during World War II. To do this, the government established the War Agricultural Executive Committee (WAEC) to ensure that farms were managed as efficiently as possible and production switched to maximise arable crop production and thereby increase the nation's self-sufficiency in temperate crops. The WAEC had the power to order the conversion of suitable grassland to arable, and the reports for the three farms in Turnastone show that between 1940 and 1941 each of the farms was required to increase its arable production by about 10 acres by ploughing grassland, and Dolward contributed a further seven acres from its lands in St Margaret's (see Table 1).

Table 1. Cropping Patterns on Turnastone Court, Cothill and Dolward - WAEC'S 1941 Survey

Areas in acres	Turnastone Court Farm	Cothill Farm	Part of Dolward Farm in Turnastone Parish	Total Dolward Farm	Total Turnastone Parish	Total 3 Farms
Cereals	22.3	20.8	25.1	62.0	68.2	105.1
Root Crops	3.6	4.8	4.5	11.0	12.8	19.4
All Arable	25.9	25.6	29.5	73.0	81.0	124.5
Of which grass ploughed up in 1940/41	(10.5)	(10.1)	(10.1)	(17.5)	(30.8)	(38.2)
All Grassland	73.2	37.6	83.8	207.0	194.6	317.8
Orchards	2.4	0.0	2.4	6.0	4.9	8.4
All Farmland	101.6	63.2	115.7	286.0	280.5	450.7

Note:
i. The Turnastone Parish figures exclude that part of Dolward farm in St Margaret's.
ii. The table also includes separate figures for Turnastone parish, the whole of Dolward Farm, and for the area covered by the three farms in Turnastone and St Margaret's parishes.

In Turnastone parish the conversion of grassland to arable represented an increase in arable land of around a third. At Cothill and Turnastone farms the land brought into cereals increased by almost a half. A further small acreage was used for roots and protein crops. Arable production continued at this level until the 1950s.

In respect of grassland management, the WAEC records in 1941 show the effects of government encouragement to increase the quality of grassland through ley farming. The aim was to enlarge the area of temporary grassland used for mowing and grazing. However, the impact was relatively minor with permanent grassland as a percentage of total grassland remaining very high in Turnastone Court and Dolward Farm (92.3%) (see Table 2).

Table 2. Grassland land uses on Turnastone Court, Cothill and Dolward - WAEC'S 1941 Survey

Areas in acres	Turnastone Court Farm	Cothill Farm	Part of Dolward Farm in Turnastone Parish	Total Dolward Farm	Total Turnastone Parish	Total 3 Farms
Temporary grass i. for mowing	2.8	4.9	4.0	10.0	11.7	17.7
ii. for grazing	6.1	-	-	6.1	6.1	
Permanent grass i. for mowing	29.1	16.2	20.2	50.0	65.6	95.3
ii. for grazing	41.3	10.5	59.5	146.0	111.3	197.8
All Grassland	73.2	37.6	83.8	207.0	194.6	317.8
All Farmland	101.6	63.2	115.7	286.0	280.5	450.7
Grassland as % farmland	72.1	59.5	72.4	72.4	69.5	70.5
Permanent grass as % all grassland	96.1	71.0	95.2	94.6	90.9	92.3

Long-term changes in land use in the three farms in Turnastone/St Margaret's – 1842/44 and 2009

The broad changes in land use for the whole period from the 1840s to the present day are identified in the two maps below which compare the land-use pattern in the 1842/44 tithe maps and a field survey of the current position. The map of land use (Fig. 10) demonstrates that in the early 19th century, land use was characterised by a significantly higher proportion of cereals and mixed farming patterns for each of the three farms, with a concentration of cereals production on the relatively flat upland

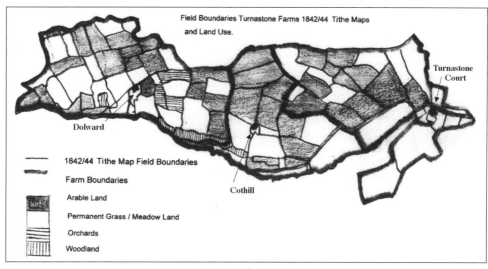

Fig. 10 Land use 1842/44

fields on Dolward and Cothill farms. Turnastone Court had some arable but was distinguished by its variety of grassland pastures with some rough pasture, grassland, and wetland meadows adjacent to the river Dore and its tributaries. Dolward retained several orchards and extensive woodlands on the banks of streams.

The land use pattern for the three farms in 2008/9 is detailed in Fig. 11, which also indicates the changes in the field boundaries since the 1840s and the new pattern of land use from a survey in 2008/09. The most significant adjustment to the field boundaries has occurred on Dolward Farm, where the change from a mixed arable/ livestock farm has induced changes to the field boundaries. Cothill Farm has shown the most complete change from mixed arable to almost total grassland farming. In

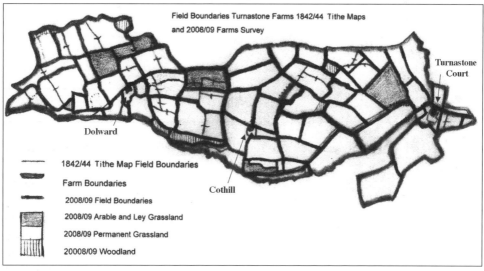

Fig. 11 Land use 2009 with changes in field boundaries

21

this case, the field boundaries of the 1840s have been retained with little modification. An unusual feature of Cothill is the retention of two small 'glebe land' fields owned by the church and rented out for grazing. Turnastone Court has also seen significant changes in land use, with only one of the eleven arable fields in the 1840s retained in arable production in the recent survey. Some of the smaller fields have also been amalgamated to form larger grazing paddocks on the upper fields of the farm.

The wider farming landscape through the 19th and 20th centuries

In 1794, John Clark published *A General View of the Agriculture of the County of Hereford*, which provides a very detailed and comprehensive portrait of farming life and practices. At this time, land ownership in the county was dominated by individual farms, which were surrounded by their plantations. The owners of estates rather than absentee landlords were generally resident in the county. This enabled them to manage their estates better and encouraged their tenant farmers to make improvements.[7] The size of the estates was in general extensive, with from 400 to 500 acres for the large farms in the fertile Wye Valley and parts of the Golden Valley, where the Whitehouse estate was recorded as 531 acres in 1833.[8]

In common with many farms in the late 18th and 19th centuries the lowland farms in Herefordshire were farmed by tenant farmers, rather than by the landowners. The tenant farmers lived on the farm, cultivated and grazed the land, maintained its fertility and retained the proceeds from the sale of their crops and livestock. The way they farmed was often constrained by varying degrees of restrictive clauses and obligations laid down by the owner in granting the leases, as at the Whitehouse estate. The tenant was often required to keep the property and hedges in good repair, and maintain the fertility of the land by spreading lime and manures, and rotating clovers and pasture and arable crops. Landowners who were interested in investing in the improvement of their estates might make a commitment to undertake long-term repairs and improvements, clear rough ground for cultivation, drain and fence the land, and maintain and improve the buildings. They also often retained the rights to all timber extraction, the fruit from some orchards and the stone from working quarries.

The 19th century
In the course of the 19th century, rural life in England, and in the rest of the UK, was to undergo significant changes as it witnessed periods of serious economic downturns, widespread mechanisation and transport innovations such as the arrival of the railway. Structural changes in the economy, with the growth of industrial production especially in the latter half of the century onwards, was accompanied by major population migrations away from the country to the town. Dolward, Cothill and Turnastone farms, like other farms in Herefordshire, would have had to respond to these developments.

No farm, therefore, could ignore entirely the range of challenges and raft of innovations in farming and the wider world that characterised a number of periods in the 19th century. Most certainly they had, for example, to respond to market prices. Such a time was the very serious post-Waterloo depression in 1815 preceded by three consecutive years from 1809-12 of bad harvests when hardships were so severe that large numbers of those who made their living from the land lost their livelihoods. The periods of bad harvests and recession in the middle of the century were also felt keenly by many farmers and farm workers. But the feared depression coming from the repeal of the Corn Laws in 1846 began to bite in earnest only in the early 1870s with the flood of cheap corn coming from America and a series of bad harvests.[9] The depression, known as the Great Depression, continued for the next twenty years resulting in upheavals across the country and once again many lost livelihoods. Herefordshire, however, with its tradition of mixed farming did not fare as badly as other counties at this time. The last quarter of the century was, in fact, a time of wage rises and increased prosperity for many in the county.[10]

As the century progressed, the more fortunate farmers were able to take advantage of the new technologies to improve the efficiency of production. It is evident that some of the farms in Turnastone were adapting to each development as it occurred. For example, new farm buildings were constructed at Dolward and Cothill in the 1830s and 1840s and Turnastone Farm's new buildings, including farmhouse, wain-house and granary, were built in around 1876 as new owners or tenants brought additional resources and enthusiasm for improvements to their holdings.

Mechanisation, in the form of the steam-threshing engine and mechanical reaper, was one of the major factors that transformed the nature of farming in the latter half of the 19th century, and was widespread throughout the country by the middle of the 1860s. All three farms were large enough to consider the use of the new mechanical means of drilling, a far speedier and in many ways more reliable system of sowing the seeds for the coming harvest. However, the expense involved in keeping up with the latest developments in this 'progressive age' was considerable. Landed estates could for the most part afford it, but tenant farms the size of Dolward, Cothill or Turnastone might not have been able to, particularly during the years of depression

and poor harvests. Nevertheless, at times the pressures to invest would have been such that few farms could ignore them altogether. With road improvements and the arrival in the 1850s of the railway in Herefordshire fresh markets opened up to farmers throughout the county. Many farms in the county and the country as a whole prospered at this time of the railway age, good harvests and the increasing demand for food from the expanding towns and

Fig. 12 Late 19th-century Ransome threshing engine (HRO)

cities.[11] While up to this point some farm produce would meet local demands, now an expanding network of supply lines were appearing, enabling the industrious and able farmer to take advantage of these developing avenues. However, challenges never seemed far away.

Phillip Dodd noted that the several periods of recession between 1815 and 1848 generated adjustments in farming expenditure. Some of the most flexible costs were wage rates and the overall numbers employed. The wage rates tended to rise and fall in relation to the quality of the harvests. Between 1819 and 1823 farm labourers' wage rates in Herefordshire fell from 10s to 8s a week. Over the next thirty years they fluctuated at around 9s up to the 1850s.[12] Towards the end of the century wage rates rose significantly due to the shortage of labour resulting from increased migration to towns, cities and overseas. By 1898 the agricultural labourer's wage in Herefordshire was in the region of between 12s and 14s a week.[13] The rise in wages throughout the country led to a general increase in the standard of living for rural workers although there were many regional variations, and wages in Herefordshire were lower than those in many parts of the West Midlands and elsewhere in the country.[14]

The impact of the steady migration to the towns and overseas which began in the 1850s was not significant until the 1870s, when the rural population across the whole country was in decline.[15] Herefordshire's population, for example, was 88,436 in 1801 and 115,489 in 1851. The population of Turnastone had peaked earlier in 1841 but declined noticeably from 1851.[16] In Herefordshire as a whole there was an overall decline of 22% of the population between 1871 and 1931.[17]

The 20th century
The decline of the rural population continued, as markets, as of old, contracted while others expanded, bringing both benefits and challenges. The demand for arable crops continued to reduce from the latter part of the 19th century through to the early 20th century. The effect on farms in Turnastone and the county generally, once again, however, was, as MP Thomas Duckham reported, not severe 'because of the great variety of crops' grown. During World War I, farms across the country were ordered to put more land under the plough. In the west of Herefordshire, however, less land was ploughed than elsewhere. This helped farmers to cope with the steep fall in arable prices in the 1920s and 30s, as much of their land was still predominantly grassland, a situation that continued until World War II.

After World War II, the government introduced an ambitious and expensive programme of farmland 'improvement' through the rationalisation of farm holdings and changes in field boundaries in order to allow the use of modern agricultural developments and machinery. There was a particular concern for the expansion of ley farming to replace low-grade pasture. A side effect of this policy was the trend to farm specialisation leading to a decline in marginal, small farm holdings. In the central Golden Valley parishes the number of farm holdings reduced from 131 in 1951 to 83 in 1971; crop diversity declined and livestock specialisation increased over this period.

However, the three farms in Turnastone had been able to maintain their economic viability as individual holdings by taking on board the government's support for agriculture, using family labour and adapting farming patterns to meet market conditions. In the case of Turnastone Court the Watkins family continued to farm in a traditional way of livestock farming which enabled them to keep the cost of inputs low.

The post-war drive meant that British agriculture in general became 'production orientated'. The changes in farming practices that resulted were encouraged by government supported intensification of farming and increased mechanisation which resulted in higher yields and greater carrying capacities for stock. These changes involved the use of increased artificial inputs (fertilizers, pesticides and herbicides) and improved

Fig. 13 Haymaking at Turnastone Court c.1930 (Watkins)

plant and animal breeding programmes.[18] Immediately after the war, with the passing of the 1947 Agricultural Act, the government's agricultural policy rested on two main objectives: to increase price stability and to improve efficiency through an agricultural expansion plan which aimed to raise output from agriculture by 60% over pre-war levels. The stability was provided through guaranteed prices and assured markets. In the 1950s the minimum guaranteed prices were replaced by deficiency payments for cereals, that is, payments were given to top up market prices. With this new level of stability in prices and guarantees, farm incomes rose on the whole, giving farmers the confidence to undertake capital investments in new technologies.

These innovations were particularly effective in increasing cereal production in eastern counties, where efficiencies in the use of labour and capital were supported by environmental factors with the result that costs were reduced as the level of mechanisation increased. Increases in incomes on dairy, upland and small farms in the west of the country, including the upland fringes of Herefordshire, were slower because the environment was less suitable to the expansion of cereal production and there was less scope for mechanisation. The Turnastone farms, over time, have found it less economic to maintain their mixed arable/livestock production as prices for cereals have made them less competitive and they have increasingly concentrated on livestock production with managed grazing.

In the 1970s, after Britain entered the European Economic Community (EEC), later renamed the European Union (EU), the system of price support was changed from deficiency payments to protection and intervention payments. This system protected EU farmers through a common tariff system of import levies and the CAP price support system. The CAP had two elements which set a target price and an intervention price which guaranteed the prices below which the Community would buy the surplus production. There was a complex system of monetary compensation payments, which attempted to equalise incomes in the different countries.

During the last quarter of the 20th century the story of farming was one of the changing fortunes of the farmers. The numbers of farms fell steadily across the country, a reduction that has accelerated in the past 20 years. However, with improved plant breeding, more widespread use of pesticides and herbicides, and the increasing intensification of livestock through the 1960s the farmers' output overall steadily increased into the next decade. But over-production of wheat in particular led eventually to a glut in yields and, as a consequence, the rise of 'grain mountains'. In due course the EU's response was to reduce the numbers of subsidies linked to production, and, because of an increase in concern about the health and wellbeing of biodiversity in the countryside, payments were introduced to encourage a more integrated approach to land management that supported agricultural production and environmental concerns. It is a system of payments that is broadly in place today. However, as the issue of 'food security' worldwide becomes more pressing, farmers are once again being encouraged to increase their arable yields.

4   Turnastone Court

Andrew Langton

Shortly after crossing the bridge over the river Dore into Turnastone a range of farm buildings comes into sight on both sides of the road. On the right is a tall red brick Victorian farmhouse and facing it across the road is a large weather-boarded barn with a cluster of other farm buildings. This is Turnastone Court Farm. It is a 247-acre traditional livestock farm compromising the eastern and low-lying part of the parish around the village centre, and bounded on the north-east by the river Dore and to the west, where the ground rises, by Cothill Farm.

The Owners

Until 1912 the farm had since at least the late 16th century formed part of the neighbouring Poston estate in Vowchurch. As already described (see page 14), the estate had been settled by Henry Somerset, 1st Duke of Beaufort, on his fifth son Lord Arthur Somerset in 1699. It then passed down by inheritance and marriage to Sir Edward Boughton, who had Poston House built on the hillside looking down on Turnastone. He died in 1794.

Sir Edward's illegitimate daughter, Eliza Davies, inherited the Poston estate and married first Sir George Charles Braithwaite in 1801, who changed his name to Boughton to meet the terms of his father-in-law's will.[1] He died in 1809 and she subsequently married Newton Dickenson in about 1836. The only surviving child of her first marriage, Frederica (1805-73), inherited Poston and married Thomas Robinson (1796-1880) in 1824. Thomas's great-uncle served George III as Master Gardener, his father as Superintendent to the Royal Farms at Kew and Windsor, and the family lived at Sheffield House, conveniently close to Kensington Palace. Thomas and Frederica's daughter, Harriet (1825-52) married in 1846 a surgeon, Francis Harrison (1811-75) in Madras, where she died in giving birth to a daughter, also named Harriet (1852-1944). This Harriet Egbertha Lucy Harrison married her cousin Edward Lewis Gavin Robinson of Poston (1837-1908) in 1872. After his death she married in 1918 another cousin, Commander William Thresher (d.1922).

The changes of name and the dates of the marriages and deaths are significant in following the fortunes of the Poston estate and its Turnastone farm. Soon after his marriage E.L.G. Robinson invested heavily both in the construction of the ill-fated Golden Valley Railway and in rebuilding Turnastone farmhouse and buildings. It was also a time of severe agricultural depression, the rent of the farm falling from £355 a year in 1878 to only £246 in 1912. After his death his son Ralph Gavin Robinson inherited the estate with little choice but to sell the greater part. In 1912, the Turnastone farm was purchased by its tenant, William Watkins, apparently by private treaty before the auction was held.[2]

The Tenants and Occupiers

The tenant in 1800 was James Jones, listed in the Land Tax records from 1789 to 1804, although as someone of that name is mentioned in the parish registers from 1758 he may well have been at the farm for many years earlier. The next tenant appears to have been William Parry Bromage, listed in 1809-10. By 1813 the tenant was Thomas Holder who was listed until 1817.

From 1818 until 1903 all tenants named in the Land Tax records had the surname Probert, and they were probably all related. James Probert held the tenancy until 1826, then Thomas until 1829, who was succeeded by Richard until 1836, when he married Ann Jenkins and moved to Abbey Dore. James Probert was the next tenant until his death aged 60 in 1862. He had married in 1837 Selina Withers, originally from Slimbridge, Gloucestershire, and they had at least eight children, two of whom were boys. The elder was John (b.1840) who succeeded to the tenancy (with his mother Selina) following his father's death. Selina died aged 73 in 1882 and shortly afterwards John Probert married Alice Jane Fletcher from Bodenham. John and Alice had nine children between 1886 and 1900, all being listed as living at the farm in the 1901 census. They moved to Hill Farm, Vowchurch in 1903, ending the family's long connection with the farm throughout nearly all the 19th century, but both were buried at Turnastone, John in 1918 and Alice in 1951. Like their successors they appear in the records from time to time, James Probert serving on the jury of the Snodhill manorial court in 1824, John Probert for failing to trim his roadside hedges, but there are no parish records or personal papers to provide information about their life at the farm during its rebuilding and the late 19th-century agricultural slump.

William Rogers Watkins (known to his contemporaries as Bill and sometimes as 'William Watkins the Green' in the Welsh style) moved from The Green Farm, Newton St Margaret's on being granted the tenancy of Turnastone in 1903. It was the beginning of another family's long occupation that

Fig. 14 William Watkins (Watkins)

28

Pedigree of the WATKINS family of Turnastone and their connections

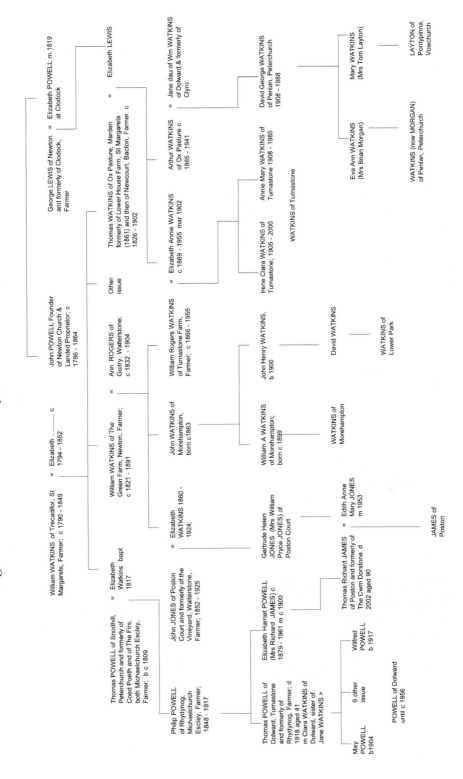

William WATKINS of Trecadifor, St Margarets, Farmer; c 1790 - 1849 = Elizabeth ...... c 1794 - 1852

George LEWIS of Newton and formerly of Clodock, Farmer = Elizabeth POWELL m.1819 at Clodock

John POWELL Founder of Newton Church & Landed Proprietor; c 1786 - 1864

Thomas POWELL of Snodhill, Peterchurch and formerly of Coed Poeth and of The Firs, both Michaelchurch Escley, Farmer; b c 1809 = Elizabeth Watkins bapt 1817

William WATKINS of The Green Farm, Newton, Farmer; c 1821 - 1891 = Ann ROGERS of Goitry, Walterstone; c 1832 - 1904

Thomas WATKINS of Ox Pasture, Marden formerly of Lower House Farm, St Margarets (1861) and then of Newcourt, Bacton, Farmer. c 1826 - 1902 = Elizabeth LEWIS

Other issue

Philip POWELL of Rhydynog, Michaelchurch Escley, Farmer; 1848 - 1917

John JONES of Poston Court and formerly of the Vineyard, Walterstone, Farmer; 1852 - 1925

Elizabeth WATKINS 1860 - 1924;

John WATKINS of Morehampton, born c1863

William Rogers WATKINS of Turnastone Farm, Farmer; c 1866 - 1955

Elizabeth Annie WATKINS c 1869 - 1955 mar 1902

Arthur WATKINS of Ox Pasture c 1865 - 1941 = Jane dau of Wm WATKINS of Dolward & formerly of Clyro

David George WATKINS of Penlan, Peterchurch 1908 - 1988 = Mary WATKINS (Mrs Tom Layton)

Elizabeth Harriet POWELL (Mrs Richard JAMES) c 1879 - 1961 m c 1900

Gertrude Helen JONES (Mrs William Pryce JONES) of Poston Court

William A WATKINS of Morehampton; born c 1899

John Henry WATKINS, b 1900

Irene Clara WATKINS; 1905 - 2000

Annie Mary WATKINS of Turnastone 1908 - 1985

WATKINS of Turnastone

Eva Ann WATKINS (Mrs Brian Morgan)

WATKINS (now MORGAN) of Penlan, Peterchurch

LAYTON of Pontypinna, Vowchurch

Thomas POWELL of Dolward, Turnastone and formerly of Rhydynog, Farmer; d 1918 aged 41 m Clara WATKINS of Dolward, sister of Jane WATKINS >

Thomas Richard JAMES of Poston and formerly of The Cwm Dorstone d 2002 aged 90 = Edith Anne Mary JONES m 1953

David WATKINS

WATKINS of Morehampton

WATKINS of Lower Park

JAMES of Poston

May POWELL b1904

Wilfred POWELL b 1917

9 other issue

POWELL of Dolward until c 1956

29

was to last the whole of the 20th century. He had married his first cousin Elizabeth (Lizzie) Anne Watkins at Madley in 1902. He was already described as 'of Turnastone' and she was housekeeping for her brother Tom Watkins at the Bacho Farm, just in Madley parish beyond the pass out of the Golden Valley. Not only were husband and wife closely related, they were also related to a swathe of other farming families. All three farms in the parish, Turnastone, Cothill and Dolward, have been occupied by members of this family network of Watkins, Powell, Herring and Morgan. Indeed, reading the unpublished account by Eva Morgan, 'The Watkins Family of Newton, Bacton, Marden, Turnastone, Vowchurch and Peterchurch', (2009 in progress), it would hardly be an exaggeration to claim that the extended family have occupied or owned most of the farms in the neighbourhood at one time or another.[3]

William had been brought up to the hardships of farming by his father, also William Watkins, who would rouse him at 4 in the morning to get the horses fed and geared before breakfast, ready for the day's work. He was well liked, a shrewd businessman and strong-minded, emphasising his views by banging the stick which he always carried. Though perhaps not showing it, he was also deeply sensitive. His first child, Annie, died in 1904 at only 15 months old, their second, Irene (Rene) Clara was born in 1905, and a third, Annie May (Nancy) in 1908. Many years later Rene told Eva Morgan how her parents, always called Papa and Mama within the family, were still arguing about Nancy's first name as they left the house for her christening at the church next door. Her father was heard to say to her mother, 'You call her what you like – I shall call her Nancy!' He felt unable to call another little girl by the same name as his lost first-born daughter Annie.

Fig. 15 Mrs Watkins with Rene and Nancy c.1915 (Watkins)

His decisiveness was evident in his determination to raise the loan to purchase the farm where he had been sitting tenant for the previous nine years, followed by purchases of land and cottages at the Slough from Lord Abergavenny's estate, in Turnastone village from the Whitehouse estate on the death of Herbert Howarth Wood in 1924, and the Langford fields near Poston Court from the Poston estate. On one such occasion, however, when asked how it came about that her father had owned Hinton Farm at Peterchurch about 1922 or 1925, Rene revealed to Eva Morgan how he had been overruled by his no less strong-willed wife:

> Rene said that a Mrs. James was living there beforehand. She must have got hard up and one day as they were getting out of the trap at the Wheatsheaf inn, Hay-on-Wye, on market day, she approached William and asked him if he would buy her farm and its surrounding fields from her. He asked his wife and she said 'No', so that appeared to be that. However when he arrived back at the end of the day to harness up the pony and trap to leave for home he said he'd met with Mrs. James again and had bought the house as a retirement home for them. However the girls and their mother (always known as Mama) wouldn't go there so he had to sell it again!

He was not a man to miss an opportunity of a bargain. The hill farmers hand down the memory that he would be at his gate as they drove their stock to Peterchurch market and would offer to buy their animals. Looking for a better price at market they would refuse the offer, but should they return with unsold stock he would again be at the gate to buy – at a lower price.

In replacing the Robinsons as the owner of the principal farm in the parish, William and Lizzie Watkins had acquired a certain standing in the community. William met some of the expenses of the church out of his own pocket and in 1950 paid for the installation of electricity. But it was Lizzie who particularly set their standards. Eva Morgan recalls:

> One of my earliest memories was of the Turnastone ladies dressed in their furs from head to toe; hats, coats and gloves, all purchased and cared for regularly by Augustus Edwards's shop in High Town, Hereford, "The Furriers of the West". Mama always wore a fur, complete with head and claws, around her shoulders, over her suit or dress, summer and winter. Of course to go out visiting or to Church they always wore a smart hat and gloves, summer or winter, as well-dressed ladies did.

Mama ruled over her family. It was she who determined that to suit their new circumstances Turnastone Farm should be renamed Turnastone Court.[4] Anxious to keep the farm in the family she also watched over her daughters, hosting Sunday suppers and organising dances at the Memorial Hall, but steering them away from boyfriends she thought unsuitable. Neither Nancy nor Rene married.

Nancy had always helped her father run the farm and is typically remembered driving tractor and hay-turner to dry the cut hay. In later years Rene became house-keeper and looked after the poultry. From the beginning William, like other local farmers, concentrated on his stock of Hereford cattle, but unlike John Pearce of neighbouring Poston Court in 1878, who had a herd of seventy Herefords, he did not aspire to join the Hereford Herd Society, whose members were mostly the gentry. But he bought from them, and the family were proud of the many prizes they won. The whole house, especially the front room downstairs, was adorned with the rosettes for their prize cattle sold at Hereford market. On the deaths of both William and Lizzie in 1955, Nancy managed the farm whilst Rene cared for the house and garden. [5] The 'girls' continued to go to Hereford market, instantly recognisable in their fine clothes and fur and feathered hats, and returned home with yet more rosettes for the walls of their bedrooms. They had little appetite for change and, as they were reluctant to do anything that their father had not previously done, the house and husbandry went on in their traditional ways.

Among the farm workers in that post-war period, Percy Woodhouse came to Turnastone in 1953 with his wife and young family of two boys and two girls. They lived in Rose Cottage for many years until he retired to a bungalow in Peterchurch. At that time a second farm worker was Friedrich Marschall (known as 'Fred the German'), who lived at Brook Cottage with his family (see page 51). [6] A later succession of men and boys, including Richard Broughton and David Jones (who came from Evesham), both bachelors and favourites of Rene and Nancy, either lived in at

Fig. 16 Rene and Nancy Watkins (Watkins)

the farmhouse or in the cottage. All the unmarried ones usually had their meals in the farmhouse. Occasionally additional help was sought. Trevor Powell and Wilfred Carberry did hedging, fencing and shearing, the Price brothers from Hinton Court and the Lloyd brothers from Abbey Dore harvesting and manure-spreading. In Rene's last years and with all the complications of the annual form-filling to meet the government's demands for its 'Integrated Administration and Control Systems', she relied heavily on her cousins David Watkins of Lower Park, Abbey Dore, and his son Robert, allowing them to work the arable land and sell back corn and straw for use at Turnastone and also help with the management of the stock.

Much responsibility rested upon two successive farm bailiffs, Tom Nichols, who had assisted William Watkins since 1953 and Herbert Dale, whilst Tom Reece, who cycled over from Hinton from 1960 to 1974, was a regular helper. During the whole of that period there were usually two farm workers living either in Rose Cottage or the smaller part of Brook Cottages. Both Tom Reece and the bailiff, Herbert Dale, who came from the Worcester area, were bachelors who lived in the farmhouse with 'the girls'. Nancy died on 22 March 1985 leaving Rene to continue farming assisted by Herbert Dale, who dealt with much of the paperwork and cared for her like a son in her final years. Rene Watkins finally died aged 94 on 10 October 2000 and Herbert Dale the following year aged 77. He is buried beside the Watkins sisters in Vowchurch churchyard.

Following the death of Rene Watkins and delays caused by the widespread outbreak of foot-and-mouth disease in 2001, the farm came on the open market, attracting alarm among Herefordshire environmentalists that its traditional way of farming, undisturbed environment and ancient water-meadows might be lost. The Countryside Restoration Trust (CRT) was alerted and acquired the farm for £1,270,000 in January 2003.

The Farmhouse

The present farmhouse dates from the 1870s, being described in sale particulars of 1878 as 'modern' with 'newly erected' farm buildings. E.L.G. Robinson had it built on a new site on the north side of the road to replace the former farmhouse, marked on the tithe map of 1842 in the south-east corner of the farmstead. In plan the earlier house was cross-shaped but no picture of it has been traced though it is said, not unreasonably, to have been timber-framed.[7]

A story that this old house was burnt down in about 1850 is questionable. The census returns between 1851 and 1871 record the large household of the Proberts, their indoor servants and agricultural labourers remaining together, apparently undisturbed, in the farmhouse. In 1851 John and Selina Probert and their five young children, maidservant and four farm workers were living there. In 1861 their eldest daughter was no longer at home but another young girl had been born and the household remained the same size. By 1871 Selina had been left a widow but her two sons, John and William and one daughter, Clara, were still at home, together with a maidservant, a groom, a farm labourer and a 12-year-old farm servant, Edwin Helmes from St Margaret's. If there *was* a fire, the old house clearly remained habitable. It is perhaps more likely that a fire occurred at the beginning of the 1870s, leading directly to the construction of the new house.[8] It is, however, equally likely that E.L.G. Robinson built it as part of his investment in the Golden Valley Railway. In that case he would have been disappointed that in the midst of the farming depression he was unsuccessful in putting the estate on the market in 1878.

The surviving mid-Victorian house is of substantial brick construction under a clay tile roof with ornamental ridge tiles. The elevations were rendered soon after William Watkins's death in 1955 but the rendering was removed in 2006-07, exposing the weathered brick beneath, with its bands of patterned brickwork.[9] There is an attractive partly glazed brick and tile porch to the south facing front door. The house stands tall, the ground floor rooms with high ceilings, kitchen, pantry and dairy with flagstone floor, a large cellar, galleried landings and two staircases leading to the three first-floor and two second-floor bedrooms, tank room and bathroom. Electricity was installed in 1952.

Rose Cottage, an early 17th-century house across the road just beyond the farm buildings, was bought by William Watkins for his farm bailiff or another worker and remains part of the farm. Its history is described separately later (see pp.39-43).

The Farm Buildings
The Watkins family believed that the new farmhouse, which was only about 25 years old when they went to live in it, had been built on the new site across the road in order to separate it from the noise and dirt of the farmyard. Around the yard is a conglomeration of buildings which were extended over the centuries, several of the extensions dating from about the same time as the new farmhouse but, owing to the conservatism of Nancy and Rene Watkins, modern stock sheds are notably lacking.

In 1842 there were only the two great barns standing parallel on either side of the yard with the old farmhouse in a far corner. The older of the two is the traditional timber-framed barn along the roadside (90ft x 24ft). This is listed as a Grade 2 building of architectural and historical interest, probably originally of four bays dating from the early or mid 17th century, which would make it the oldest building in the parish apart from the church; some of the framing panels retain the original cleft oak wattle infilling. The eastern bay was later rebuilt in brick and an extra bay, and then two further timber-framed bays, were added as a stable to the east end of the barn in the late 18th or early 19th century. There is a 19th-century shelter shed with feeding racks attached to the south wall. The roof is now covered in 20th-century asbestos sheeting.[10]

Across the yard the large four-bay stone barn (55ft x 24ft) with lean-to additions is also listed Grade 2 and dates from the late 18th century. There is a stone threshing floor with brick 'dwarf' walls on either side supporting central and raking shores from sill to tie beam. The steeply pitched roof, covered in 20th-century asbestos sheeting, has collar beam and queen struts. The north doors allowed draught adjustments when flail threshing, and space below for a 'lift' (a planked barrier confining

the crop on the floor during threshing, and allowing the doors to open above accumu-
lated manure in the yard). The western gable end was rebuilt to a high standard using
traditional materials in 2007-8. At its eastern end is a much altered timber-framed
former stable with wattle panels, the footings of which extended farther east. It is
marked on the tithe map but contrary to Rene Watkins's belief this is not the site of
the old farmhouse, which is clearly marked on the 1842 tithe map several yards to the
south-east.[11] Old timbers from the house may well have been re-used in building or
repairing the stables.

All the other farm buildings are of a later date and, with the exception of the early
19th-century privy standing close to the site of the original farmhouse, most of them
are associated with the reconstruction of the whole farmstead and new farmhouse
in the period shortly before 1878. Within the farmyard these comprise a long range
containing a brick stable and building to house the chaise with hay loft above, an
eight-bay open-fronted cattle shed with feeding passage, and a further stable with loft
above. A small freestanding brick stable lies to its south.

Close to the new house stands an open fronted wainhouse with granary above (40
ft x 30ft), brick-built with a slate roof and of the same date as the farmhouse. The
wainhouse or waggon lodge consists of three open-fronted bays and a fourth enclosed
bay with doors to form a garage. There are external brick and stone steps to the four-
bay granary above, having five bins with low two-plank high partitions. The floor is
supported by stout posts with long 'jowls'. Nearby, behind the house are two brick
pigsties built between 1878 and 1886.

The only important more recent addition to the farm buildings is a six-bay Dutch
barn (known in Herefordshire as a 'French' barn), which dates from the mid 20th

Fig. 17 Turnastone Court c.1960 (Watkins)

century and was supplied by Dales of Leominster. It is constructed with steel stanchions, timber tie-beams, and steel king rods under a curved galvanised corrugated iron roof, with three metal ventilators. Large lean-tos with fibre cement roofs were added to both sides of the barn in 2008.

The future of both the farmhouse and the farm buildings is uncertain. In the autumn 2009 issue of *The Lark,* the newsletter of the Countryside Restoration Trust, the Trust announced that it was planning over the next two years to sell the Victorian farmhouse, and convert the stone barn into a new farmhouse and other farm buildings into a shop, education centre, Forest Farm School and accommodation for visitors. At the time of writing no decision has been reached, but such developments to such a prominent site will clearly have considerable effects on the appearance and life of both the farm and the village.

Land Use Past and Present

Turnastone Court is a rare surviving example of a Herefordshire mixed farm which has continued to be farmed by traditional methods, without resorting to the use of chemical fertilisers, herbicides and pesticides. The extensive meadow and pasture support stock-rearing, with enough arable to provide grain and roots for feed and, at least up to fifty years ago, for sale. The records show how this area of arable land has steadily declined over the last two hundred years, due to external, even global, pressures and the decisions of the Probert and Watkins families.

The earliest survey of the farm dates from 1812 when it consisted of 204 acres, of which about 48 acres were part of the meadows stretching into Vowchurch parish. There were still 37 acres of woodland on Turnastone Hill, but in the following 30 years the trees were cleared, probably to supply fuel for the lime kiln nearby, fed on limestone from the quarry that has left humps and hollows on the hillside. By 1842 the wood had been converted to a new pattern of fields of rough pasture and arable. Elsewhere there were a few changes in the field boundaries during that period, and the hopyard near the farmstead was given over to orchard.

The tithe apportionment and map of 1842 clearly shows for the first time the field numbers, names and areas of the farmland, and whether they were arable, pasture/meadow or woodland. The total area had been increased to 233 acres of which 95 acres were arable, 127 acres grassland and 11 rough pasture. The late 19th-century agricultural depression, partly caused by imports of grain from North America, was met by a further conversion of arable to grazing and the marked reduction in the rent, already mentioned, from £355 a year in 1878 to £246 in 1912. By then, when the farm was sold by the Robinsons of the Poston estate, only about 60 of its recorded 256 acres were scheduled as arable.

The Ministry of Agriculture and Fisheries (MAF) census return dated 4 June 1941 provides a fascinating snapshot of the farm during the Second World War.[12] In addition to the Watkins family, three full-time male workers over the age of 21 were employed. There was one Fordson tractor and four working horses. There were 21 milking cows, a bull and 73 beef cattle; 2 rams, 74 breeding ewes, 71 lambs, and

60 young ewes and other sheep; a breeding sow and 17 young pigs; 250 chickens, 29 geese and 13 ducks. The cropping in 1941 was 181 acres of pasture, 6 acres of orchard, and 64 acres of arable (27 of wheat, 20 of oats, eight of barley, four of potatoes, three of turnips and swedes, and two acres of mangolds).

In order to increase wartime food production grassland was ploughed up under the War Agricultural Committee's directions for growing arable crops. The tale that William Watkins successfully refused to accept these directions is unfounded. Members of the Watkins family who worked with him after the war affirm that such an attitude would have been out of character. More irrefutable, the MAF census recorded in 1941 that 26 acres of grass fields were ploughed as requested. These were the part of the former Turnastone Hill Wood and Seven Acres, which had been arable in 1842, and the Upper and Lower Cross Field which were partly meadow in 1842.[13] The claim that the meadows have never been ploughed is similarly suspect. The only meadows on the farm that can be said with some certainty not to have been ploughed since 1800 are Turnastone Meadow and Bridge Meadow alongside the bank of the river Dore, the Long Meadow in Turnastone and West Meadow (Weethes Meadow 1842) in Vowchurch. Of the rest, nearly all the fields north of the road to Michaelchurch were arable in 1842 and the aerial photograph of the Eskleyside Ploughing Match on 3 October 1947 indicates that much of that same land was under the plough then. Faint traces of ridge and furrow are recalled on the rising ground of Turnastone Hill. Weethes (or Weiths) Orles was ploughed and combined in the 1950s.[14] In the last fifty years, though, the area of grassland has been increased further so that by 2001, when the total area was 247 acres, the arable area had fallen to just 18 acres.

After the war the family's fine herd of nearly 100 pure bred Hereford suckler cows continued to produce prize-winning store cattle. They also had a flock of Clun Forest

Fig. 18 Ploughing match at Turnastone Court 1947 (Watkins)

sheep. All their livestock was home-bred and fed entirely on grass or hay produced on the farm. Basic slag was rotationally applied to the grassland until the mid 1980s, but farmyard manure and the occasional application of lime were the only fertilisers used.

The delays in the sale of the farm in 2000-2003 broke the continuity in the life of the farm and the new owners, the Countryside Restoration Trust (CRT), had to make a fresh start. As a farming and conservation charity the Trust has the bold aim to protect and restore Britain's unspoilt countryside through commercially viable and wildlife friendly land management. Founded in 1991 it is committed to promoting the importance of a living and working countryside, and to this end has acquired several farms which, by utilising sensitive farming methods, demonstrate the production of high-quality seasonal food alongside the conservation of wildlife in order to preserve our countryside for future generations.[15]

In late 2003 Robert and Chrissy Fraser, who had little previous farming experience, were granted a 10-year Farm Business Tenancy by the Trust. Living in Rose Cottage with their two children, Gus and Grace, they are farming according to the CRT's principles. In 2009 their stocking was a breeding flock of 142 ewes (74 Ryelands and 68 Shropshires), 5 rams, 45 Hereford single suckler cows and 4 Gloucesters, 7 Berkshire and 4 Tamworth breeding sows and one Tamworth boar, and a mixed bunch of approximately 50 free-range chickens kept for egg production. To market their produce and that of other local suppliers the Frasers for a time in 2008-09 ran a farm shop at Poston Mill Caravan Park in Vowchurch. They also operate a local delivery service and a monthly 'meat box' scheme, and participate in the monthly Country Market at Vowchurch Memorial Hall and farmers' markets elsewhere. They currently use a self-employed contractor, Stuart Thorpe, to assist them with work on the farm, with Chrissy Fraser's mother Liz March and her partner David Phillips helping with jobs around the farm and farm shop.

About six volunteer working party days take place during the year for CRT members to assist with fencing, bank-side coppicing, planting new orchards and hedges, and various ongoing conservation projects on the farm. There are also occasional farm walks and 'open' days. In September 2008 the farm hosted the sheepdog trials, hedge-laying competition, produce and livestock sections of the Eskleyside Agricultural Society's annual show, and in October 2009 hosted the National Hedgelaying Society's annual championships, held in Herefordshire for the first time in over 50 years and attracting some 140 competitors from all over England and Wales.

An unexpected threat to the farmland arose with plans for a national-grid gas pipeline to run from Milford Haven in Wales to Tirley in Gloucestershire. The CRT opposed the proposed route of the pipeline, owing to the damage it would cause to the water meadows, and after negotiation the route was altered to avoid the most sensitive areas. The large diameter high pressure gas main was eventually swiftly laid beneath only a small southern portion of the farm during the summer of 2007 and today the scar is marked by little more than some lengths of clean fencing to protect newly planted hedging.

5   VILLAGE HOUSES (EAST)

ROSE COTTAGE
Cynthia Comyn

Rose Cottage, sometimes called Church Cottages, has been owned with Turnastone Court since the early 20th century.[1] It was described by the Royal Commission on Historical Monuments in 1933 as

> Cottage on the S side of the road 40 yards SE of the church is of one storey with attics; the walls are timber-framed and partly refaced with brick; the roofs are covered with stone slates. It was built in the 17th century. There is a stone chimney stack at the N end. Inside the building are some exposed ceiling beams.

The interior of the cottage has been described by Margaret Disley née Woodhouse, who lived there as a child from 1953. The kitchen (16ft x 11ft 3ins) was entered from a door on the front path and had a pump in one corner. Above the kitchen

Fig. 19 Rose Cottage 2009

Fig. 20 Rose Cottage interior c.1930 (Mrs C.J.F. Comyn)

was a bedroom to which the only access was gained by a staircase shut off from the kitchen by a door; this room was cut off from the rest of the house. Next to the kitchen was a rather low ceilinged room which was very damp – things left in there for any length of time would begin to grow mould. Beyond that was the main sitting room (16ft x 12ft), which had not changed a great deal since the photograph (see Fig. 20, above) was taken about 1930.[2] Between the middle and sitting rooms was an enclosed staircase leading to the bedrooms – during the Woodhouses' tenancy Mr and Mrs Woodhouse slept in the room over the centre of the house while their four children used the end room. Later on, the girls moved into the room over the kitchen leaving the two boys to themselves.

Margaret Disley also remembers that Rose Cottage already had electric light – something they had not had in their previous home in Kingstone. Their water came from a well near the front path and from a pump in the kitchen. There was no internal sanitation but a privy was sited at the end of the garden. Nowadays, the accommodation on the upper floor consists of two bedrooms with limited head-room and a bathroom.

The cottage is Listed Grade II, in greater detail as:

Probably late C17 to early C18 with later extensions. Timber-frame, partly cased in brick, brick extension, stone slate roof, external stack with bread oven and detached brick shaft to north gable end. Two-bay,

2-cell cottage extended one bay south in mid C19. One storey and attic. East elevation, rebuilt in brick has two 2-light early C20 metal casements under segmental heads, one either side of entry; door to C19 brick extension is contemporary with it and ledged. First floor has wide gabled dormer with 4-light metal early C20 casements to left of main entry. Rear elevation to west is timber-framed; C19 part has mock framing painted on brickwork. Frame is 3 panels high from low cill to wall-plate; two symmetrically placed C20 2-light metal casements under timber weatherings to ground. North gable has heavily jowled post to north-west corner.'[3]

Several building alterations have taken place recently – one before the tenancy of Marcus Lloyd (1996) and another on the arrival of the present tenants Robert and Chrissy Fraser in 2003. The chimney at the end nearest the road has been rebuilt, once during the tenancy of the Woodhouse family *c.*1970 and most recently since 2003, but not according to its previous three-stepped pattern despite the building's listed status.

The owner of the cottage in 1842 was William Seward Wood (1793-1862), who had inherited the Whitehouse estate in 1833. It seems likely that Rose Cottage had been part of the estate prior to that date as the tenant from about 1827 was David Lewis, a carpenter, who was almost certainly employed by the Woods. He had been born in about 1790 in Michaelchurch Escley where he married his wife, Hannah Williams, in 1819. Of their children the first to be baptised at Turnastone was James Lewis in 1827. David, who was parish clerk,[4] died in 1859 but his widow continued to live in Rose Cottage until her own death in 1871. For a short period in David Lewis's lifetime, a minister of the local Primitive Methodist chapel, Thomas Hall from Little Hereford and his newly married wife Mary (probably née Lawrence from Kingsland), apparently also lived in Rose Cottage. Thomas Hall filled in the 1851 ecclesiastical census of his congregations for each of the parishes of Turnastone, Vowchurch, Peterchurch and St Margaret's but like all those in the local nonconformist ministry, seems to have been moved on fairly quickly. He was in Cheshire in 1856, in Staffordshire in 1858 and by 1861 he was described as a City Missionary living in Marylebone, London.

The next tenant after Hannah Lewis was Thomas Williams, also a carpenter, who had been living in the Whitehouse estate's cottage at Ladywell with his first wife Frances Jenkins. She was almost certainly a servant at Whitehouse, one of her children being named Alice Herberta after Mr and Mrs Wood, and her family had been long-term tenants at Ladywell. After she died in 1873 it seems likely that Thomas and his two children soon moved down to the carpenter's accommodation at Rose Cottage where they were listed as living in the 1881 census. He might in fact have been obliged to move if Ladywell Cottage was needed to accommodate a tenant with a wife who could work at Whitehouse. In 1882 Thomas Williams married Jane, the widow of James Cornelius Morgan, a miller at Poston Mill, who had died in 1872 aged only 41. The Morgans with five children had been living at The Villa in 1871 but on Jane's remarriage she moved into Rose Cottage with Thomas where they lived for a further twenty years. They had probably been replaced soon after the 1891 census by George Jones and his wife Jane, née Lewis.[5] The Jones family had come from St Margaret's with four children but a fifth, John, was apparently born at Turnastone in 1892 and in 1901 they were living at Rose Cottage, then sometimes referred to as Church Cottages. George Jones was described as a waggoner and possibly worked at Turnastone Farm though more probably he was employed by William Wood. The Joneses were still there in 1924 but both he and his wife died that year.

At about that time, William Watkins of Turnastone Court bought the cottage from the Whitehouse estate, possibly on the death of Herbert Howarth Wood in 1924. In that case his first chosen tenants were George and Caroline Cole, already in their 70s when they came to Rose Cottage about 1925 and both dying four years later. Horace Dyde was listed as living in the cottage next in 1930, a labourer who had married Myfanwy Jones, a schoolmistress, in 1926. They began their married life at Slough Cottage, but were at Rose Cottage from 1930 to 1938; they had left by 1946 when the house appears to have been empty. The next two known tenants did not stay long, William and Elizabeth Weaver occur in 1948 and Charles Lewis, a labourer, with his wife Nellie and seven children, was the tenant from about 1950 to 1952.

In March 1953, Percy and Catherine Woodhouse became the next tenants. Mr Woodhouse was born in Bishops Frome in 1909 and came to Thruxton to work for Edward Lloyd, father of W.E.V. (Verdi) Lloyd.[6] Soon after 1944 he and his wife moved to Kingstone to work for a family at Dunswater before coming to Turnastone Court to work for William Watkins. Mrs Woodhouse helped in the farm-house and also cleaned the church. They had four children all born before the move to Turnastone – Patricia Mary (Mrs Sidney Gardner of Peterchurch), Margaret Ann (Mrs George Disley of Peterchurch). William John (unmarried) and Jeffrey Charles. Percy Woodhouse retired in about 1974, when he and his wife moved to Peterchurch; she died in 1989, and Percy in 1991.

Margaret and her sister Mary were already pupils at Kingstone School when they came to Turnastone in 1953. Mary went up to Fairfield school in Peterchurch while Margaret used to catch the bus down to Kingstone each morning. However, when John reached school age, he was enrolled at Vowchurch school and Margaret was moved there too. All the

Fig. 21 Woodhouse and Disley families 1969
(Mrs G. Disley)

42

children eventually went on to Fairfield joining Mary. Margaret remembers how the walk to Vowchurch school could be hazardous as they had to negotiate the Watkins's sheep-dog which lay in wait for them and would attempt to round them up. Another terror was the fear of the geese which roamed loose in the farmyard and would dart out hissing loudly when they spotted the children. Most frightening of all perhaps was Miss Robinson, who lodged at the Old Rectory and would flit around the churchyard in her nightclothes at dusk.

Among the later tenants, Marcus Lloyd is one of the sons of Lindsey and Barbara Lloyd of Abbey Dore; he came as a young bachelor and was so exceptionally hard-working and efficient that most of his farm work was completed by lunch time, and in the afternoons and early evenings he ran a mobile fish-and-chip van. This became so popular that not long after his marriage he gave up his labouring job, moved back to Abbey Dore and now runs his own business full time.

c.1827-1842	David Lewis	Carpenter	
1851	David Lewis	Carpenter	Had Thomas Hall, Methodist minister, as a lodger
1859-1871	Hannah Lewis	Widow of David Lewis	
1881-1892	Thomas Williams	Carpenter	He had come from Ladywell Cottage
1892-1924	George Jones	Waggoner	
1925-1929	George Cole		
1930-1938	Horace Dyde	Labourer	
1948	William Weaver		
1950-1952	Charles Lewis	Labourer	
1953-1974	Percy Woodhouse	Farm labourer	
c.1990	Raymond Davies	Farm labourer	From the family at The Stensley, Peterchurch
c.1992-1995	Robert Turner		
1996	Marcus Lloyd		From Abbey Dore
1997/8	Les Attwood		
	Martin Lawrence		Had a family of three children
c.2000-2001	Paul Smith		Labourer at Turnastone
2003	Robert and Chrissie Fraser		Tenants of the Countryside Restoration Trust

GLENDORE (THE SHOP)
Sylvia Teakle

On the roadside between two right-angled corners in the centre of the village stands a dwelling which is Turnastone's most striking landmark. Now a shop with old fashioned 1950s Avery Hardoll petrol pumps, it is quoted whenever directions are given to destinations beyond Turnastone – 'you turn off at Vowchurch Turn, pass two churches, pass the petrol pumps and ...' The dwelling is brick-built, probably early 19th-century, with a stout decorative front door, slate roof and a small 'Gothick' window upstairs similar to windows at Brook Cottage next door, made in imitation of the extension to Whitehouse which was erected in about 1812-13. The accommodation consists of shop, sitting room, dairy and scullery downstairs, and two double bedrooms, landing and storeroom upstairs. This is comparatively large for the period and it is said that it was once an inn called the Coach and Horses.[7]

It is likely that the property is the unnamed 'cottage or dwelling house' in Turnastone which in 1800 was mortgaged by Benjamin James, a sawyer whose father had lived in the house, to William and Samuel Davis, husbandmen (tenant farmers).[8] Forty years later in 1841, when it had probably been rebuilt, the property was owned by a William Davies, who could be the same person but more certainly was also the owner of Brook Cottages. It appears that at that time the house was divided in some way because it was occupied by William Turner, an agricultural worker, and his wife and two children, together with Mary and Frances Davies who had a separate household on the same site. In the following year a William Jones occupied the section previously held by the Davies sisters and in 1851 the house was apparently still divided between George Jones, a miller aged 36, and his wife Frances, probably the Frances Davies living there in 1841, and William Davies, an agricultural labourer, who may have been the owner. In 1861 Benjamin Lloyd or Loyd was living there with his wife Mary Ann and their daughter Dinah, who on the day of the census was apparently staying at The Rectory as a dressmaker.

In 1871 the house was empty. Five years later James Christopher, a wheelwright, and his wife Ann were living there, and by 1881 the property was described as a shop with the shopkeeper being Ann Christopher, James's widow, together with her daughter Mary Ann and a visitor, one Charles Hatton. Another part of the house was occupied by two unmarried brothers with the local name of Mapp. The frequent changes continued. In 1891 the property was occupied by Robert Brown, a shepherd, and his family, and in 1901 by John Griffin, a miller, and his wife and baby daughter aged five months.

The ownership of the house in the fifty years since the time of the Davies family has not been traced, but it is probable that like other village houses it came to belong to Whitehouse estate. Then some time in the early 20th century, most likely after he had acquired Turnastone Court in 1912, the property, together with Brook Cottages, was bought by William Watkins for the sum of £150.

The tenant from 1907 was James Charles Wilding (always known as 'Charlie'), who had married Zipporah Lockley in 1899. Although her father was from Liverpool she came to live with her maternal grandparents at the Slough forge and attended Vowchurch School. After she and Charlie married they lived at Corgum on Vowchurch Common, a house that has now been demolished. Charlie and Zipporah set up business at the shop in Turnastone, but were somewhat restricted because of the existing shop at Brook Cottages. And so began the connection between his family and the shop that continues to this day.

Initially Charlie was a builder, carpenter, motor mechanic and cycle repairer, but being self-taught he would turn his hand to anything. He made his own 'cat's whisker' wireless set and it is told that he rebuilt Cwmddu, a cottage at Vowchurch, in six weeks with the help of a plasterer who could only work when he was drunk and then was so fast that it took three labourers to keep him supplied with material. Charlie's carpentry work included making coffins, and one of his best customers was the Dore Poor Law Union. The cost of a coffin about 1930 was £5 delivered anywhere in the area.

In 1921 Charlie was granted a licence to store petrol in two-gallon drums and in 1927 a licence for the installation of a petrol pump and 500-gallon tank. It is believed that about this time he started to call the business 'West End Garage'. In the 1930s Randolph Trafford of Michaelchurch Court would land his Gipsy Moth biplane in the field opposite the rectory, and the Wildings refuelled it by lugging cans with 28 gallons of fuel from the shop over to the aircraft – but Trafford insisted on filtering it into the tank himself.[9] There can be few garages in the country that have been run by the same family for over a hundred years, and that can claim that they have fuelled aircraft. Charlie added motorcycle and wireless repairs to his list of occupations, along with insurance agent, tobacconist, newsagent, coal merchant and clerk to Vowchurch Parish Council. In 1917 he became an agent for Raleigh bicycles and sold Hercules bikes on hire-purchase for two shillings and sixpence per week. In 1937 he was given a silver plaque by Raleigh, now fixed on the front door, to commemorate his twenty years' unbroken service, and the Raleigh sign still on the front of the house dates back to those days.

Charlie died in 1948 at the age of 78. Zipporah had predeceased him by 28 years, dying in 1920 at the age of 41 just five days after the birth of a daughter, Doreen. There were ten surviving children – five boys and five girls. All the girls, with the

Fig. 22 Hedley Wilding refuelling Gipsy Moth c.1930
(Ewyas Lacy Study Group and Baxendale family)

45

Fig. 23 Mary Wilding in the shop 1958
(Hereford Evening News, courtesy of
Hereford Times)

exception of Doreen, moved away from Herefordshire when they married. Doreen lived on Vowchurch Common and married Eric Lewis, a long-serving parish, district and county councillor. Of the boys, Rowland had been a prisoner of war in World War I and died in 1957 aged 58, Arthur Trevor lived for some time at the Old Rectory, moved in 1960 to Sutton St. Nicholas and died in 1973 aged 67, and Raymond lived at Thruxton where he and his wife Betty had a shop and post office. Percy and Hedley remained in Turnastone working in the business until Hedley went into the army in 1940.

Hedley Hensley Wilding joined the King's Shropshire Light Infantry in 1940. He became a Lance Corporal Instructor and taught men to drive Heavy Goods Vehicles and Bren gun carriers before transfer to the Royal Electrical and Mechanical Engineers. He saw service with anti-aircraft batteries in Norfolk and eventually ended his service in Germany before being demobilised in 1946. He had already in 1940 married Mary Jones of Garway, whose grandfather Private Robert Jones won a VC at Rorkes Drift in 1879 whilst serving with the South Wales Borderers during the Zulu War. Mary stayed in Garway during Hedley's war service but once he was back home they moved to Turnastone with their three children, Rosemary Ann, Diana and Robert to join Percy at the shop. In 1949 the post office was closed at Vowchurch and its business was transferred to Turnastone with Mary as postmistress. Hedley and Percy ran the workshop at the back of the Rectory until 1950 when Hedley bought Commerce House in Vowchurch with a view to having larger premises (see Fig. 63). Two more children were born – Michael in 1952 and Hedley junior in 1962.

The business continued to encompass everything – taxi service, motor repairs of all kinds and the tiny shop. Mary stocked most groceries and if what you wanted wasn't in stock it would only be a few hours before she would get it for you. The petrol sales flourished and in 1960 Hedley bought the disused Primitive Methodist Chapel in Vowchurch from Jack Bowyer of Peterchurch. As Trevor Wilding had put the rectory up for sale, the brothers had to move their workshop from there, and the redundant chapel, after some necessary alterations, suited their purpose well. Looking back, Roger Colling of Thruxton spoke at Hedley's funeral:

> There are local tales of engines being hoisted out of cars with the winch tied to an apple tree bough. The orchard was full of gear boxes and cider apples; of back axles and beehives; of wheels and washing on the line. The little place hummed 18 hours a day with little rest except for Sundays.

Fig. 24 Brook Cottage and petrol pumps at the shop

And Sundays, his son Robert remembers, meant church at Turnastone in the morning and Sunday school at Vowchurch in the afternoon.

In later years Mary, Hedley and Percy got involved in all sorts of committees. Hedley was churchwarden at Turnastone for 39 years, a parish councillor, member of the Vowchurch and Turnastone Hall Management Committee, and member of the Vowchurch Sports Committee. Mary served on the Parochial Church Council, was at one time president of Peterchurch Women's Institute, was on the Hall Committee, Sports Committee and involved with the organisation of the "Vowchurch Ball". Nothing was too much trouble for her and she was a true friend with a great sense of humour. From personal experience my Saturday afternoon shopping sprees at the shop would take a couple of hours whilst we jawed and Mary sliced the bacon, chopped off a lump of cheese, found some windfall apples for a pie for the next day, and so on. It was both an experience and a pleasure.

In 1996-7 they were in danger of losing the petrol pumps, as the Fire Authority considered them to be too near the highway and for safety reasons ordered them to be closed and the tanks filled in. With the help of Roger Collings, a past President of the Vintage Sports Car Club, a petition was organised and signed by nearly 1,000 people. At the appeal in Hereford, after a day of furious argument and opposed by half a dozen barristers and lawyers, Hedley's personal appeal was upheld by the inspector, who congratulated him and his team, and ruled that the pumps should remain and that petrol should continue to be sold in gallons, not litres, a ruling that exists to this day.

Mary was taken ill and eventually died in 1985. Hedley and Robert carried on with the business, Hedley getting more and more frail and bent with arthritis, but we still could have a good giggle and his mind had total recall – he remembered everything – every car anybody had ever bought from him, the year and how much is cost. Who bought every house in the area and how much they paid for it. How old everybody was and most of the birthday months – it was incredible! He eventually died in February 2008 in the bedroom in which he had been born ninety years before.

His son Robert, who lives on Vowchurch Common, carries on the tradition, runs the shop and repairs vehicles at the converted chapel.

Fig. 25 Robert Wilding at the shop 2009

BROOK COTTAGES
Cynthia Comyn

The two Brook Cottages were converted into a single house in about 1990. Soon after then their Grade II listing describes them:[10]

> House – early 19th century, extended later 19th century. Painted stone rubble with dressed stone quoins. Concrete tile roof with gabled ends. Stone central axial stack, rebuilt at top in brick; brick gable-end stack to later range. PLAN: Original house 2-room plan with lobby entrance in front of central axial stack with back-to-back fireplaces. Later 19th-century rear outshut and parallel range at rear projecting at south end, possibly added as separate cottage but now one house.
> EXTERIOR: 2 storeys. Symmetrical 3-bay east front; centre first floor blind; windows and doorway have four-centred arches, the 2-light windows with iron casements and Y-bars. The doorway has flush-panel double doors and similar Gothick fanlight with Y-bars. Later range set back on left has similar Gothick window on first floor and, below, a casement with cambered arch and French casement to right. Rear [W], main roof is carried down as catslide over outshut and 2-storey gable-ended parallel range to right. INTERIOR: not inspected.

It is not known exactly when these cottages were built but a building on the site is marked on the drawings made in 1814-15 for the first Ordnance Survey one-inch to one-mile map and they were shown at a larger scale on the tithe map of 1842. The rather charming Gothick windows on the frontage facing Glendore Shop resemble those of the shop itself. It is likely that they deliberately imitate the windows of the Strawberry Hill Gothick wing of Whitehouse built in 1812-13.

The cottage nearer the road (No.1) may originally have had only two rooms on each floor whilst the other smaller section (No.2) was of only two rooms in all. A later rear outshut was added to No.1, almost doubling the accommodation, but the second cottage remained small and during Mrs Naylor's occupation c.1974 consisted only of two rooms with a kitchen situated in a lean-to at the far end of the building.

No.1 had a door onto the road, bricked up by the Patience family in the 1990s after several floods, but still visible; the main door leads onto the garden, facing the side of the Shop. No. 2 was entered through the lean-to but also had a garden door.

When David and Caroline Phillips lived in No.1 (c.1985-87), the garden entrance was the door used. It opened onto a tiny hallway with a door at right angles on each side of the entrance. The right hand door led into a small room in which Mrs Phillips had installed a little manual printing press on which she produced cards, programmes and tickets for local events. The left hand doorway led into a small sitting room (with a fireplace and Victorian grate) from which there was a door into the passage and then to the kitchen at the rear of the house. The passage led off to the right and gave access to the ground-floor bathroom, a hallway with the door onto the road and to a staircase (which was in a rather parlous state) leading to the three or four rooms above.

Each cottage had had a privy in the garden but by about 1970, No.1 could boast internal sanitation, with an 'Elsan' cabinet sited just inside the road-side door. By the time that David and Caroline Phillips moved in fifteen years later, there was a bathroom in place of the 'Elsan' closet but the water supply was rather temperamental as it was shared with that of the Cross House. If a tap was run in the latter, the supply to No.1 would cease until the Cross House tanks had refilled – often leaving someone stranded in a rapidly cooling bath or with unrinsed hair.

At the time of the tithe apportionment in 1842 both cottages were owned by a William Davis (or Davies) who appears also to have owned the house that is now the shop. He was the occupier of No.1, but it is difficult to be sure of his identity as the census of 1851 describes the occupant of that name as an agricultural labourer, which seems an unlikely occupation for a man of considerable property. In general, until about 1966, the cottages were occupied by agricultural labourers and their families with ownership held in the later 19th century by either the Poston or, more likely, Whitehouse estates. However, at some point and probably about 1920, they were acquired by William Watkins of Turnastone Court and he regularly used No.2 to house one of his farm workers.

The larger cottage was rented by John Jones and his wife Harriet from about 1880; he was a roadman or general labourer, born in 1849 in Blakemere and married in 1873 to Harriet Hughes in St Margaret's. Their early married life was spent in Clodock and then in Vowchurch, when John worked for a while at Shegear, and then they settled in Turnastone, where they spent the rest of their lives. They raised nine of the ten children born to them.[11] Their second son, George, enlisted in the South Wales Borderers and died in 1898 at Charata, Bengal aged 22, whilst their youngest child, William, was killed in France in 1918 aged 23 – the only one of the Turnastone men who enlisted in the Great War to die in action. Both are commemorated in Turnastone Church and the latter is also named on the War Memorial inside the church.

One of the Jones daughters, Harriet (Addie), married Arthur James Brookes who was born in Brilley, the son of Thomas Brookes, a labourer of Eardisley by his wife Julia Ann Skyrme of Vowchurch. Thomas Brookes's brother Edward was a farm servant at Vowchurch Court in 1881 and married Elizabeth Skyrme in 1883 in Vowchurch, so this local connection may explain how Arthur Brookes and his parents met their eventual spouses. Harriet Jones died in 1930 and John had left by 1932 when his daughter Harriet Brookes and her husband took over the tenancy until about 1966, when the family's occupancy of nearly ninety years came to an end.[12] For some time Mrs Brookes ran a little shop. According to her granddaughters, Mrs Jones and Mrs Woolhouse, this shop continued almost until Harriet's death and was sited in the front room nearest the road, in which there was a wooden counter over which she dispensed cigarettes, sweets and other household goods. It was only after her shop closed that the Wildings opened theirs.

Thereafter, as can be seen in the table below, tenants came and went. David and Caroline Phillips came from the Old Cider House on Vowchurch Common; David Phillips was a schoolmaster at several schools in turn while living in Turnastone, for the most part at Picklenash School, Newent. The Phillips would have liked to buy their cottage (the smaller half was then still occupied by Tom Manuel) but Miss Watkins refused to sell it, so eventually they moved away to Broad Oak. This was a considerable loss to the village as David Phillips used to play for the church service (and sing

Fig. 26 Tree felling outside Brook Cottage c.1930; J.C. Wilding on left (M. Jones)

encouragingly) every Sunday in Turnastone Church and sometimes in Vowchurch as well. Eventually in about 1990 Miss Watkins decided to sell up and the Patience family bought both cottages. It was at this point that the two were made into one house, the interior considerably re-modelled and the door onto the road bricked up.

Little is known about many of the tenants of the smaller cottage but we do know that James Griffiths and his wife Ann (Walters) had three children baptised in Turnastone, two of whom died young, and that James himself was killed while working in a quarry and was buried in Vowchurch in 1868 aged 67. It is not entirely clear why the family is called Griffiths alias Tanner but this style is sometimes given to a child whose surname has been changed, for instance when the mother marries again.

Arthur Challoner, born at Lydham in Shropshire, the son of an agricultural labourer; was a groom to the Revd Frederick Green, rector of Turnastone. In 1888 he married Martha Tipton of Leintwardine, who was a servant at the vicarage there, where the rector of Turnastone's father lived. Her sister Annie is named as a servant to the rector in Turnastone in 1891, so it seems likely that it was through Annie that Arthur met his future wife and came to live in Turnastone. The Challoners were living here, probably in the smaller of the two Brook Cottages, by 1889 when their only child, Annie Lilian, was born and they were still in the cottage in 1891. By 1901 they had moved to the Villa (now Yew Tree House, see pp.64-8).

William Brown is named here in 1911 when he is described as an agricultural labourer. He and his wife Susannah (née Watkins) had been married for ten years without a child. Although their household included a Thomas Watkins aged 11, described as Susannah's nephew, he may have been adopted by them as he appears in the registers of Vowchurch school as Thomas Watkins Brown.

Friedrich Marschall, known locally as 'Fred the German', had been serving in a tank regiment in North Africa in about 1941-2 when he was captured and brought to Britain. He was held in the prisoner-of-war camp at Hay-on-Wye and put to work as a farm labourer. He stayed on after the war, married a nurse in Llandrindod Wells and later came in 1953 with their two children, Erwin and Pauline, to work at Turnastone Court. Erwin (born 1951) retains clear memories of the two-bedroom cottage, its little living room and kitchen with an open fire and two side ovens and the outside toilet at the bottom of the garden. He writes 'I also remember that every time it rained the lane flooded and the only way out was by going through next door, where a very old man and his wife lived.' He went to the school and he and his friends played on the railway line and in the meadow where his father built them a

Fig. 27 Friedrich Marschall c.1940 (E. Marschall)

bridge over a waterfall in the Slough brook. A second daughter, Lillian, was born at Turnastone and four other children after they left here.[13]

Large Cottage (No.1)	Small Cottage (No.2)
1841 William Davis Owner & Occupier [from perhaps as early as 1800]	1841 James Griffiths *alias* Tanner 1851 Catherine Jones, widow
1851 William Davis 1861 ?William Davies 1871 ?Herbert Skyrme	1871 ?Mapps
1881 John & Harriet Jones	1881 Thomas and Sarah Ann Williams
1891 John & Harriet Jones	1891 Arthur and Martha Challoner
1901 John & Harriet Jones 1911 John & Harriet Jones 1932 Death of John Jones	1901 Ann Williams 1911 William and Susannah Brown 1930-38 Wm H. and Susannah M. Taylor
*c.*1932-67 Arthur Brookes and Addy (née Jones). He died 1973, she in 1975	1932 JW Ball with dau Gwendoline; left 1934 1938 John Stinton 1939 William and Ethel Blainey, John Stinton 1940 Gwendoline Margaret Lewis (later Mrs Robert H. Gwilliam) 1946 Robert H. and Gwendoline M. Gwilliam and Sarah A Davies 1946 John Jones and Marjorie (Neighbours) parents of Derek Jones, the baker's roundsman 1947 Cyril James Beavan 1948 Daisy and William G.H. Price *c.*1950 Andrew Groffner
1968 Peter Philip Beavan and his wife Ann Irene née Cook (niece of Eirlys Thomas of Slough Forge) *c.*1970 Mr and Mrs Malcolm Teece 1977,78 Carl and Jennifer Shutt	1952 Frederick and Lilian Dykes 1953-*c.*1957 Friedrich Wilhelm Marschall, his wife Betty Aline (née Watkins) and children *c.*1959 Bill ?Price (retired roadman) and family 1966 Denzil C and Dorothy J. Phillips *c.*1973 Lena Laura Naylor died 1978
1979 Mr and Mrs Colin Joy who were followed by his mother Florence; Mr Joy was then the butcher in Peterchurch 1984 Timothy and Davina (née Joy) Newton; she was the daughter of Mr and Mrs Colin Joy	1980 Thomas H. Manuel uncle of Mrs Colin Joy; died 1988
*c.*1985 David and Caroline Phillips 1989 Philip and Janet Price	1988 Philip & Janet Price
1990-1998 Iain and Janet Patience *c.*1990 Both cottages sold by Turnastone Court and remodelled into one house	*See opposite column*
1998 Steve and Debbie Leary	

6   VILLAGE HOUSES (WEST)

The Cross House
Cynthia Comyn

The Cross House, so named from the wooden cross in one of the panels in the timber framework at the front of the house, is the second of the only two dwellings in Turnastone mentioned by the Royal Commission on Historical Monuments in 1933.[1] It is described as

> House adjoining the Rectory, 50 yards SW of the church, is of one storey with attics; the walls are timber-framed and the roofs are covered with slates. It was built in the 17th century and has a larger modern house added. The timber-framing is exposed on the SW and SE. Inside the building, a room on the ground floor is lined with re-used early 17th-century panelling.

Construction
The house has three sections – a half-timbered black and white section, a stone and brick section and a modern brick one. The oldest part of the house, which may have been constructed late in the 17th century, is of two storeys (not one) and built of timber frames infilled with wattle and daub and roofed in stone tiles. In later years, the wattle and daub sections were faced with brick and painted white.

This building consisted of a long panelled downstairs room (now used as a drawing room) with a stone fireplace at each end and a curving staircase in one corner leading to a similar-sized space above, which had been divided into two interconnected rooms. Halfway up the staircase is a secondary set of stairs leading to a room over what is thought to have been the original kitchen at the opposite end of the house to the long room. Alongside the long room and at the rear of the house was a row of little interconnecting low-ceilinged rooms used for storage.

The house has been altered considerably. At some time, it appears there was a passage leading straight through the house from the front door to the rear onto which one of the long-room fireplaces and the kitchen fireplace (built of stone) with their attendant chimney stack both backed. It is still possible to discern signs of a filled-in doorway at the rear of the house but the passage itself is no longer accessible, which caused considerable difficulties when the house was re-wired in 2001. Neither of these fireplaces is now in use and one has been made into a cupboard.

The second section of the house consists of a stone and brick two-storey addition with a date stone of 1885 and the initials HHW (for Herbert Howarth Wood of Whitehouse). It is believed that the extension was built during the tenancy of one of the series of doctors who lived here *c*.1883-*c*.1901 and that the architect was one of the sons of the Wood family of Whitehouse. Although it provided two welcome extra rooms, this addition was hardly in keeping with the rest of the house. It was on a higher level and, as it had three outside walls, was extremely difficult to heat. Access to the upper room is by a staircase which is not connected to the rest of the house.

It is possible that one or two of the little rooms behind the long room were altered or enlarged at about this time as there is a late 19th- or early 20th-century photograph showing several lights in the low-leaning rear half of the roof and also a large and ornate French window at the end adjoining the Old Rectory. From some of the early 19th-century maps, it would appear that this house was joined to the Rectory and, whether or not this was the case, there is evidence of a bricked up doorway in the Rectory wall facing the end of this house.

Mrs R.A. Comyn bought the house in 1950 from Col R.G.R. Thompson, RA and some time later made considerable changes. During the First World War, she had suffered a car accident whilst driving officers behind the lines in France and in later life she became extremely lame. At one time, she had a pulley attached to the ceiling of the staircase and would swing herself up and down the stairs using a

Fig. 28 The Cross House from the rear (Mrs C.J.F. Comyn)

rope. It eventually became apparent, however, that she could no longer climb the spiral staircase to her bedroom in safety so, after several years of sleeping behind a curtain at one end of the drawing room, she embarked on a major reconstruction to convert the chain of small store rooms into a ground-floor bedroom, bathroom and larger store room. At the same time, most of the tiled roof at the rear was taken off and a modern section of brick was built on to create accommodation for a live-in nurse or companion above the newly remodelled rooms below.

At the same time, the two bedrooms above the long room were altered. The room nearer the stairs was walled off, making a passage to the further bedroom and new part of the house, and an airing cupboard was constructed. Mrs Comyn also made alterations to the kitchen. The door from the garden at the rear of the house had opened into a scullery and thence into the kitchen. A new brick kitchen was built onto the Victorian stone section, and the old kitchen became a morning room with a new external door and window opening onto the driveway at the side. The range (which had been in the position of one of the old fireplaces described earlier) was removed and the chimney closed off, an Aga was installed in the new kitchen, and a hatch was cut through the two-foot thick stone wall to the dining room. Mrs Comyn also added the porch at the front to cut down draughts.

Since her death in 1976, when the house was inherited by her son John Comyn, little building work has been undertaken apart from taking off the tiles at the front in 2000 to allow for roofing felt to be inserted and repairs to be carried out, some remedial work to exterminate dry rot in one of the storerooms and, in 2001, some long overdue re-wiring.

History
It is said that this house, which formed part of the Whitehouse estate until 1943, had originally been used as a dower house by the Howarth and Wood families when required. However, this seems unlikely. Not only is Whitehouse large enough for two households, while the original Cross House was modest in size, but for much of the 19th century at least, the Cross House was a public house. It was named the Red Cross Inn in the census of 1841 and it has therefore been assumed that it was the alehouse referred to in a receipt for rent to the Whitehouse estate in 1743.[2] The death in 1803 of a publican named James Matthews was described by a visitor to Turnastone, J.P. Malcolm:

> As the dying man's bedside is a scene for his relatives only, I chose to wait under the shelter of the church porch for my friend's return. The sexton in answer to my inquiries, said that 'John [sic] Mathews was a little koind of publican, as sold yeale [ale] and cyder'; and was an industrious well-disposed man; that he had a wife equally indus-trious, who was the mother of two children, one a year and a half, the other but three weeks of age. Fever seized Mathews, and a delirium followed. He now lay exhausted, quiet, and sensible.'[3]

Later publicans are listed in a volume of licensees dating back to 1818 as follows:

Date of Licence	Licensee	Surety
13 September 1819	Thomas Hancorn junr	Thomas Hancorn senr
4 September 1820	Do	Do
3 September 1821	Do	Do
18 September 1822	Do	Do
9 January 1823 (by certificate)	Matthew Gough	Charles Russell
8 September 1823	Charles Vaughan	Robert Davies, St Margaret's
6 September 1824	Do	Thomas Matthews
26 September 1825	Do	Matthew Gough, St Margaret's
18 September 1826	Do	John Davies
24 September 1827	Do	John Wilson, Vowchurch
30 September 1828	Do	John Lewis, Vowchurch
1833, perhaps 1835	Do	
1841 Census	John Wilson	Public House
1842 Tithe Map	William Garrett	Public House
1851 Census	William Garrett	Public House
1861 Census	William Garrett	Public House
1862 (June)	John Seaborne	Public House

Publicans and Tenants

Thomas Hancorn junior was the son of Thomas Hancorn senior (1764-1846), a member of the Peterchurch family now represented by Stephen Hancorn of Trenant Farm. Of the many Thomas Hancorns in that family's pedigree the licensee was almost certainly the Thomas Hancorn living in 1851 near the church in Vowchurch, born c.1793 in Peterchurch and a wood-dealer employing 10 men. His son John, born in Turnastone and then aged 27, was a carpenter employing one man. Thomas died in 1873 and John in 1903.

Charles Vaughan 'of Vowchurch' died in 1836 and in April 1837 his widow Margaret and their several children, then still living in Vowchurch, were the subjects of a poor law removal order quashed three months later.[4] She subsequently married Thomas Garrett of Peterchurch, whose brother William became the licensee of the Red Cross Inn c.1842.

John Wilson was a shopkeeper in Vowchurch where he had been born c.1814 and married in 1838. In 1851 they were living at Vowchurch Common when his wife Harriet was described as a schoolmistress. Both were still alive in 1891 when John was described as a farmer.

Compared with most Turnastone residents, Eli Edwards led an unsettled life. He was born in about 1841 at Penn Common, near Wolverhampton, the son of Timothy Edwards, a brickmaker, later turned grocer, and named with his parents and siblings in 1841 at Bishops Cleeve, Gloucestershire and in 1851 at Withington,

Plate 1 The meadows looking towards the Black Mountains

Plate 2 Walking the bounds at Dolward, looking east

Plate 3 The church

Plate 4 The Elizabethan mansion of Whitehouse

Plate 5 Poston House

Plate 6 The upland farms

Plate 7 18th-20th-century buildings at Turnastone Court

Plate 8 Hereford cattle at Turnastone Court (Watkins)

Plate 9 Farmhouse in 2009 after removing rendering

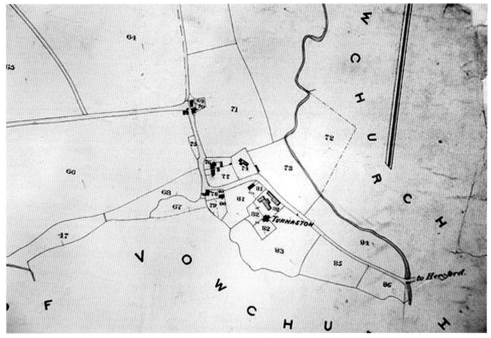

Plate 10 Turnastone village 1842 (HRO)

Plate 11 The Shop

Plate 12 Brook Cottage 2009

Plate 13 The Cross House

Plate 14 Yew Tree House (The Villa)

Plate 15 Whitehouse

Plate 16 Ladywell House 2009 (C.Drury)

Plate 17 Ladywell Cottage

near Hereford. In 1866, when he married Dinah Loyd of Vowchurch, he was a police officer and living in Turnastone, but was in Hoarwithy when his daughter was born in 1869. In the 1871 census he was named again in Turnastone, but as a coachman aged 30, apparently living with his family not in the former inn but probably in the coach-house in its garden, which has a small room with a fireplace and small range and two rooms above. If Eli was in fact the coachman at the Rectory, this might explain the doorway between the two properties. He and his family moved to Stockton-on-Teme, Worcestershire, c.1873 and by 1881 were in Clifton-on-Teme where he was again shown as a policeman aged (inaccurately) 38.

Later Occupants	Tenant/Owner	Occupation/Status
1871	Eli Edwards	Coachman
1881 Census	House empty	
1885	House extended	
1889 Medical Directory	Thomas Reuel Atkinson	Doctor
1890 Parish Register	Thomas Reuel Atkinson	Doctor
1891 Medical Directory	Edwd A.G. Dowling	Doctor
1892 Medical Directory	Edwd A.G. Dowling	Doctor
1895 Parish Register	Arthur Wm McMichael	Doctor
1901 Census	(McMichaels away from home)	Doctor
1902	Henry Percy Jones or Percy Jones Henry	
1905	House empty	
1911 - 1930	Miss Emma Chambers	Tenant
c.1932	Mr & Mrs T.G. Wood	of Whitehouse family
1938	Ernest Alfred Berry	Tenant
c.1939	William Stanley & Gladys Hellyer Heath	Tenant
1943 Sold by Whitehouse estate	Mrs Heath's Trustees	Owners
1947	Col R.G.R. Thompson, RA	Owner
1950	Mrs R.A. Comyn	Owner
1976	Mr J.R.G. Comyn	Owner

The Doctors[5]

According to the *Post Office Directory* of 1879, the nearest medical practitioners to the Golden Valley were David Evans of Kingstone, John Powell of Ewyas Harold and Charles Price and Leslie Thain of Longtown. In Turnastone the recent extension to the former alehouse in 1885 and the modernisation of the older timber-framed part had created a house to suit a professional family.

The local medical practice dates from about 1889 when Thomas Reuel Atkinson arrived in Turnastone.[6] Born in 1856, he trained at Guy's Hospital 1881-82, had been a ship's surgeon and became medical officer of health for the Madley area of the Rural Sanitary Authority from about 1885. He was married in Peterchurch by his wife's brother-in-law, the Revd Willis Lambert, the vicar there, in 1889 but soon after the birth of his eldest child in 1890 they moved away to Sherborne in Dorset and thence to Essex.

The next doctor here, Edward Dowling, also stayed for only a short time. Born in Kensington *c*.1865 he qualified as a medical practitioner in 1888 after training in London at St Bartholomew's Hospital. After about two or three years at Turnastone he was at Forest Hill, Oxfordshire by 1893 and in 1901 in Bristol as a dental surgeon rather than a general practitioner.

He was succeeded in about 1895 by Arthur William McMichael, born in 1869 when his father was a Baptist minister at Bourton-on-the-Water, Gloucestershire. He qualified as a medical practitioner in London in 1893 and after a short time at the Jaffray Hospital, Birmingham, married Mary Amelia Nott of Great Malvern in 1894 and set up home in Turnastone where their first child (George) Boraston McMichael was born the next year. Boraston was educated as a boarder at Lucton School where on his entry in 1909 it was noted that he suffered 'some weakness of heart and was not allowed violent exercise'. Nevertheless, he went on to serve in the First World War, then trained as a doctor and set up his own practice in Much Birch before succeeding his father at The Croft in Vowchurch, built in 1902.[7] As the doctor's family they were amongst the first to have a

Fig. 29 Dr A.W. McMichael (Miss M. McMichael)

telephone installed – their number at The Croft was originally 'Peterchurch 26'. Boraston McMichael's sister, Helen, is thought to have been the last child to live in The Cross House from a very early age until the births of Emily and Hugo Comyn in 1977 and 1980 respectively.[8]

Both father and son are remembered as caring and effective practitioners. Like other country doctors at that time Dr Arthur McMichael performed operations. When, as a boy, David Powell of Dolward fell beneath a timber carriage and crushed his foot the doctor reset it and got the local wheelwright to make a wooden support to fix the leg; the foot quickly mended. Because travel was difficult and country people were poor, the doctor was rarely called out and then he was often paid in kind with a piece of home-cured ham, a chicken or a saddle of lamb: an example of the self-sufficiency of the old community.

Miss Chambers & the Aultons

During the decade after the departure of the McMichaels, there were several tenants of whom little is known.[9] Then in about 1911, a Miss Emma Chambers moved in and lived here until her death in December 1930 aged 86. Over that period, the house was known as The Cottage or Turnastone Cottage.

For much of her life, Emma Chambers, born in 1844, lived with her elder sister Elizabeth, who had married first Thomas Aulton, a farmer at Whitbourne in north Herefordshire with whom she had eight children, and secondly John Cadle, her farm bailiff, when they all lived together in Staffordshire. One of her nephews, Frederick Aulton (1876-1934), married Constance Webb in 1906, and Constance's sister Dorothy, who was living at Turnastone Cottage by 1911, married Percy Wyatt Wood of Whitehouse in 1914. This provided the link between the Aulton family and Emma Chambers, herself still unmarried, and Turnastone and its neighbourhood. Until her death in 1930, Emma Chambers occupied the house, with a variety of nephews and nieces joining her at intervals. Her eldest niece, Emma Margaret (Maggie) Aulton (b.1871), became an artist and lived sometimes with her aunt and sometimes at Clatterbrook on the Peterchurch road. Emma's nephew, Frank Howard Aulton (b.1879), joined the South Staffordshire Regiment from which he retired with the rank of Lieutenant Colonel to live at Wellbrook Manor in Peterchurch. Another niece, Ethel Mary (b.1874), remained unmarried and shared the house with her aunt. Members of the family have signed the church visitors' book in 1976 and 1986.

After Miss Chambers's death, some of the Aultons possibly continued to live in the house for a few more years until Ernest Alfred Berry of Messrs Ratcliffe and Berry, corn merchants, leased it in about 1938. The following year Arthur Seward Wood and Percy Wyatt Wood, as trustees of the Whitehouse estate, leased the house to Mrs Gladys (Babs) Heath and her husband William Heath, a farmer from Blockley, Gloucestershire, until 1943, when the Woods sold it for £1,300 to Mrs Heath's trustees. She is said to have been a tennis champion and may be credited with having had a tennis court made both here and at Whitehouse, where they moved after selling Turnastone Cottage to Colonel R.G.R. Thompson of Grosmont for £3,300 in 1947. He sold it to Mrs R.A. Comyn for £3,650 in 1950.

Mrs Comyn (née Cecily Blanche Burney) bought the house to be near her widowed sister-in-law Dorothy (Mrs A.E.C) Burney, who lived at Hay. Mrs Comyn was born in Dymock in 1893, the youngest of the five children of Arthur George Burney, a barrister, and his wife Annetta Forbes (née Cave-Browne). For many years, from when she was about seven, the Burneys lived at The Weir on the bank of the Wye in Kenchester. In 1925 she married her cousin Robert (Robin) Atherton Comyn, who was a schoolmaster at Hurstpierpoint in Sussex, but after a few years they decided to try their luck by participating in a government-backed 'homesteading' scheme to farm in Southern Rhodesia (Zimbabwe), where Mrs Comyn's brother Geoffrey had farmed before the First World War. They were granted land near Salisbury (Harare) rent-free on condition that they cleared it, built themselves a house and started growing crops, mainly tobacco. After ten years, they would be allowed to buy the land at a substantially reduced price.

The Comyns' two children, Jean and John, were born in 1929 and 1932 respectively and things were at last beginning to look up when Robin caught Spanish influenza and died in 1937 aged only 36. Cecily realised that it was impractical to continue alone, came back to England and, after a rather nomadic life staying with relatives, settled in Hay-on-Wye. Eventually she managed to buy Turnastone Cottage, which, she said, 'was cheap enough for me to afford because it was so inconvenient'. And here she remained until her death in 1976, despite her struggles with lameness and arthritis. She had one of the earliest hip replacements, which transformed her life for several years.

Although life was difficult for her, it was considerably smoothed by deliveries from Keylock (the butchers in Hay), milk from Pat Robinson of Poston and later from Ken Rogers of the Nag's Head in Peterchurch, bread from Hallard of Poston Mill (who was succeeded by his roundsman and nephew Derek Jones) and groceries from the shop in Peterchurch. If no-one came to the door in time, the shop's delivery man would leave cheery notes advising, for instance, that the ice-cream had been safely put away in the freezer.

The Cross House, as it was now known, was inherited by her son, John Robert Geoffrey Comyn. Immediately on leaving school, he was conscripted for national service, and served as a second lieutenant with the Gordon Highlanders who were on active service in Malaya; there, in the jungle, he captured a *dacoit* (a Malayan bandit or insurgent) but then (after questions in the House of Commons concerning under-age soldiers on the front line) had to be rushed back to base camp as he was still a minor. After his two years' national service he trained as a manager on a tea garden in North Bengal, later moving down to Calcutta and then to Madras before returning home. His mother, reinvigorated by her hip replacement, was able to go out to sail home with him, stopping off in South Africa and travelling up to Southern Rhodesia to visit her husband's grave. Back in London in 1970 he joined Hambros Bank where he remained until his retirement in 1992.

In 1982, John Comyn bought the 10-acre field opposite The Cross House from David Bulmer's sale of the Whitehouse estate; on the tithe map of 1842, this field was shown as part of the holding of the Red Cross Inn and, possibly after the alehouse closed, it was apparently allocated to Cothill.[10] When Mrs C.J.F. Comyn came to Turnastone after her marriage to John in 1974, Rowland Vaughan's 'Trench Royal' was still an open ditch on the field side of the hedge opposite the house but shortly afterwards it was piped as it is today.

Fig. 30 John Comyn, subaltern in the Gordon Highlanders 1950
(Mrs C.J.F. Comyn)

60

THE OLD RECTORY
Sylvia Teakle

The Old Rectory took over a year to build mainly because of the unsatisfactory way the Governors of Queen Anne's Bounty dealt with the funding. The contract was signed by Henry Cooke, surveyor and builder of Vowchurch, on 4 April 1837 and the estimated cost amounted to £411 12*s* 10*d*. At the time the value of the benefice was £86 per annum and there were 80 inhabitants in the parish. The house was to comprise four bedrooms and dressing room on the first floor and a dining room, drawing room and two kitchens downstairs, together with a cellar and coalhouse.

Cooke had surveyed the previous rectory and found it to be in such a state of dilapidation – he called it 'just a mud cottage' – that in his opinion it could not be repaired to serve any useful purpose and should be taken down. He valued the old materials at £5 and recommended that these should be used where possible in the new house. The previous rectory is said to have been half-timbered, like the house next door, and as the incumbent had not lived in the parish it had fallen into decay. The Revd Thomas Powell, the newly appointed incoming rector, certified to the Governors of the 'Bounty of Queen Anne for the augmentation of the maintenance of the poor clergy' (which was formed in 1704 using the Crown's resources arising from monies confiscated by Henry VIII) 'that he had not received any dilapidation money for the living nor would he receive any in consequence of the late Rector dying intestate and a bankrupt out of the Kingdom'.

Work on the new house proceeded. The builder submitted interim invoices to the rector and he in turn sent them to the Governors of Queen Anne's Bounty for payment. There were considerable delays in the receipt of these payments and some bills were paid by Powell himself to ensure that the work could proceed without interruption. Writing from his home at Hardwicke he sent pleading letters to the Governors for reimbursement, saying in July 1837 that work had been brought to a halt for lack of payment. The final letter, when the contract was completed on 17 May 1838, stated that he was owed £400, a large sum in those days. Presumably this was paid eventually.

There was a small amendment to the agreed plans for the top floor of the house. A back bedroom was shown with the door leading off the passage at the open side of the staircase. As first planned, presumably by Henry Cooke and approved by the bishop of Hereford 'to the best of my judgement', this would have made access to the top floor impossible as the stairs ran straight up to the ceiling below the back bedroom. When the house was built, however, the party wall between landing and bedroom was altered to fit the staircase.

Further alterations were made to the house at the turn of the century. The Revd Frederick Green, incumbent from 1887 to his death in 1918 (see page 127), added bay windows to the rooms on the south-west elevation. He also had a large stable block built at the rear of the garden to house his horses. He was a very keen rider to hounds and was known locally as 'The Hunting Parson'. He extended the house on the north-east elevation by adding a further scullery and saddle room and enlarging the coalhouse to make an extra room. He died in 1918, the last rector to live in the rectory.

After putting in a series of tenants the diocese sold the house in 1937. The purchasers were Hector Munro Chadwick (1870-1947) and his wife Norah (1891-1972). Both were outstanding literary scholars and historians, and they are the only people to have lived in Turnastone who feature in the *Dictionary of National Biography*. He taught at Cambridge University from 1893, and in 1912 became Professor of Anglo-Saxon, a post in which he advanced the study of the English language and literature at Cambridge. Among his publications the most notable are *The Origin of the English Nation* (1909) and *Growth of Literature* in three volumes (1932-40), written with his wife, his former student and a powerful scholar in her own right. He spent all his adult life at Cambridge, where he died, and they seemed to have used the Old Rectory as a country retreat. The house was sold when Professor Chadwick died in 1947.

It was bought by Trevor Wilding, brother of Percy and Hedley Wilding at the Shop. He was a champion rose grower and won over one hundred first prizes and the National Rose Society's Bronze Medal. The large stable block was used by his brothers as a car repair workshop until 1962, when the house was bought by Gordon and Sylvia Teakle, who ultimately used the stables as a workshop for the repair of horticultural machinery.

In these more recent years several alterations have been carried out. A small extension was built on the south-east elevation to extend the downstairs sitting

Fig. 31 Unknown horseman at the Rectory (possibly Revd F. Green) c.1900
(Mrs S. Teakle)

Fig. 32 Groom Charles Croft with Revd F. Green's hunter c.1910
(Mrs S. Teakle)

Fig. 33 The Old Rectory 2009

room and provide a box room and lavatory upstairs. Mains electricity was installed, mains water piped into the house, and the extensions for saddle room and scullery were taken down and a wall in the downstairs passage removed to make a sizeable hall. In 1995-6 the house was completely refurbished, with new double glazed windows, extensive repairs to the roof, electricity installation renewed, loft insulated, chimney rebuilt, together with other work to bring the house up to modern standards.

In 2002 Mrs Teakle purchased a small piece of land opposite the house. Over the years this garden had been rented out to the various occupiers of the rectory by the owners of Turnastone Court, and when the farm was sold to the Countryside Restoration Trust the garden was offered for sale separately.

YEW TREE HOUSE (THE VILLA)
Cynthia Comyn

This is a handsome stone and brick house, built in the 19th century, with a large modern one-storey extension to the rear, which includes a spacious kitchen and ground floor bathroom.

The earliest information we have comes from the draft maps made by the Ordnance Survey in 1815, which show two buildings on the site. In the 1841 census two households are shown here – those of Thomas Matthews and of Samuel Jenkins – and the tithe map of 1842 gives us a little more information. From this we learn that Thomas Matthews owned the whole property (which appears to have been two separate cottages) and that he lived in one whilst a tenant occupied the other.

Thomas Matthews stood surety for Charles Vaughan, the licensee of the Red Cross Inn, in 1824. He died in 1847 and was buried in the April of that year in Turnastone aged 86. He left no will and it is not known to whom the ownership of the property passed. Samuel Jenkins, who was born in Peterchurch, continued as tenant after Matthews's death, was listed there in the 1851 census and voted as 'of Turnastone' in 1852 but by 1861 had moved to St Margaret's from whence he was brought for burial at Turnastone in 1865. In 1851, Matthews's cottage appears to have been empty. It is possible that it was at about this time that the cottages were acquired by the Poston estate, as they were marked on the relevant sections of the map when the estate was put up for sale in 1878.

By 1861 the inhabitants were William Turner and family in one cottage and William Davies and family in the other; both were described as agricultural labourers and were widowers with families. At some time between this census and that of 1871,[11] it seems likely that the houses were demolished and a new one rebuilt – or perhaps one was demolished and the other enlarged. This latter theory is perhaps the correct one, for when Calvin Brockhurst was the tenant, he was told that The Villa (as the house was then known) appeared to have been two cottages that had been extended and joined together. After 1871, only one house is listed on this site.

It is not yet possible to say with great assurance who lived where in several of the houses in Turnastone in 1871 but it is likely that James Cornelius Morgan and his family were living here. James was a miller and was born in Grosmont in about 1841; he was in Much Dewchurch in 1851 where the next year, a Cornelius Morgan[12] (also a miller) was listed as one of the trustees hoping to build a chapel and school there for the Primitive Methodists.[13] James married Jane Pritchard in 1857 and their children were born in Much Dewchurch (in 1862 and 1864), Weston under Penyard (in 1865), Grosmont (in 1868) and Abergavenny (in 1869). This suggests that James was a journeyman miller and worked as a miller's assistant rather than on his own account. He died in 1872 aged only 41 at Little Polston [*sic*] so he was probably working then at Poston Mill.

After James Morgan's death and certainly by 1881 his widow lived at Park Gate at the top of Vowchurch Common, where she was described as a laundress aged 44. With her were three of the five children listed in 1871 and one more child, a son Philip born in 1872 in Vowchurch two weeks before his father's death. In 1882, Jane married Thomas Williams, a widower formerly from Ladywell Cottage, and they moved into Rose Cottage where the 1891 census shows them living.

By 1881 Mary Ann Price, widow of William Maurice Price (formerly the tenant of Dolward before his death from pneumonia in 1879), was living in what had then become known as Yew Tree Villa; as the five Price children were all under 12, it seems likely that Mary Ann could not manage Dolward alone or had not been able to have the tenancy transferred into her own name. On vacating the farm, she moved into The Villa with her children (three of whom were pupils at Vowchurch School). One of these, Arthur, was removed from the school on 1 January 1890 when the family probably left the village as by 1891 Mary Ann had gone to Kington to keep house for an uncle. In that year The Villa was empty.

By 1901 Arthur Challoner, groom to the rector, the Revd Frederick Green, had moved into the house from Brook Cottages, with his wife Martha and their young daughter Annie Lilian. They must have left a few years later as in 1909 they were in Michaelchurch Escley, where Arthur Challoner was described as a general carrier. He is listed in various local directories thereafter as a carrier passing through Turnastone on his way to and from Hereford on Wednesdays (market day) and Saturdays, returning the same day.

The Villa seems to have been another of the village houses which William Watkins acquired after he had bought Turnastone Farm in 1912. It would appear that it continued to be rented out though William and his wife may have intended to live there themselves in old age. While by 1908 the Watkins had only daughters, William may well still have been hoping for a son to take over the farm later.

In 1911, the tenants were Charles Croft, another domestic groom, and his wife Eliza Jane, both of whom had been born in Dorset. Charles had obviously moved about quite a bit after his marriage as one of his children had been born in Dummer, Hampshire and the other two in Tring, Hertfordshire. All three attended Vowchurch School from 1905, which probably indicates their arrival in Turnastone at about that time. Their eldest child, Arthur Charles, served in the Royal Field Artillery during the First World War and is named on the war memorial in Turnastone Church. The youngest child, Harold, was still attending Vowchurch School in 1918 but soon afterwards the family moved to Ross with Mrs Green, the rector's widow.

Between 1920 and 1930, Tom Percival Realey (born in Michaelchurch Escley) lived here. He was the son of Thomas Realey of Michaelchurch, who was a miller. In 1911 T.P. Realey was living in three rooms somewhere in Michaelchurch and described himself as a farmer. According to Hedley Wilding, he had only one arm so his sister Bertha Adeline lived with him and kept house. It is not known what happened to T.P. Realey after 1930, but in that year his sister was living at the Slough before she moved about 1938 into Glendore to help look after James Charles Wilding.

The electoral roll of 1930 lists Myra June [more correctly Myra Jane, née Addis] Watkins and her step-daughter Sophie Watkins as the occupants (just before the latter's marriage) and in 1931-32, Myra was still there with (from 1932) Daisie Minnie Hancocks (who later moved up to Dolward to look after the young Powells). Myra had been the housekeeper to David Watkins at Llanfihangel and married him after the death of his first wife; they lived for some time in Abbey Dore.[14] David Watkins was a cousin of the Watkins of Dolward.

The next tenant we know of by name was Elizabeth Mary Watkins in 1938. She was born one of the Herrings of Cothill, was the widow of Thomas Watkins of the Green Crize Farm, near Aconbury, and mother of Cynthia Clare Watkins, later Mrs O.C. Powell of Locks Garage in Allensmore. By 1946, the tenants were John B. Farrell and his wife Marjorie (née Atlas) who, with their children, had come from Vowchurch and were still at The Villa in 1948-49. However, in 1953 and 1954, the tenants listed in the electoral roll were Harvey Joan Broughton and her husband Richard Charles Broughton, who had three children; in 1961 Alan Geoffrey Cook, a solicitor, was on the electoral roll with his wife Pamela Ann; their daughter Rosemary Joy was born in May 1961 and baptised at Turnastone the following November. Reginald and Joyce Spode were the tenants from about 1962 and Sylvia Teakle remembers Mrs Spode and her children (one of whom, Jonathan, attended Vowchurch School and Sunday school). At that time, the house had two bedrooms and a third made out of part of the landing. Space was cramped and there was little room for storage.

The Spodes were followed by Ralph P.J. and Margaret Sheffield, listed in 1966, and they were followed in turn by Michael H. and Kathleen Watkins. Mrs J.R.G. Comyn remembers visiting the house in about 1976, when it seemed rather small. On entering the front door, which faces south, there was a passage running front to back with doors off to left and right. Immediately on the left was a small sitting room which was almost completely filled by a sofa. On the right was an equally small room furnished as a dining room. Beyond each front room were similar small rooms, one of which was a kitchen. When Calvin Brockhurst lived there in 1989, the rear of the house had been slightly altered so that the kitchen (then behind the dining room) appeared larger than previously.

Calvin Brockhurst was rather an exciting tenant as he was a co-owner of a firm specialising in commercial anti-espionage which was based in Peterchurch. His expertise did not alas prevent his house from being burgled during his tenure (*c.*1989-97). He had a German partner named Hank and they possessed a number of vehicles adapted for espionage and surveillance purposes. One of these was a large black 'General Purpose Vehicle' that was fitted with every possible device including retractable antennae and hidden cameras; but Hank managed to write it all off one day by driving it through a flood and completely ruining the electrics.

Calvin was followed by William (Bill) Wood, who bought the house from Miss Watkins and, to local amazement, re-roofed it in the space of an afternoon. He sold it to Charlie Williams, a major in the Army, who about a year later married Claire Ridger. After he was posted to Afghanistan, she moved to be nearer her parents and their two or three sons were born thereafter. The Williams extended the ground floor considerably by adding a kitchen/dining room and a bathroom; they also knocked the rooms facing the road into one large room. They continued the practice of letting the property – one couple rented the house for about nine months whilst looking around locally for a house big enough for a bed and breakfast establishment. Then there was Alastair Beattie, a London journalist, who came to ruralise with his American partner Maura. They were followed by a youngish couple, Adrian and Julia, with very young children, and then by Mark Howarth, a builder from Madley. When the Williams eventually decided that Yew Tree House (as they had renamed it) was too small even as a second home, it was put on the market. Mark Howarth moved out and John Carter, the present owner, moved in. He has continued the process of change and in the summer of 2009 removed one of the chimneys over the door facing the drive.

1871	James Cornelius Morgan and family	Miller. Died 1872
1881	Mary Ann Price and family	Widow with children
1891	Empty	
1901	Arthur Challoner and family	Groom at Rectory
1905-1918	Charles Croft and family	Groom at Rectory
1920-1930	Tom P Realey and sister Bertha	
1930-?-	Myra Watkins and step-daughter Sophia Watkins	Daisy Minnie Hancocks as lodger in 1932
1938	Elizabeth Mary Watkins	Née Herring (of Cothill)
1946-1948/9	John and Marjorie Farrell and family	Warrant Officer, RAF in 1945; later clerk and telegraphist in GPO
1953, 1954	Richard Charles Broughton and family	Adviser, Ministry of Agriculture
1961	Alan Geoffrey Cook and family	Solicitor
1964	Reginald and Joyce Spode & family	
1966	Ralph & Margaret Sheffield	
	Michael H. Watkins and wife	
1976	Reginald E. and Evelyn Marshall	

1977	Edward and Lucy J. Hammond	
1978	Empty	
1979	Hester E. Pendino	Mother of Thomas
1995	Calvin Brockhurst	Tenant
1997	Philippa Lydford and Calvin Brockhurst	Perhaps slightly earlier
	William (Bill) Wood	Owner
	Major Charles Williams	Owner
	Charles and Claire Williams	Owners
	Alastair Beattie, Maura and Bashi	Journalist and tenant
	Adrian and Julia	?Estate agent and tenant
	Mark Howarth	Builder and tenant
	John Carter	Owner

7 THE WHITEHOUSE ESTATE AND LADYWELL

Sheila Harvey

The Whitehouse Estate

The great timber-framed mansion of Whitehouse stands just outside the Turnastone parish boundary. The story of the house from its building by Symond Parry in Elizabeth I's reign to its sale by his descendants in the reign of Elizabeth II has already been written by Arthur Seward Wood in 1954, extended and enlarged by Timothy Wood in 2000.[1] It would lie outside the bounds of our study had not its estate included cottages and the two hill farms of Cothill and Dolward in Turnastone and had not its owners been so active in local affairs, especially from the early 19th century.

In 1800 the Whitehouse estate had for a quarter of a century been the subject of a series of vexatious lawsuits between the heirs of Herbert Howorth (1675-1728). He had seven children, enough, one might have thought, to ensure the safe descent of the estate. But five were girls and the two boys died unmarried. As a result, by the end of the 18th century and two generations later there were three legitimate claimants, George Pardoe (Herbert Howorth's grandson), John Havard Apperley as trustee to the children of Bartholomew Haselden (another grandson) and Frances Haselden, daughter of Herbert Haselden (a third grandson). Frances Haselden is the key family figure during the ensuing chaotic inheritance. Her father had died when she was a toddler, and she was only 24 when, on the death of her uncle Bartholomew in 1783, she was persuaded by her Hereford solicitor, William Bird, to waive her rights in the estate to her two cousins in exchange for a lump sum of £500. She was, however, uneasy about the arrangement and turned for advice to her future husband, William Wood, whom she married in 1787, a well-connected and Hereford-born cider merchant then living in London. He found a second Hereford solicitor, William Downes, to act for her, but with unfortunate misjudgement chose an even more dishonest lawyer. Within the next few years Downes succeeded in buying George Pardoe's share, then Frances's share and finally had Apperley ejected.

Frances Wood, however, realised that the family had been outwitted by Downes and in 1803 she pressed her husband to engage a third solicitor to act on her behalf

Fig. 34 Whitehouse c.1813 (St Margaret's PCC)

in investigating the loss of her inheritance.[2] This time William Wood made a better choice. Benjamin Fallowes was the fourth man of that name in a dynasty of Herefordshire land agents and lawyers. His father had been clerk of the peace of Herefordshire for almost half a century from 1752 to 1797, a post which he himself filled from 1804 to 1817. Using the loophole left by Downes in failing to pay the full sum that he had offered for Frances's share in the estate, he advised William Wood to sue Downes and recover the estate. The lawsuit was eventually heard by the Lord Chancellor in 1811 and the Woods won, with the result that Downes was turned out of the property and ordered to refund the monies he had made during his occupation. William and Frances Wood moved into Whitehouse, built a large new wing in the fashionable Gothick style in about 1812-13 and continued the recovery of the estate, funded largely by continuing the profitable sale of timber, in much demand for the Navy during the Napoleonic War.[3]

They came into possession at a bad time. Although Downes had introduced changes in his own interest, the divided and disputed ownership since the mid 18th century make it unlikely that the estate had benefited fully from the surge of improvements in agriculture. With the end of the Napoleonic War in 1815 farming went into a slump. The responses of four Herefordshire landowners, consulted for an enquiry by the Board of Agriculture published in 1816, spoke of tenants unable to pay their rent, bankruptcies and high levels of taxation (the land tax, the poor rates and tithes). The Revd John Duncumb, the Herefordshire agriculturist and historian, writing from Hereford but knowledgeable about conditions in west Herefordshire as incumbent of both Mansel Lacy and Abbey Dore from 1809-10 until his death in 1839, revealed that conditions were especially bad in the west of the county. He commented that among eight named landowners whose farms were in hand because they could not find tenants were Lady Dickenson (formerly Boughton) of Poston for four farms, Edward Lewis of Michaelchurch Escley and Mr Wood of Whitehouse. William Wood was therefore perhaps fortunate that in 1816 he could prepare a seven-year lease of Whitehouse and Cothill at £410 a year to Richard Skyrme, a neighbouring farmer from St Margaret's.[4]

The two eldest daughters of William and Frances were born in London but by 1793, when their only son William Seward Wood was born, the family was living in Leominster, where five more daughters were also born. In 1814, with the lawsuit won and the new part of the mansion rebuilt, they moved into Whitehouse. William kept his other properties in Hereford, London and Leominster but now, despite the uncer-

Fig. 35 William Wood (1758-1833)
(T.J.R. Wood)

tain state of agriculture, turned his attention to improving the estate, a long process which his son was to carry forward with new buildings at both Whitehouse and Cothill. He also entered public life with zest, becoming both a magistrate and a deputy lieutenant of the county. Frances died in 1830 and William in 1833, leaving £12,000 to be divided equally between his six surviving daughters, of whom only one was then married, and all his property including Whitehouse to his son William Seward Wood. Later that same year, at the age of 40, William Seward Wood married Mary Ann Hardwick of Lulham in Madley. They too had only one son (and two daughters) and like his father he also served the county as a magistrate and deputy lieutenant as well as being admitted a freeman of the city of Hereford. He was said to have been an exceptionally large man, weighing 19 stone (some 120 kilos) in middle age; he died in 1862, his wife in 1884.

Their son, Herbert Howarth Wood, after education at Shrewsbury School and St John's College, Oxford, spent his whole life at Whitehouse. He married Alice Wyatt Carrington of Cheltenham in 1867 and their family consisted of nine sons and three daughters. Aged 50 when he inherited the estate, he was notable for his public service. Like his father and grandfather he was a magistrate and deputy lieutenant of the county and an hereditary freeman of the city of Hereford, but additionally he was a member of Herefordshire County Council from its beginning in 1889 and he served on the Dore Board of Guardians (see p.158), the Dore Rural District Council and local charitable trusts. His earliest such achievement was to help in the foundation of the Vowchurch and Turnastone School in 1872, with the assistance of a grant from the National Society of the Church of England and financial support from other local landowners. Unsurprisingly, Herbert Howarth

Wood served on the managing committee as its first chairman and was a frequent visitor to and practical supporter of the school. Likewise he was one of the landowners in the valley involved in the promotion and building of the Golden Valley Railway. On its re-opening in 1885, the first ticket was issued at Pontrilas Junction to his eldest son William. The local churches also benefited from his generosity, including the restoration of St Margaret's and the foundation of Newton church. His lifetime coincided with long periods of stagnation and slump in the fortunes of English farming and country estates, and Whitehouse must have been under considerable strain, not helped by the financial collapse of the Golden Valley Railway in the 1880s. His sale of Dolward in about 1920 to its tenants, the Powell family, may be a sign of financial retrenchment but also suggests a sympathetic practical solution to the problems then facing the Powells (pp.103-4). As five of his sons had left Whitehouse to work abroad by the time of his death in 1924 he appointed his two sons living in Britain, Ernest the second son and Arthur the fourth, to be his executors.

The arrangements in his will for the future of the estate, though unusual, were designed to leave it to the son most committed to its survival but at the same time ensuring a share for the others. He instructed that, on the death of his widow Alice, the estate should be offered for purchase to each son in turn. The proceeds were then to be passed on to the whole family. From 1925 until November 1938 the widowed Alice Wood continued to live at Whitehouse with her unmarried daughter, Evie. They were the last members of the family to do so, for although Ernest and his wife moved into Whitehouse after his father's death he himself died in 1935 and his younger brother Arthur and his wife Honora had ten years earlier built themselves a new smaller house, Ladywell House.

On Ernest's death Arthur took on the management of the estate. He had been born at Whitehouse in 1880 and was educated in Hereford and at the School of Mines, Camborne. He had married Honora Penelope Madan in 1921 and their two children, Lilia Frances Penelope (known as Penelope), born in 1924, and Geoffrey, born in 1927, were brought up at Ladywell House. After his mother died in 1941 he bought the estate but Whitehouse was used as a school throughout the war years. Although it was to remain in the hands of the family for another forty years, none of them would again live in the old mansion. Penelope's interest in her ancestral home was expressed in a university undergraduate thesis on Rowland Vaughan's 16th-century scheme for drowning the Turnastone water meadows, whilst Geoffrey followed the example of other male members of the family in his interest in rare trees and forestry, taking degrees in forestry and botany at Oxford. His tragic death in 1957 in an accident in the forests of Brunei devastated his parents. After her husband's death in 1968 Honora became increasingly lonely and dependent upon Jean Jones (see p.105), who worked and later cared for her for a total of 22 years.

Honora had been a familiar figure in Turnastone, visiting her tenant farms and bringing treats to the schoolchildren, but Penelope had left the Golden Valley long before her mother's death in 1980. In 1950 she married John Digby Bletchly and they lived for most of their married life near Aylesbury with their two sons Lawrence Arthur John, born in 1952, known as Arthur, and Francis Edward John, born in 1956. Their links with the estate and especially with the mansion of Whitehouse were weakened by their absence. In the late 1970s they moved to The Court House at Dorstone with a view to looking after the estate but Penelope became ill and they returned to Aylesbury. Soon afterwards in 1981 she decided, without consulting other relatives, to sell the estate, reserving only the extensive woodland for her younger son Francis. Arthur had already been left Ladywell House by his grand-mother and, on Francis's death in 1997, he also inherited the woodland.[5]

The purchaser of the estate in 1981 was David Bulmer of Brilley Court who, to the family's dismay, broke it up by selling Whitehouse, Cothill and the estate cottages. Today, only the woodland remains in the possession of the family that has held it over the centuries.

Ladywell House

Following the death of Arthur's father in 1924 and the decision of his elder brother Ernest to move to Whitehouse, Arthur and Honora Wood built Ladywell House. It became their home for the rest of their lives. The house stands on what was part of the estate's farmland of Cothill, next to Ladywell Cottage but set farther back from the road between Vowchurch and Michaelchurch Escley. Gardens and a small orchard were created around the house, which faces south, looking across the meadows and up to Chanstone and Whitehouse Woods. To the west it looks out on to the rising pastureland of Cothill Farm.

Its design and structure are both typical of new houses in the 1920s, built of brick, probably made fairly locally, with a red tiled roof. The brickwork has since

Fig. 36 Ladywell House 1925 (T.J.R. Wood)

Fig. 37 Datestone in the porch

been painted. A lot of wood, most likely taken directly from the estate's extensive woodland, was used in the building. In layout it is fairly symmetrical with a central large stone porch and wooden front door. In the wall to the right of the front door is a stone dated 1740 bearing the Howorth coat of arms, a cross crosslet gules, and also a sun argent in splendour gules, the arms of Delahay of Hay Urry (Urishay in Peterchurch). The front door opens into a reception hall from which doorways lead to the ground floor rooms. The largest and most important of these are the drawing room on the left and the dining room on the right. Originally there was some oak panelling to the walls of the hall but over the years this has been removed. The wooden floor boards have been retained and, where exposed, form an attractive feature. Outside, at the lower end of the little orchard, is a corrugated iron barn which is possibly of the same age as the house, but the other outbuildings – garages and summer houses – have been added in more recent years.

As already mentioned, Arthur and Honora Wood lived in the house until their deaths – Arthur in 1968 and Honora in 1980, having made no changes to modernise the house itself. The latter left the house to her elder grandson, Arthur Bletchly, who visited and lived in it from time to time although his main home was in Wales. Jean Jones, who worked in Ladywell House for Mrs Arthur Wood for many years, is still in touch with Arthur, who comes down at intervals to oversee the Whitehouse wood-land. He eventually sold Ladywell House in about 1987-88 to Dilwyn Jones, reput-edly for £45,000, but Dilwyn, Linda his wife and their young daughter only stayed for about a year as Linda died unexpectedly. Dilwyn sold it to the Ashton family, Denis and Deborah, Iris and Jason, but they too only stayed for a short time for by

1992 Richard and Belinda Templeton were the owners. They were based in London and had two daughters, one of whom was baptised at Turnastone Church. The next owners were Geoffrey and Madeleine Harrington, who bought the property in about 1994-95 and added a large conservatory to the back of the house at the north-west corner during their ownership. They moved to Lugwardine in 2004, having sold the house to the present owners, Charles and Sarah Drury. They have installed solar panels on the south-facing roofs as energy-saving water heaters.

Ladywell Cottage

Ladywell Cottage was part of the Whitehouse Estate until 1981. It had been built on the estate in 1806 as a tied cottage for estate workers, standing away from the main part of the village but conveniently near to the big house, where most of its occupants worked, and close to a powerful natural spring head only a few metres away. The cottage was, during the first half of the 19th century, actually called Wellhead Cottage. However, during the first part of the 20th century the cottage was renamed Ladywell Cottage. The local explanation for this is that nearby there is a "lost" Lady Chapel. As yet, no evidence has been provided to support such a theory. In the late middle ages there had been a chapel of St Leonards somewhere in Turnastone and possibly nearby on the small plot of glebe land just below the Slough bridge. Alternatively, wells were frequently named after Mary, mother of Jesus.

The cottage is in the western part of the parish, fronting the C road between Vowchurch and Michaelchurch, facing south and with Ladywell House as the neighbouring property on the west. It is surrounded by half an acre of garden with boundaries to Turnastone Court fields on the north and east sides. Across the road are the old water meadows belonging to Cothill Farm. On the western boundary is a pretty little orchard belonging to Ladywell House.

The original cottage has thick walls (about 460 mm) made from local stone that probably came from the estate quarries in Whitehouse Wood. The roof was constructed with a low double pitch sloping on the north and south sides. It was probably tiled with traditional Welsh grey slates that have gradually been replaced over the years so that today the whole roof is tiled with natural slates from Spain. Although thinner than slates from Wales, they are not as brittle and do not weather quite so quickly. The cottage was built with two red brick chimneys, originally one at each end of the building but, as explained later, an extension now puts the western chimney towards the middle of the roof line.

The shapes, sizes and positions of the original windows have all been retained on the south side of the cottage. The frames are still of wood with segmental-arched lintels and sills of stone. The arched lintel and door step of the south-facing front door are both of original stone, indicating that the position of the front hardwood door has not been altered. However, at one time a wooden open-sided porch surrounded the front door, but it seems to have been removed many years ago. There is evidence internally to show that there was originally a back door opening out from the north side, towards the west end. A lot of wood, mainly hard wood, was used in the building of the cottage and presumably came from the estate woods. Most has been well preserved and is exposed, especially in internal partition walls, ceiling beams and roof rafters.

The layout of the original cottage was two rooms downstairs, with a small passageway behind these, and then two rooms upstairs with a narrow landing over the passageway. It is thought that a lean-to may have been at the back, providing a kitchen-washroom area. No evidence remains of a staircase but Mrs Ethel Reece remembers that there used to be an outside stairway at the back of the cottage. There was an outside privy and the remains of a small stone wall can still be seen today which apparently reveals its position. It was certainly 'down the garden', being 110 metres from the cottage.

The downstairs room on the left of the original cottage, that is the west end, is slightly larger than that on the right. The front door opens out into the larger room, where the position and size of an exposed stone chimney breast, oak mantel and fireplace seem to indicate that this was the main living area of the cottage. Upstairs, the two bedrooms lead off from the narrow landing with the original low doors and frames remaining. The doors are still the old wooden plank style with wrought iron latches and hinges. The timber-framed partition wall with brick infilling between the two bedrooms has been exposed (see Fig. 38) as has a similar wall in the larger bedroom, which is a continuation of the partition wall of the main living room below. Perhaps the most attractive feature of the two bedrooms is that, in each, they are open right up to the apex of the roof. There is no loft space above them and the

Fig. 38 Exposed timber-framing upstairs

ceilings follow the sloping south and north sides of the roof. Oak roof trusses and beams are therefore exposed and stained with a light oak varnish.

In 1960 Ivor Howells, then the tenant, was granted planning permission to create vehicular access and he probably also added a modern garage to the west side of the cottage, which was soon moved when the first extension to the cottage was made about 1983 by new owners, Mr and Mrs Michael Avis. They also built the two-storeyed extension on the west end of the cottage. This gave an extra room downstairs as well as a room upstairs for possibly a small bedroom and a bathroom. Both south and west elevations of the extension are stone-faced and match well with the original stone of the old cottage. The roof line has just been continued and the roof slate tiled so that from the front of the cottage it is not obvious that an extension has been added.

The second extension which has been built across the whole of the north side is much more obvious though hidden from the road. It was built between 1994 and 2000, probably in small stages, by Mr and Mrs Colin Taylor who were the owners at that time. In fact, Colin Taylor himself carried out a lot of the work with the help of his father-in-law, who was a builder. Downstairs this extension provides a kitchen, utility room and staircase, with a large bedroom and a bathroom upstairs. The external walls are of traditional cavity blockwork, which are not stone-faced but rendered smooth and painted. The rendering has been extended over the stone wall at the east end of the cottage and likewise painted. All new windows in both extensions match the style and are more or less the same size as those of the original old cottage. All the new window frames are of wood.

Ladywell Cottage, even today, has always obtained a fresh water supply from the natural spring close by in the adjacent field. Since the 1920s, the spring water has been collected in underground tanks and it is one of these, the overflow tank, that provides water for the cottage. The water is piped indoors via an outdoor access "well" and, once in the cottage, is electrically pumped to a storage tank in the loft over the north side extension. There is a mains electricity supply but, as with all the other properties in the area, no gas supply.

Very little reliable information has been discovered about the early occupants of Ladywell Cottage. As it was used as a tied house, there was probably a very frequent change of tenancy. Some workers may have been employed for only a few months at a time or just seasonally.

Records show that in 1835 it was occupied by John Richard Cheshire or Chesher but from 1836 to 1873 it was lived in by various members of the Jenkins and Williams families. They were related by marriage and it is not entirely clear as to who belonged to whom. There seem to have been illegitimate daughters on the Jenkins side, one of whom only survived for three weeks. In 1841 there were some members of three generations of the families living in the cottage at the same time. The men, it seemed, worked as farm labourers although a Thomas Williams was registered as a carpenter. Jane and Frances Jenkins worked as servants, possibly at Whitehouse though Frances, when aged 13, was working at Vowchurch Court. By

1887 all the Jenkinses and Williamses had left or died and the cottage was occupied by Francis Morris, aged 23 and his wife Elizabeth, also 23, and their 11-month old daughter Elizabeth, who had been born in Vowchurch. Francis was a stonemason, born in Raglan, and his wife was from Bodenham.

From about 1887 until the early 1900s the tenants were George and Hannah Howard and their young family. Their son Robert died soon after they moved in, aged 8 years, and is buried at Turnastone. George and Hannah also had two daughters. Margaret, the elder, came with them from Michaelchurch Escley where they had been married. Florence was born in Turnastone in about 1890. George first worked as a stable-boy for W.S. Wood and lived in at Whitehouse when he was 14 years old. He then became a labourer, living nearby with his brother Thomas and family at Slough Forge. By the time he was married and with a family he was working as a coachman at Whitehouse and eligible for a long tenancy of Ladywell Cottage. However, he died in 1902 aged only 56, and Hannah, his widow, then moved to St Margaret's, where she died in 1924 aged 71.

The next recorded tenant at the cottage was a Thomas Bold (or Botel) in 1904, but by 1905 the occupants were James (Jim) and Alicia Margaret Jenkins, who may have stayed until 1920. He too was H.H. Wood's coachman. In the register of the Vowchurch and Turnastone School of that time a young Ernest John Jenkins, born in 1903, was at the school from 1908 until 1916, and was probably their son.

Fig. 39 John William Reece with family members 1929/30 (Mrs R. Morgan)

During their time the Land Valuation of 1910-11 gave the gross value of the cottage as £76 and the rateable value £4 5s.

In 1921 the cottage was occupied by Annie Jessie Evans and it was presumably her husband Thomas John Evans who was a gamekeeper on the estate. They were followed by Becca Doris Hatton in 1924. She had married George James Jenkins, the son of James and Alicia James, who was a gardener. It is not known for how long they stayed in the cottage for there is a gap in the records until 1930 when the lease had passed to William John Reece. At this point, for the first time we have evidence from a family who used to live in the house.[6] The previous tenant had been William John Reece's father, John William Reece, who died of cancer at the age of 70 in 1930, having been a carpenter working for the Wood family. His wife, Emily, took in laundry. Both were much involved with St Margaret's Church, where John was the sexton and Emily was involved in 1930 in the proposed unification of the benefices of St Margaret's, Michaelchurch Escley and Newton. Their son William Reece, known as Bill, worked as a gardener at Whitehouse and in 1937 married, in Turnastone Church, Ethel Neate, the daughter of Harry Neate, the blacksmith at the nearby Slough forge. She too worked for many years at Whitehouse and Ladywell House, looking after the children of Arthur and Honora Wood. The Reeces then went to live in Gloucestershire except for a few years during the war when Ethel and her two boys were with her parents at Upper Rock, St Margaret's while Bill was serving in the Army overseas.

At Ladywell Cottage the next known tenants were John Adams Leake and his wife Alice, possibly from about 1938 but certainly by 1952 when Alice Leake first appeared on the church electoral roll. She and her husband had been married in 1910 at Stoke Prior. He was a retired sign writer, born in Hereford in 1874. They both died in 1956, he at Ladywell Cottage and she a few months later at Allensmore. Both were buried at Turnastone. By 1960 the Howells family was occupying the cottage. George Ivor Howells was a tractor and lorry driver, born at Newton in 1923. He also worked in the garden of the Cross House for Mrs Comyn. He and his wife Elizabeth Mabel (née Price) had five children, Freda, Graham, Ellen, Sheila and Patricia. Freda and Ellen were married at Turnastone in 1963 and 1970 respectively. The family seems to have moved to Kingstone in the early 1970s.

By that time Arthur Wood had died (in 1968). His widow Honora seems to have had some internal improvements made to the cottage in the mid 1970s. On her death in 1980 the ownership of the cottage passed to her daughter, Penelope Bletchly, who in the following year sold most of the estate, including Ladywell Cottage, to David Bulmer. He sold Ladywell Cottage and its half acre of ground in January 1982 to Michael and Judith Avis from Devizes.

Michael Avis was a craftsman, engaged in horological work and specialising in decorating clock faces with vitreous enamelling for which he constructed a purpose-built workshop in the garden. His wife made small pieces of jewellery.

In May 1985, they sold the cottage to Anthony and Sandra Tabb. Sandra was from Kingstone, a daughter of Brian Teague, a builder. After their divorce in 1992

Sandra and her new husband, Colin Taylor, became joint owners of Ladywell Cottage and in 1994 they began extensive alterations to the back of the cottage. Their daughter, Beatrice Gail, was born in 1999 and baptised at Turnastone.

In about 2003 or 2004 the Taylors moved to the Isle of Man and in April 2005 sold Ladywell Cottage to Sheila Harvey, the present owner. Originally from London, she had lived in Herefordshire for ten years during the 1970s and 1980s, and loved the countryside so much that she decided that it would be the place in which to spend her retirement.

8   COTHILL FARM

Sheila Harvey and Brian Smith

Cothill Farm, owned and run primarily as a sheep farm by Robert and Alison Lloyd, stands on the tip of the spur of high ground that pushes into the Golden Valley from Dolward. It is in a prominent position with wide views over the valley and across the dingle of the Slough brook to the mansion of Whitehouse. The sturdy stone farmhouse is partly rendered and whitewashed, a bold landmark on the hillside, surrounded by its traditional stone buildings and large modern stock sheds. The old farm buildings, which are listed as of historical or architectural importance were described in 2006 as 'a complete and remarkably unaltered early to mid 19th-century farm complex'. But they are unsuitable for use in modern farming and at the time of writing (2009) are for sale for conversion into dwellings. Cothill's story over the last 200 years is closely linked with the Whitehouse estate, of which it formed a significant part in the 19th and 20th centuries.

The name Cot Hill, or Cothill as it has for long been known, indicates that the first building on this hillside promontory overlooking the Turnastone meadows was a sheepcot.[1] Its name recalls the traditional Herefordshire practice of cotting sheep. The cot was described by the agriculturist William Marshall (1745-1818) as the ground floor of a building large enough to allow each sheep a space of a square yard. Feeding racks lined the walls and ran suspended from the ceiling down the length of the cot so that they could be hauled higher as the level of dung and litter rose. A lease of Whitehouse in 1744 specifically reduced the rent of George Haines by £6 'to be laid out in fencing in a fold and putting up cratches [racks] and other conveniences at the sheep cot'.[2] Here the sheep would have been fed hay, barley straw and their favourite fodder, peas haulm/halm. Over the cot, at a height of five or six feet, were chambers for storing the fodder and possibly for the shepherd to sleep in. The sheep were kept dry and warm, lambs were safe from predators, the wool became finer, and manure of the best quality was obtained, cleaned out once or twice a year and spread on the arable land.

From the Middle Ages the local breed of sheep was the Ryeland, so called after the poorer rye-growing land around Ross for which the sheep was especially suited. The medieval wealth of the monasteries of Leominster Priory and Dore Abbey was reputedly based upon their flocks, the breed being nicknamed 'Lemster Ore' by the poet Michael Drayton (1563-1631). It was a white-faced and hornless small sheep with long-stapled wool, outstanding among English breeds for its fine wool, which was exceeded only by that of the Spanish merino. In 1783 and 1788, when the common coarser English wool was selling for a mere fourpence a pound, Ryeland wool was fetching two shillings and Spanish wool three shillings.[3] The Ryeland was also appreciated for its 'sweet meat'. In the days before fertilisers, however, sheep were valued less for their wool or meat, than for their dung and it was the usual practice to fold sheep in the open on arable land, moving the hurdles steadily uphill to ensure that the whole field was evenly manured. All sheep, but perhaps especially the small, long-fleeced and delicate Ryeland before it became crossed in the early 19th century with more robust breeds, were prone to the rot (liver fluke) from the cold and wet of dew-laden pasture. Herefordshire farmers therefore continued to house sheep at night and feed them in sheepcots.

During the years between 1789 and 1811, when the Hereford solicitor William Downes had seized control of the Whitehouse estate, he set about restoring and improving it in line with the recommendations of the agricultural reformers. The terms of the leases to his tenants were drawn up with attention to the details of their husbandry clauses, vast quantities of timber were taken out of the woodlands, then in much demand for naval ship-building during the Napoleonic War and sold for his own benefit. He had the estate valued by William Wainwright of Hereford and James Turner of Bockleton (Worcestershire, formerly part of Herefordshire), land surveyors, before he drew up an agreement on 8 February 1796 for a seven-year lease of Whitehouse and Cothill to a new tenant, Benjamin Phillipps of Shegear, the adjoining farm in Vowchurch.

It is a long document, setting out the terms of the lease in minute detail. Downes plainly intended to restore the estate from the neglect it had been suffering, and was ready to invest in long-term repairs and improvements. He undertook to clear the land from thorn and bushes (presumably gorse, much of which remained until the beginning of the 20th century), drain it and erect floodgates in the meadow, make new ditches and plant new hedges.[4] He retained for himself the rights to all timber and quarries, to plant fruit and other trees and to hold manorial courts (though no evidence survives to prove that these were ever held). Additionally he demanded that a bedroom and sitting room at Whitehouse should be reserved for his own use. More specifically he might take the Seven Acres, the field at the foot of the road to Cothill, as a nursery and require the tenant to lay down the adjacent Slough Field to pasture; in both cases he offered compensation for the loss of these two arable fields.

It is not entirely clear how far these improvements affected Cot Hill directly but it appears that at 'the Cot' itself Downes undertook to erect a barn and sheds within six months and it seems likely that this refers to the existing barn on the north side of its farmyard. The barn is of late 18th- or early 19th-century date with walls built in stone up to some three feet high and weather-boarding above. It has a threshing floor and lean-to extensions, at least one of which in later times was used as a pigsty. Downes also agreed to build a limekiln, for which he would look to the tenant to pay 2% interest on the costs that he incurred but he would pay for half the coal used for lime burning and for seed for Slough Field. The lease also mentions his intended repairs to the dwelling house, but in ambiguous terms that leave it unclear whether these refer to Cothill or Whitehouse. [5]

For his part Phillipps, who had to reside at Whitehouse, was required to keep the property and hedges in good repair and also oversee Downes's builders working on Whitehouse and the labourers planting his trees. He had to spread lime on the arable at the rate of thirty barrels to the acre, manure the hopyard (in part of Slough Field), sow one-quarter of the arable with turnips, another quarter of the holding with clover and grass, and spend the hay and straw on the premises, not, it is inferred, cart it away to Shegear or for sale. He was to pay £10 for every acre sown with flax or hemp, presumably to deter him from sowing a crop of short-term benefit. He also had to be prepared to do quite a lot of haulage – of material for repairs, fencing and drainage, of young tree or quick for hedging within a twelve-mile distance, and of coal for the limekiln which was fetched either from the nearest wharf six miles away at Canon Bridge in Madley, a few miles upstream from Hereford, or from Abergavenny. He was allowed to put stock into the woods provided that these had not been fenced off for felling or coppicing. Special arrangements were agreed for him to take off his harvest at the end of the term, including the assignment of a room for two farm servants, two barns to house and thresh the corn together with a corn chamber for the grain and use of a beasthouse and land for him to spend the hay, straw, fodder and turnips until the April or May following expiry of the lease. The lease was to run for seven years from the end of February at an annual rent of £200 a year with the tenant paying all taxes except the land tax. The rent reflects the undated valuation of the estate by Nathaniel Price when it included 'The Cot, Barn Fold &c'. [6]

Having recovered possession of the estate in 1811 and rebuilt the east wing of Whitehouse in the latest architectural fashion, William Wood prepared in 1816 a seven-year lease of the Elizabethan wing of the mansion and 'all that cottage or tenement with the barns and buildings at the Cot hill' for a new tenant, Richard Skyrme from the neighbouring parish of St Margaret's. This is the earliest clear record of a dwelling house at Cothill, showing that the estate was following the trend for replacing a seasonally occupied sheepcot by a permanent farmstead. The original sheepcot must have been rebuilt, for none of the surviving buildings or the oldest part of the present farmhouse accords with the style or dimensions of a Herefordshire sheepcot as described by Marshall and Duncumb. [7] The rent was doubled to £410 a year, reflecting the improvements that had been made since 1796, with an additional charge of £10 for every acre converted into tillage or hop ground without consent in writing. [8] But by this date the post-Napoleonic War slump in farming was already being felt and Skyrme may have rejected the terms, for only the draft document, ready for signature and sealing, has survived.

This first house at the Cot Hill remains embedded in the existing larger house, built in thin courses of the local sandstone dug from the quarry immediately to the west of the farmstead. It was basically a cottage of two rooms downstairs, two upstairs and, probably, a lean-to outshut or dairy at the rear. It faced the farmyard and now consists of a single large room with exposed roughly shaped beams and a low ceiling. At the west end, originally the kitchen, is a large open fireplace, flanked in traditional style by the bread oven on the right and a steep newel staircase on the left. As in the earlier lease, Skyrme was to be allowed at the end of his term to house wheat sown the previous Michaelmas (29 September) in the corn barns at Cothill and to have a room there to lodge two farm servants until the following 1 May to look after and thresh the corn and 'to lay it down in the said room or granary' or to carry it away. The straw or chaff was to remain in the barn. The corn chamber may not have been in an outbuilding, for when the bedroom floorboards in the old part of Cothill were recently taken up the area between the rafters was found to be packed with grain – perhaps for insulation, or perhaps because grain had been stored upstairs.[9]

Cothill, with its traditional sheep-farming practices, provided a useful balance in the management and profitability of the estate as a whole, which relied heavily on the sale of timber from its woodland, although by this time the original Ryeland breed was declining fast, largely because of its small size for meat and the availability of imported Spanish wool for manufacture. It is likely that the traditional 'cot and meadow' practice of moving the sheep between the Whitehouse meadows and the night-time cot was already going out. An undated survey, probably made about 1833 when William Seward Wood (1800-1868) inherited the estate, records that the whole estate amounted to 531 acres.[10] Of these, about 189 acres were wood-

Fig. 40 Cattle shed 2009

84

land, 154 arable, 67 were described as rough pasture or called 'Broomy' (21 acres), presumably gorse-covered land, 63 were pasture, 55 meadow and 3 acres were roads. If we exclude the woodland and roads, the working farmland of the whole estate was 339 acres. The area of Cothill was about 205 acres, of which about three-quarters was pasture.

Between 1816 and the survey of *c*.1833 the only change in the use of the farm land appears to have been the conversion from arable to pasture of Cot Field on the Dolward side of the farm buildings. Now, however, it seems that W.S. Wood embarked on a long programme of improvement and investment. The earlier leases and the 1833 survey show that Cothill and Whitehouse were held and farmed together by tenant farmers, and over the next fifteen years the farmstead at Cothill was substantially expanded, perhaps with the intention of removing farming activities from the precincts of the mansion house by making it the home farm of the estate. Certainly the new buildings were of a size and variety that would hardly seem to be justified for the 208-acre farm recorded on the 1842 tithe map.

A date stone of 1839 marks the large addition to the east end of the small 'two-up two-down' cottage, turning it into a substantial two-storey house. The extension, now rendered and whitewashed with a slate roof and apparently planned to become the main living area, is reached through a wide doorway from the downstairs room. Clearly it was intended to upgrade the dwelling very considerably to the benefit of the tenant farmers, so much so that Elizabeth (Poppy) Lloyd, who has carried out

Fig. 41 Great barn, cattle stalls and wattle ceiling

her own research into the history of farm and family, surmises that it may have been added by William Wood for extra accommodation for shooting parties or on other social occasions at Whitehouse.[11] An uncommon feature is the barred dairy window which still bears the external label 'Dairy' to signify that it was not a living room and therefore was not liable for Window Tax.[12]

A further sign of the changing use of the farm from sheep to cattle is the addition by 1842 of more farm buildings designed for housing cows. The most striking is the great six-bay barn, 26 metres long, containing at the east end nearest the farmhouse cow housing with a hay loft above and at the farther west end a threshing barn with the traditional tall, wide doorways facing each other to let the waggons into the well-paved threshing floor. It is built in a style of about 1830.[13] The low 'dwarf' walls flanking the threshing floor are of massive rectangular stone slabs, the two largest each being three metres long. Digging these from the quarry, hauling and setting them into position must have been a formidable task. Between this new barn and the old one a long, low cattle shelter of six bays with feeding racks was built to face south-east with the roof on its open side supported by stout oak posts in the local style. This completed the rectangular enclosure of the yard, but the building programme was still not finished.

In about 1845 a stone-built stable was erected at the entrance to the yard. Among the estate papers is the specification for the stone building of 29 by 18 feet with foundations one foot deep, three-foot thick walls, two doors with ventilation space above them, but no windows. Toothing was to be left at the upper end with space allowed for a small hackney stable. The estimate was for 92 perches of walling at two shillings a perch (adding up to £9 4s) and 8 square [perches] of [stone] tiling at 7s each (a total of £2 16s), making a total of £12.[14] Alongside it is a weather-boarded wain house and on the opposite side of the entrance a supplementary stable was later built for a horse and trap, its door furniture, hinges and latches of cast iron having been made at the Slough forge immediately below the farm. To the left of the entrance gateway an open-fronted shelter stood from at least 1887 until about 2005.

Like most Herefordshire farmhouses and many cottages Cothill had its own small apple orchard. Conveniently close to the farmhouse on the north side and apparently also dating from soon after 1842 stood the cider house, situated to allow barrels to be rolled straight into a wide back door leading to the cellar beneath the 1839 extension of the farmhouse. On the first floor above is the granary with a wide external stairway. Opposite the cider house-granary but attached to the house itself were workshops, wash-house and a well, fed from the spring on the site but run dry by the mid 20th century.

The tithe award of 1842 names William Wood's tenant at Cothill as Daniel Burnett (more correctly Francis Daniel Patrick Burnett), who was probably the

Fig. 42 Stable built in 1845

86

son of William and Eleanor Burnett, née Patrick of Burghill. He had been working Whitehouse Farm since about 1837 and his household at Cothill in 1841 is more fully revealed in the census return. He was then recorded as 35 and his wife Sarah (née Goode) as 30. They had daughters Tabitha aged 6 and Sidness aged 3, and sons Daniel aged 5 and Jeremiah, aged 2. The eldest, Tabitha, and the youngest, then called Isaiah, died within a few days of each other in June two years later.[15] Also within the household were a 20-year-old domestic servant, Mary Keys, and five young lads working as farm labourers, Thomas Mason, John Carver and John Merrick, all aged about 15 to 20, and John Layton and Henry Walker aged 10 to 15.

Ten years later the 1851 census provides more precise details but so contradictory as to leave doubts as to the accuracy of the census and suggest waywardness or suspicions on the part of the people supplying the information. They were often vague about their age and inclined to change the favoured names of their children; similarly in official documents the acreage of the farm varies, although no change in its boundaries has otherwise been recorded. Even allowing for the limitations in the information requested – the 1841 census, for example, did not require precise ages or place of birth of adults – and the novelty of being officially asked these personal questions, the variations are sometimes remarkable. Daniel Burnett gave his age in 1841 as 44, in 1851 as 48, in 1861 as 65, and at his death in 1869 he was said to have been 72. Sarah, said to have been 49 in 1841, was given as 43 in 1851, 59 in 1861, 69 in 1871 and 85 on her death in 1877. Daniel had been born at Sutton, just north of Hereford, and Sarah at Amberley in the adjacent parish of Marden. In 1851 the name of their oldest child, Daniel, was given as Glaynes, aged 14, but we learn later that he had the two Christian names and was usually known by the second. Sidness, later named as Sidness Ursula, was now 13, both of them had been born in St Margaret's and there was also a new young boy aged 7 called Israel, born in Turnastone and presumably at home at Cothill; later, we find that he too had two names, Israel Aner. All three children were listed in 1851 as 'scholars' though at that time there was no statutory 'school age' and in any case apart from Sunday schools the only school in the whole area was Goff's charity school in Peterchurch, which had been started by the Baptists in 1819. The children were not christened at either St Margaret's or Turnastone and their parents' choice of Old Testament names for them suggests that they were a bible-reading family, perhaps members of either Baptist or Methodist congregations.

In 1851 the Burnett family still had a servant in the house, Selina Thomas, and five farm servants aged between 20 and 14. The oldest, Abraham Deem, also came from Sutton but the others had been born rather nearer, at Allensmore and St Devereux and the two youngest, both aged 14, from nearby St Margaret's. It was the usual practice to engage farm hands by the year, and the young unmarried lads probably moved on after two or three years at the most. It was rare for a labourer to be recorded in the parish in two consecutive censuses. The Turnastone farmers may have hired farm hands in the traditional way at the autumn or spring hiring fairs and mops in the nearby market towns of Hereford and Hay or at the smaller hiring fairs at Peterchurch on 16 May and Longtown on 21 September, but it would seem from the evidence in the censuses that they also relied on a network of family and neighbourly connections in choosing farm workers who would be living in the farmhouse with the family. The 1861 census strengthens this supposition. Daniel is described as a farmer of 210 acres employing two men and a boy. Only one of the men lived on the farm, the 20-year old carter John Powell, together with the 17-year old carter's boy, Moses Portman from Peterchurch. The unnamed other farm labourer must have lived in his own home and come in to work. With his two unmarried sons on the farm, Glaynes now recorded as 23 and Israel 16, Daniel Burnett no longer needed to employ more labour regularly. As before, there was a servant in the house, a girl of 17 from Cusop called Catherine Jones. There was also, on the day of the census, a visitor in the household, 22-year-old Hannah Mathy; she, like the carter, had been born in Holmer, near Daniel and Sarah's birthplaces of Sutton and Marden.

After Daniel was buried in Turnastone churchyard in 1869 at the age of 72 Sarah became the formal head of the household, with her son Glaynes, then 33, taking on the tenancy of the 209-acre farm. By 1871 the immediate family had been reduced to Sarah, Glaynes and Israel, with the addition of her 7-year-old granddaughter Emily and grandson William, the children of Sidness Ursula and her husband Thomas Andrews, who was briefly the tenant of Dolward before moving to Chanstone, just across the meadows in Vowchurch. They subsequently went to live out of the valley, for Sidness died at Lower Bullingham, now part of Hereford, in 1894 and Thomas Andrews was of Stretton Court at Stretton Sugwas, also near Hereford; they evidently kept in close touch with the Turnastone family as both of them were buried at Turnastone. Back at Cothill, Glaynes, still unmarried, was now left with his bachelor brother Israel to run the farm with a couple of living-in workers, the carter 21-year old William Prosser (born in Burghill where old Daniel Burnett had come from) and a cowman, Staffordshire-born William Hill, aged 18. A 16-year-old domestic servant, Ann Davis, helped Sarah run the house.

Ten years later in 1881 little had changed except for the servants. Glaynes and Israel remained in partnership with a couple of young men to work on the farm, William Griffiths, aged 19, and Joseph Scandrett, aged 18. They were both Herefordshire-born, respectively in Norton Canon, a few miles away across the river Wye, and in the more distant north-east of the county in Thornbury. There was more change in the house, as Sarah was now 79, 19-year-old Harriet Godsall had been engaged as a domestic servant and they had obtained a 27-year-old housekeeper, Christine Campbell, who also acted as their book-keeper. It would seem likely that her duties included the care of the elderly Sarah. A few years later Sarah must have returned to her own childhood home, for she died at Withington in 1887 at the age of 85. Buried at Turnastone, her death marked the end of the 50-year connection of the Burnett family with Cothill. Daniel and Israel Glaynes had also left by 1891 to end their days at Higford Farm in Yatton, near Ross-on-Wye in 1910 and 1917 respectively.

Plate 18 The great barn, Cothill 2009

Plate 19 Tithe map showing
'Cot Hill' 1842 (HRO)

Plate 20 Great barn
threshing floor and walls

Plate 21 Cothill 2008

Plate 22 National grid gas pipeline 2007

Plate 23 Dolward from the south-west

Plate 24 Dolward farmhouse

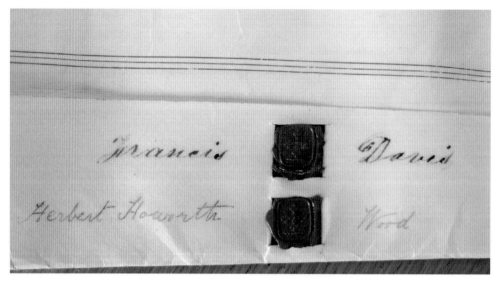

Plate 25 Sealed conveyance 1856 (HRO)

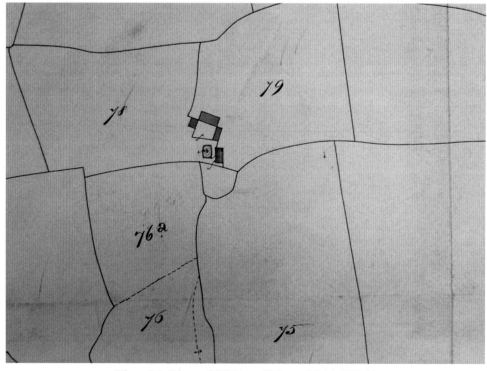

Plate 26 Plan of Whitewall farm 1844 (HRO)

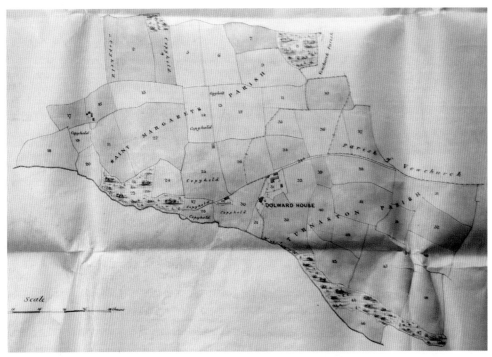

Plate 27   Map of Dolward estate 1856 (HRO)

Plate 28   Modern hedgerows

Plate 29 The church interior

Plate 30 The church

Plate 31 St Leonard's window in memory of Revd F.R. Green

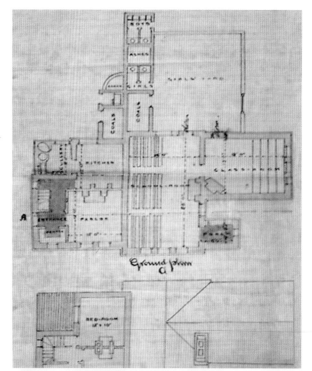

Plate 32 School plan (HRO)

Plate 33 Country market at village hall

The Burnetts were succeeded as tenants by a family that originated from Llowes in Radnorshire on the other side of the river Wye from Hay. James Herring was not a young man when he took on the lease as in the earliest record of his presence at Cothill, the census return of 1891, he was registered as being 65. He arrived with his grown-up family, David (27), Jane (24), Thomas (22) and Edward (20), all of whom were born in Llowes, remained unmarried and were employed on the farm. A (William) Arthur Herring, at that time aged 19, was the youngest son and Elizabeth, then aged 9, the youngest daughter, both also born in Llowes but they, like James's 56-year old wife Susan, were not at home on the day the census was taken, though we shall meet them later. In addition the family had a general labourer, 40-year old William Fletcher, originally from Shrewsbury, and a 14-year-old domestic servant, Ellen Hughes, born in nearby Clodock. As an example of the closely related farming community James Herring's younger sister Ann Gwilliam, a widow, married secondly William Watkins and subsequently went to live at Dolward.

Much happened in the following ten years up to 1901. James died in 1894 aged 69 and was buried at Llowes. His widow Susan, although recorded in directories and electoral registers as the tenant up to 1906, was not at Cothill on the day in 1901 when the census enumerator called, and all the older children had left home, David James to farm at Shenmore in Madley and Edward probably the farmer of that name at Rowlestone. At Cothill, Arthur Herring and his sister Elizabeth were running the farm with only a single 15-year-old girl, Ada Stephens, living in for domestic help. Their baby niece, Margaret, who had been born two years earlier in Clodock, was staying with them. Any farm workers must have been coming in from their own cottages, either daily or as needed. By 1911 Arthur Herring had been joined in the tenancy of the 188-acre farm by his elder brother Thomas, according to the Land Valuation carried out in the aftermath of Lloyd George's 1910 budget, which had proposed a tax on land to finance social reforms and build up the armed forces. They also rented from the rector the adjoining 4-acre piece of glebe by the road at the Slough (the possible site of the medieval chapel of St Leonard). They had a 40-year old waggoner, John Jones, and a young girl as a servant living in the ten-roomed house when the census was taken that same year. The three of them, Thomas, Arthur and Elizabeth 'Bessie' Herring, continued to live at Cothill until at least 1925.[16]

Soon after 1925 the tenancy passed to Arthur Crofts. His family had been hosiery manufacturers in Leicestershire until his father came to farm in the Golden Valley at Peterchurch in about 1900. Arthur was 23 when he went to Cothill and reputedly worked hard to improve the farm, clearing the gorse on the bank below the farmstead to provide more grazing. The effort and expense are said to have been the cause of his depression and suicide in 1927 on the land that eventually he had successfully cleared.[17] There are still a few brightly flowering yellow gorse bushes on the now neatly cropped sheep pasture of the hillside, deliberately retained by the more recent farmers at Cothill as a reminder that if neglected it would not be long before the gorse began to spread across the pastures again.

In 1929 George J. Pugh became the tenant.[18] He had been born in 1875 and for a period as a young man between about 1905 and 1912 was a milk-seller in Hereford. Little else is known of his background and there is no known connection between him and Thomas Pugh of Allensmore, who had been a young farm labourer at Cothill in 1851; the surname is not uncommon in the Welsh Marches. George Pugh and his wife Ann (née Williams) had at least five children, Hilda Annie (born 1907), George Stanley (born 1909, both in Hereford), Harold, John and Wilfred. The last named was still living with his parents at Cothill in 1945 and they were farming there throughout World War II. Indeed, according to a farm survey for the Ministry of Agriculture, in June 1941 George Pugh was renting 237 acres at £257 a year, although the breakdown of the area under crops or grass only adds up to 156 acres. Of this area 33 acres were growing wheat, 15 oats and 3½ barley; 66 acres of land were permanent grass and 27 temporary grass. Root crops for fodder and potatoes took nearly 12 acres. Perhaps he was also working the Whitehouse fields and they were included in the larger total but not analysed. Although his farmland was assessed at no more than 'fair' the condition of the land (both arable and pasture), fences, buildings and house were all good. The livestock included 94 cattle (44 calves intended for slaughter), 122 sheep (50 ewes, 40 yearling ewes to be put to ram, 2 rams, and 30 lambs) and 200 fowls. The farm was worked by just two men, George Pugh himself and one of his sons, probably Wilfred, with one seasonal worker, using a Fordson tractor and ten horses. At the War Agricultural Committee's direction, as part of the drive to grow more food for the nation, he had ploughed up seven acres of grassland for wheat in 1940 and 20 acres in 1941. George Pugh died in 1952 and his widow Ann then went to live with her son George Stanley Pugh,

Fig. 43 Verdi, Mary and Robert Lloyd 1981
(R. Lloyd)

who had earlier left Turnastone to farm at Bellamore in Preston-on-Wye, where she died six years later. She was buried alongside her husband in Turnastone, where in the parish burial register she was erroneously recorded as a spinster, formerly of Dolward. Her son George Stanley died in 2004 and was also buried at Turnastone.

Arthur Seward Wood's new tenant in 1953 was another Radnorshire farmer.[19] William Edward Verdun Lloyd, always known locally as 'Verdi', was born at Rhulen near Builth Wells halfway through the Great War in June 1916 and named after the heroic French defence of Verdun that year. His father took the tenancy of Thruxton Court on the Whitfield Estate in about 1924 but Verdi left home to work elsewhere – during World War II at Grosmont and at Turnastone Farm (where he worked in 1941-2). He then went as farm bailiff to Mrs Margaret Millichamp at Norton Brook Farm, Hereford where he married her daughter Mary. Together they moved to Little Whitfield farm on the Whitfield Estate. Finally, seeking a larger farm for their family, they settled in January 1954 at Cothill, at that time reduced to 134 acres, bringing with them their three young daughters Elizabeth (Poppy), Christine and Denise, together with one of the farm workers, George Disley. From early on Verdi engaged a second worker, John Lewis of Kingstone, from his brother-in-law at Thruxton., both young men living in at Cothill until George Disley married Margaret Woodhouse of Rose Cottage in 1964. The Disleys set up home in Slough Cottage close by the Slough bridge and formerly used as the laundry for Whitehouse, where they remained until 1976 before moving to a modern house in Peterchurch. George continued working at Cothill until 1981 and may still be found doing gardening and other jobs for people in Turnastone. John Lewis went on working at Cothill until 1999 and now lives in Kingstone. These same four people, Verdi and Mary Lloyd, George Disley and John Lewis worked Cothill for almost thirty years.

Cothill Farm in the 1950s

On St Valentine's Day 1942 at the age of six George Disley was evacuated from Bootle to a farm at Erwood near Builth where he spent the rest of his boyhood. He stayed on that farm until 1952 when his 'uncle' Richmond Watkins told him that a nephew, Verdi Lloyd of Little Whitfield in Herefordshire, was looking for a farm boy. George took up the job and the next year moved with Verdi to the larger 134-acre farm of Cothill in Turnastone.

In those days, despite wartime directives and mechanisation, farming was still determined by traditional practice and hard physical labour. George routinely worked from 7.30 in the morning to 5.30 at night with a half-day off on Saturdays and only light work on a Sunday morning, for a wage of 25 shillings a week. He and his fellow worker John Lewis, both lived in, sharing an upstairs room in the farmhouse and taking meals with the family, regularly and punctually provided by Verdi Lloyd's wife Mary, a notably good

Fig. 44 George Disley (Mrs C.J.F. Comyn)

cook. The disadvantage was that customarily live-in workers did not receive any overtime pay. Lighting was by oil lamps and there was only one tap in the house, though there were two in the yard where the two farm workers washed.

Like the others in the valley, Cothill was a mixed farm, growing cereal crops in a four-year rotation on five of its eight fields – wheat, roots, oats and barley, and grass. Although wheat grain, barley for malting and seed potatoes were sold much of the produce, oats, mangolds and some wheat was retained as feed for the livestock. They regularly fed 100 cattle for slaughter and 200 breeding ewes for lambs for the fat market, buying from neighbouring farmers and selling at Hereford or directly to the Meat Marketing Board. The cattle were usually Hereford cross and the sheep Clun and hardy Kerry to withstand the raw winters at Cothill, crossed with Suffolk rams. Additionally, for the household five milking cows and a couple of pigs were kept. Mary Lloyd, as traditionally on many farms, kept poultry – up to 150 laying hens and a few ducks and geese reared for the Michaelmas and Christmas trade. The old barn was converted into a chicken house and she had a good trade in selling hens' eggs, with the Egg Marketing Board collecting some 30-dozen eggs a week.

George's special interest is farm machinery and in his reminiscences he can recall every one of the succession of machines that progressively lightened the manual work. In 1953 these included two Fordson Major tractors, together with a two-furrow trailer plough, 15-spout corn seed drill, spring-tine cultivator, roller, a tractor-drawn harvester, Massey-Harris baler and a corn-grinder fitted to the tractor; a Bamford mower and a two-head water-cooled Lister engine for shearing. Potatoes were lifted by a single-row tractor-drawn kicker that threw potatoes and dirt everywhere and were sorted on a petrol-driven riddling machine. This basic and cumbersome equipment left much work to be done manually. The root cutter was worked by hand, grass sown broadcast, potatoes planted and sorted individually, mangolds singled by hoe, the ditches cleared and hedges pleached in winter and trimmed in summer with handbills, bags of grain and potatoes manhandled, cows milked manually. Right up to 1982, when George left the farm, the potatoes were still planted by hand, John driving the tractor whilst George and Verdi or Mary sat on the planter dropping potatoes into the furrow and smothered under the dust blown up by the tractor.

Hampering this annual round of labour were the persistent water shortages. In summer the water supply pumped by hydraulic ram from a spring below the farm would run dry; in winter the taps in the yard and the drinking troughs froze up. Over the years Verdi installed both a petrol engine to pump water from the spring that had shifted after a borehole was dug at Dolward in 1955 and a generator for electricity in 1958. Mains electricity came a few years later but a mains water supply was much more recent. Every few years in the better times – 1960, 1966, 1970, !978 – a new tractor was bought, with power take-off for use with additional equipment and eventually (1970) with power-steering: the days of wrestling to steer a tractor straight along sloping ground were over. In

1960 were added a new potato-planter, a combine corn drill that fed fertiliser and grain down the same spout and their first tractor-drawn Massey-Harrison combine harvester, a still comparatively crude machine. It was a further ten years before Verdi bought a self-propelled bagger combine harvester and not until 1975 that he replaced it with a tanker combine. 'This made life a lot easier', comments George. 'It saved us a lot of work, see. We didn't have all those bags to pick off the ground, load on to a trailer, and carry off into the shed or up the granary steps. Bags of wheat weighed two hundredweight, oats one-and-a-half hundredweight.'

'It might have been a hard life,' concluded George, 'but if I had the chance to do it again I would take it. I loved it'.[20]

Such long and loyal service is in contrast to the migration of both farmers and farm workers noted frequently in the leases and census returns, revealing the movement of farmers from the neighbouring parts of Wales and of farm workers from a radius of some ten miles in both Wales and Herefordshire. It also masks further changes in farming life at Cothill in the last half century. One more child was born to the Lloyds, a son Robert, and in 1982 Verdi Lloyd bought the farm from David Bulmer in the course of the break-up and sale of the Whitehouse estate, the first time that Cothill had been parted from Whitehouse for at least four centuries. He then extended the farm by buying additional meadows opposite Ladywell to bring its total size up to 177 acres. For years it had been a traditional mixed farm in which the arable was laid down to mangolds and root crops, including four or five acres for growing seed potatoes, safe from blight because of its height above sea level. The main emphasis, though, was on sheep and beef cattle. Stock was driven down to Peterchurch market until its closure in 1956, after which the farmers had no choice but to go farther afield by road. Verdi Lloyd's motto was 'Buy in Hay, sell in Hereford'.

The wider post-war changes in farming and farm incomes, and most especially the cost of labour, led Verdi Lloyd to put down more land to grass from about 1981 and to increase the sheep flock. A modern shed had already been added behind the granary in 1973 and in 1982 he erected a new freestanding shed for the sheep. He phased out the root crops so that the farm could be managed by him and his son Robert working together, although this process was not completed until after his death in 1988. Robert has therefore spent all his life working Cothill, at first with his father, afterwards with his mother Mary, who died at the age of 86 in 2006, and now by himself with the support of his wife Alison. In 2008 he still had up to 40 cattle, which included some Belted Galloways, a small and easily managed breed, but he now concentrates on his flock of 300-400 breeding ewes. For these a new shed was built above the farmhouse in 1994-5 and the 1982 shed enlarged in 1997, leaving the mostly unused old buildings to fall further into decay. Every year, George Disley could recall, weeks had to be spent in the endless task of keeping them in repair.

The old buildings were, however, a rare resource for a new venture to diversify the farming business, whilst coincidentally in 2007 the construction of the national grid gas pipeline from Milford Haven to Tewkesbury, cutting through Cothill's farmland, provided an unexpected opportunity to plan for the future. During the summer months of that year the 40-metre wide route was fenced off and the topsoil removed before the trench for the 4-metre wide pipes was dug. No archaeological features were expected to be disturbed here and none were found. The route was diverted up the hillside to avoid the grounds of Fairfield School in Peterchurch and the Turnastone water-meadows but the massive excavators had troubles in digging through the rock underlying the shallow turf at Cothill. After welding the pipes together teams of giant caterpillar-tracked cranes dropped them into the trench and within twelve months the only sign of the scar across the face of Cothill is the fencing to protect newly planted hedges in the gaps created by the excavations.

At the time of writing and with the farm's peace restored Robert Lloyd is aiming to reduce the number of sheep to an organic flock of about 200 and to restore and convert the old stone-built farm buildings into a variety of dwellings and holiday accommodation. The plans have been drawn up, the buildings emptied and the advertisements published. In preparation for this scheme a new approach drive to the farmhouse has been made and internal work within the house is in progress to preserve its privacy within the group of homes around the farmstead. The consequential effects on the life of the farm and family as well as on the buildings will begin a new chapter in the history of Cothill.

Tenants of Cothill

1796 for 7 years	Benjamin Phillips	From Shegear Vowchurch
c.1816	Richard Skyrme	Of St Margaret's
1841	Daniel and Sarah Burnett	From Whitehouse Farm
1851	Daniel and Sarah Burnett	
1861	Daniel and Sarah Burnett	Daniel died in 1869
1871	Sarah Burnett and son Glaynes	
1881	Glaynes Burnett and brother Israel	Sarah Burnett died 1887 at Withington
1891	James Herring	From Llowes, co Radnor; he died 1894
1894-1906	Susan Herring	Widow of James Herring
1901	Arthur Herring and sister Elizabeth	Children of James Herring
1911	Arthur Herring and (elder) brother Thomas	
1925-1927	Arthur Gardner Crofts	From Peterchurch
1929-1952	George Pugh	From Hereford
1954-1982	W.E. Verdun Lloyd	From Little Whitfield; tenant
1982-1988	W.E. 'Verdi' Lloyd and wife Mary	Owners; Verdi Lloyd, d.1988; Mary Lloyd d.2006
1989-present	Robert Lloyd and wife Alison	Owners – Lloyd family syndicate

9 DOLWARD

OWNERS AND FARMERS
Alison Smith

The third farm in the parish is Dolward, with its farmhouse sheltered by a fold of the hill at a height of 200 metres at the western limits of the parish and, with its holdings of Little Dolward and Whitewall, extending well into St Margaret's. The farmhouse backs on to the parish boundary with St Margaret's at the very centre of its 295 acres of land.[1] Both its site on the ancient pastures of Dore Abbey's medieval grange of Whitewall and features within the house are historically interesting. Since 1955 it has been owned by the Price family, and it is currently farmed by Cliff and Hazel Price with their elder son Michael.

A photograph, probably taken in the 1930s, shows the stone house before its modernisation and alterations by the Price family. The two-storeyed house had a three-storeyed cross-wing at the lower end and was attached at the upper end to livestock housing and a cider house with a granary over, sheltered by trees. The two-storeyed central part of the house and the granary share the same roof line and appear to date from the 18th century. Inside, the back wall of this old part has an exposed timber beam, possibly a relic of an even earlier building dating back to the 17th century. Dolward is first recorded in 1643 as a farm on the Whitehouse estate, almost a century after the upheaval in landholding caused by the dissolution of Dore Abbey and change of ownership of Whitewall Grange (see page 10).

This older part of the present house probably originally extended to the left of its entrance

Fig. 45 Farmhouse c.1930 (Mrs M. Powell)

doorway in the traditional design developed from Welsh long houses. Possibly, though less likely, there might have been a previous cross wing.[2] In either case this end of the house was replaced in the late 18th-century by a three-storeyed cross-wing with higher ceilings and larger windows. The windows were of a distinctive design, each with three small and almost square lights above three lights double their length, of which the middle one was an opening window. Two dripstones run horizontally across the face of the wing as a decorative and practical feature.[3] Unfortunately, because little is known of the ownership of Dolward after the death in 1647 of Epiphan Howarth of Whitehouse, who bequeathed it to his two daughters, there is no documentary evidence to identify who might have been responsible for rebuilding and enlarging the farmhouse in the 18th century.

At the time when our story begins the farm had recently been bought as an investment, probably in the 1790s, by Philip Davis or Davies of Leominster with money left to him and his children by his father.[4] Deeds of Whitewall Grange of 1793-4 reveal that it was a separate farm mortgaged by John Jones, a Ross timber merchant, so it may have been Philip Davis who brought the two farms together as one holding.[5] On his death in October 1798 he left the rents and profits from the Dolward estate in trust to his wife Rebecca to support her and their children until their coming of age. Philip and Rebecca had at that time five children, the eldest, Philip being baptised on 13 October 1790, but she must have already been carrying their son Francis, who is not mentioned in his father's will and was not baptised until 12 June 1799.

When their only daughter Sarah (born 1792) married the Revd John Pierpoint Taylor in 1832 it appears that she gave her mother the use of her share of the income of the farms. Sarah's younger brother John, who was described in 1835 as of Chepstow and the 'owner' of Dolward along with John Pierpoint Taylor, died intestate in March 1837.[6] At that time Philip and Rebecca Davis's only surviving sons were John and his younger brother Thomas. Both were expected in due course to inherit a moiety, or half interest, in Dolward after Rebecca's death. This, however, did not occur until 1842, by which time she had outlived all her sons and even some of her grandsons.[7] Sometime before his death, her son Thomas had sold his moiety to William Seward Wood of Whitehouse[8] and now John's remaining moiety descended to his third son Francis, then aged 10. As a young man Francis became a chemist and druggist in Bath and so was even further removed from his Herefordshire roots.

Philip Davis and his family regarded Dolward purely as an investment, but at Whitehouse the Wood family wanted to recover it. There was now an opportunity for them to do so. As far as is known Francis Davis had no direct interest either in farming or with Dolward, which was mortgaged. He lived far away, and his own career and life lay ahead. Therefore, when he came of legal age in 1853 it seems that Herbert Howarth Wood, also a young man, saw this as an ideal time to buy back Dolward for the Whitehouse estate. The purchase was sealed in 1856 when H.H. Wood bought the farm and its mortgage.[9] The map attached to the conveyance clearly shows the extent of the then 306-acre farm in Turnastone and St Margaret's, distinguishing its division into the freehold lands of Dolward and Whitewall and the 36 acres of Little Dolward held as copyhold of Lord Abergavenny's manor of Ewyas Lacy. Half a century later, in 1903, Herbert Howarth Wood bought the freehold of Little Dolward from Lord Abergavenny's estate.[10]

When Philip Davis died in 1798 Dolward was occupied by his tenant Richard Jones, who continued to live there until 1817 when it passed to Richard Jenkins and his wife Margaret.[11] Their baby son John was baptised at Turnastone in May 1819 and the family remained at Dolward until 1831, Richard Jenkins being among the men who perambulated the boundary of the manor of Snodhill in 1824. They were followed in 1832 by another young farmer, William Bishop from Stokeley, Shropshire. A William Bishop of Dolward, from Stoke St Milborough, Shropshire, who was buried at Turnastone in 1839 aged 66, was probably his father. William Bishop the younger married Catherine Mainwaring from Huntington in 1835 at Turnastone and by 1841 they had one son and two daughters. Also living with them at that time was Catherine's uncle, Edward Mainwaring from Huntington who, although aged 62, is described as an agricultural labourer and so probably helped on the farm. Another member of the household was 65-year-old James Mainwaring, described as a pensioner, suggesting that he was a man of some private means. The family had two young house servants, Susanna Gethin, aged 15 and Maria Wistance, aged 18. As well as Uncle Edward to help on the farm there were two agricultural labourers, 15-year-old William Bradley and 14-year-old William Berrington.

By 1851 William and Catherine's family had expanded with the addition of a second son. Uncle Edward had now become a pensioner but was still living with them and no doubt helping with less arduous tasks on the farm until he died in August 1852 at the age of 80. In his will he left Catherine the generous sum of £350, much the largest of his bequests. The household then also consisted of one 16-year-old house servant Susannah Powell from Peterchurch and two farm servants, 25-year-old William Cole from St Margaret's and 17-year-old Thomas Morris from Llowes, Radnorshire.

William Bishop died in 1855 at the age of 50, but Catherine continued to run the farm for the next six or seven years with the help of her 19-year-old son William. At the time of the 1861 census she also employed a carter, Charles Loyd from Vowchurch, a shepherd, John Jones from Peterchurch, and two younger labourers, George Waring another carter aged 17, and a 13-year-old carter's boy from Kingstone, John Watkins. There would also have been help from the tenants at Little Dolward and possibly Whitewall. Catherine's 21-year-old unmarried daughter Rhoda was also living at home, making it quite a large household. Visiting them was a 70-year-old widower, Francis Bishop, a farmer from Shropshire and presumably a relative, and there was also one hard-worked house servant, Jessy Price from St Margaret's. Catherine was the first of three widows to run the farm. She died in 1885, aged 78, and both she and her husband William are buried at Turnastone.[12]

The two other dwellings on the farm, Little Dolward and Whitewall, both in St Margaret's parish, were occupied by farm workers and their families. Little Dolward, formerly known as Teer (Tir) Sheppard or the shepherd's house, is a small isolated stone-built cottage across the field behind Dolward farmhouse, which has not been lived in since 1955.[13] In 1841 it was occupied by James Brown, an agricultural labourer from Peterchurch and his wife Catherine together with Caroline Mandle or Randle (aged 17), a milliner, and 9-year-old Hariot (or Harriet) Jones; ten years later both Catherine Brown and Caroline Mandle were described as dressmakers. James and his wife were still at Little Dolward in 1861, an unusually long time, but they had left by 1871. The tenants who followed them did not stay so long. In 1871 James and Mary Hughes and their two-year-old daughter were there, in 1881 George White, a 42-year-old bricklayer and stonemason from Peterchurch, with his two sons William (14) and John (10) and in 1891 the house was described as uninhabited. By 1901 it was again occupied, this time by George and Annie Davies and their three young children, Alfred (11), Clara (8) and Charles (1); George, who was 38 and came from Vowchurch, was a waggoner on the farm. By 1905 Thomas Webb and his young daughter Louisa, who attended Peterchurch School, lived there, followed by a farm bailiff, Alfred Watkins, in about 1919. Most of the more recent occupants have not been traced but by 1936 James Blyth was there with his family. His daughter Kathleen married Cyril Price in 1937 and their son Robert Price was christened at Turnastone the following year.[14] At least two evacuee boys from Bootle were lodged there in 1942. Following the Blyth family was Ted Powell (unrelated to the Powells of Dolward) who stayed until the sale of Dolward in 1955, after which the house fell empty. It was described in the sale particulars as having two living rooms, a pantry, two bedrooms, a closet and piped water.[15]

Fig. 46 Little Dolward

Whitewall, the other dwelling, has disappeared almost without trace relatively recently, a sad fate for the sheep-grange of Dore Abbey. It stood a lonely half mile west of Dolward across gently rising windswept pastures and could be reached by City Lane, the track running from Coed Poeth by Whitewall and a field with old buildings called in 1844 the Cities, and on past Dolward to come out between Ladywell and Yew Tree House in Turnastone. The lane is said to be haunted and has a witch who rolls a cheese down it. Whitewall had its own homestead, smaller than Dolward but consisting of the house by a large pond and an open square of barns and farm buildings. No drawings or photographs of its appearance have been traced, and today it is marked only by the snowdrops from its garden which still grow in the field hedge. Tenants came and went quite quickly, agricultural labourers in their 20s and 30s with their children. There is no record of inhabitants for 1861 but by 1871 it was occupied by the Bowens, a large local family. By contrast in 1881 there were only two adults there, Thomas Williams, a farmer-bailiff and his sister Eliza from Llanbedr. Before 1891 Luke Layton arrived, a farm worker from Peterchurch with his wife Harriet from St Margaret's and their three young sons. Harriet their first daughter was born in 1891. They were still there in 1901, by then with another daughter. Luke Layton died in April 1908 aged 49 but his daughter Harriet was in August of that year working as a servant at Dolward and was still there in 1932.[16] Her childhood home at Whitewall, a ruin in 1936, had been demolished to provide stones for making the track up to Dolward from where the bungalow Brynanwen now stands. By 1955 only a barn remained, and this, having been blown down by the wind, has since been demolished.[17]

Back at Dolward itself the tenant in 1864-65 was Thomas Andrews, who had married Sidness Burnett from Cothill. He had come from Dorstone and in about 1866-67 moved on to nearby Chanstone, to be succeeded at Dolward by William Morris (or Maurice) Price, a youngish man from Riddox Farm in Eardisland. A year or two later he married Mary Anne (Marianne) Davies from Newchurch, Radnorshire. He became a churchwarden at Turnastone in 1871 and from 1870 he and Mary Anne had five children, the youngest and only girl, Bessie, being born in 1879. That same year, and still only 39, William was taken ill with pneumonia and died when at the Red Lion Inn, just outside the Eign Gate in Hereford, an inn popular with the farming community. His widow Mary left Dolward after his death and with her children went to live at Yew Tree House, finally leaving Turnastone in 1890.[18]

The new tenant at Dolward was William Watkins (not related to the Watkins family of St Margaret's, Turnastone and Peterchurch). He too was an example of the migration of Welsh farmers into west Herefordshire from the Radnorshire countryside which the Revd Francis Kilvert, the curate at Clyro from 1865 to 1872, described in his diaries. William Watkins was the son of James Watkins of Croesfaelog in Llowes and of Hester (née Lloyd) of Crossolly in Clyro, both farms that are mentioned in Kilvert's diaries. In 1865 he married a 32-year-old widow, Ann Gwilliam (née Herring), from Penyforest in Clyro.[19] At the age of 19 she had married John Gwyllim or Gwilliam, with whom she had five children, all born in

Clyro between 1852 and 1860, John, Thomas, David, Elizabeth and Eliza.[20] After her husband died about 1859-60 she must have been relieved to marry William Watkins, three years older than herself, and to move with her children to Lower Cwmgwannon, Clyro, the home of William's widowed mother and her elderly brothers John and George Lloyd; soon there were also two more little children.

Dolward had many advantages over Lower Cwngwannon – its extensive open pastures and, not least, a big house for their large household. In 1881 William and Ann had with them not only their four younger daughters, Emily Ann, Catherine, Jane (all recorded as 'scholar') and Clara (7), but also William's 86-year-old uncle John Lloyd, now described as a retired farmer, and 43-year-old Eliza Watkins née Herring, Ann's sister with her son Thomas, who may have been staying with them..[21] William's three stepsons, John (now 29), Thomas (26), and David (27) were recorded as 'indoor servants' living in the house.

William died in 1890 aged 61 but, like Catherine Bishop thirty-five years before, Ann carried on at Dolward, though in practice her son, David Gwilliam now 37, who was described as a farm servant and bailiff, was probably in charge of the husbandry. The following year Catherine, Jane and Clara were still living there, and the farm workers were John Hughes, a 28-year-old cowman from Michaelchurch Escley, and Lewis Powell, 23, from St Margaret's. Ann Watkins's death in 1892 brought about a series of changes. The tenancy passed on to her son David Gwilliam and by 1901 the household had become much reduced. His two half-sisters Jane (30) and Clara Watkins (25) remained at home, no doubt housekeeping for him, but the rest of the family had gone and there was only one farm worker living in, the cowman Edward

Fig. 47 Clara Powell (Mrs M. Powell)

Lewis (23) from Llanbedr. Luke Layton at Whitewall and George Davies, then living at Little Dolward, would, of course, have provided additional help on the land.

Then, in March 1904 a whole new chapter in the story of Dolward was opened with the marriage at Turnastone Church of Clara Watkins to Thomas Powell of Rhydynog in Michaelchurch Escley.[22] He came to live at Dolward and soon afterwards took over its tenancy from Clara's half-brother David Gwilliam, who himself got married in 1905 and settled with his wife Martha (née Prothero) in Dorstone.[23] Clara's sister Jane also left Dolward in 1905 when she married Arthur Watkins of Ox Pastures, Marden and went to live at Cornel, the farm above Dolward. In 1912 Jane and Arthur, who now had two sons, moved to Penlan the adjoining farm to the north-east of Dolward. She therefore still lived close to her sister with whom she had spent so many years of her life.[24]

For the next fifty years Dolward and the Powell family were inextricably bound together. Before his marriage Thomas had competed in the Eskleyside Agricultural Society's 3rd Annual Ploughing Match in 1899 and now at Dolward in 1905 he won a third prize in the Local Champion swing plough class. At both those matches George Davies of Little Dolward had also won prizes and in 1911 the farmhand Lewis Powell, still working at Dolward after twenty years, was first in the Servants and Waggoners swing plough class.[25] In 1909 Thomas hosted the 13th annual match at Dolward.[26] Meanwhile Thomas and Clara had started a family. Their firstborn child in 1904 was (Elizabeth) May, and between 1905 and October 1917 a further ten babies were born – three girls and seven boys.[27] Despite the live-in help of 18-year-old Harriet Layton from Whitewall, known as Addy, who came for the birth of the fifth baby in 1908 and remained with the family for over twenty-two years, life must have been hard for both Thomas and Clara with so many mouths to feed. According to May there were seven school-age children who every schoolday had to be got ready with lunches in their satchels. They had no macs or wellies for the two-mile walk to Vowchurch school mostly through the fields, while she was held responsible to see that no gates were left open and to stop the young ones getting up to mischief, tasks she did not relish. [28]

A COUNTRY CHILDHOOD

In her unpublished memoir *Life on a farm in the uplands 1904-1986* May Powell recalls her childhood days at Dolward nearly a century ago.

The Farm Dairy and Kitchen
At the side [in the kitchen] was a large boiler, bigger than the wash boiler, where we brewed our own beer for the farm men as well as made our own cider. About this time [about 1918] Mother started cheese making again, she had given up as there was so much to do with small children ... She had the vats and the cheese press etc. Milking sheep was started too, 20 fat lambs were sold, mothers were penned by their head in a farm ladder which was stretched across a cow stall and secured there. An extra hole was bored in the ladder and an iron stay was slipped down in front of the sheep and [we] milked away, what a job on a hot summer sunny morning. As soon as twenty lambs were sold a fresh batch of ewes were brought in, this went on until the pantry shelves were covered with home made cheese.

Through the summer months as well as extra men to feed churning was done once a week – one day baking, and cheese was made another day. These were

---

pressed and hardened and had to be turned each day on a wooden shelf in the pantry. Previous to this they were rubbed with butter and bandaged; poultry was dressed every two weeks to be taken into Hereford. At Christmas time some forty geese were dressed as well as turkeys and chickens for the Christmas market. The goose feathers were kept for making feather beds and pillows, the goose down was kept separately.

Butter was always more plentiful in the summer so a good portion was given extra salt, potted and kept for winter, about 1 oz of salt per pound, to increase its keeping quality.

About this time a new baby arrived each year, [so] there were fifteen in the household. Home baked bread, when the bread came out of the brick oven in went cakes, rice puddings and when available ducks well past their youth were put in the oven to cook overnight and browned off next day. What a meal they made, yet again what a mother – fifteen people to feed at one time.

Bacon was cured for our own consumption and also lard for the homestead, six bacon pigs were slaughtered for home consumption. Large bars of salt had to be crushed ready for salting, the flitches of bacon were laid on a large stone slab in the dairy. Brown sugar was spread on the hams and shoulders also some saltpetre and peppers, then the salt was piled high for two and a half weeks. The flitches were reversed, the bottom was brought up and the top one laid under-neath, then came all the lard melting this was cut into cubes put into a large cast iron boiler and melted until it turned a deep cream colour and strained off; the remains were called "scratchings" if that's the right name for it. All the odd bits of meat were put into a large earthenware pan, the pan was placed underneath the slab. The 'rime' off the salted bacon dripped down onto the salted trotters, tongue, heart etc and after two weeks these items were washed to remove the salt and boiled for five or six hours, cooled, chopped and packed away in basin – the result a brawn.

Still in our schooldays [before 1917], often we arrived home after a two-mile trek, the washing still not finished, but on baking days it was a real treat during the season, with hot apple cobs straight from the baking oven. Each weekend we had our usual joint of beef, unless it was during the pig killing season. Then it was that super meat that I have never tasted since. A sheep was slaughtered once a month for home consumption which helped out. Twice a week rabbit was on the menu, I have never tasted anything like my mother's rabbit stew. At binding time (corn cutting) masses of rabbits were caught in the corn, some were sold about 8 or 9d a piece; others kept and that was a real rabbit, baked rabbit, baked pies or any other way that mother could think of serving up rabbit.

Schoolchildren's Treats
The chapel tea was one of the highlights in our lives as well as May Fair about May 5th at Peterchurch. That and the school party attended at Whitehouse, Vowchurch and Poston, the home of the Robinsons, were the highlights of our

season. Mrs Green, wife of the Revd Green, Rector of Turnastone, was the daughter of the noted Trafford family of Michaelchurch Court and apart from her unfailing kindness to mother she will be remembered for the tea parties held on the rectory lawn at Turnastone. As children we had very few outings, what we did have we really enjoyed because they were so few. Peterchurch pleasure fair was one outstanding event. Once we made a trip to Urishay Castle. It was being dismantled, we were anxious to see what was there. The moat and drawbridge were still in view and the steps up to the castle. We had been told there was a dungeon and went into the basement. We found an opening and were dropping bottles down and it was quite a time before they landed – this could have been wishful thinking.

One great treat was to visit an aunt, Dad's sister who lived at Cwm Farm, Dorstone. Harriet [my mother's helper] would take my sister and me to Vowchurch station to see us on the train. At Dorstone we would be met by my aunt's help and some cousins. We would stay for a week or two, when the journey would be repeated in reverse.

Clara suffered poor health but May remembers how both Clara and Harriet would be washed and changed by 3 o'clock with all the major tasks completed except on washday or when poultry had to be dressed. The afternoon would be spent window cleaning, sewing, patching and darning probably dozens of socks. The children suffered with croup, measles and whooping cough which Thomas also caught when the baby, Bill, was only eight weeks old. Eight of the children had scarlet fever in turn and spun it out so they were off school from December to Easter. Over the years both Dr A.W. McMichael and later his son Dr Boraston McMichael would have visited the family many times, at first by pony and trap, and then by motor-cycle and sidecar, the last part being always on foot as there was no road.

Disaster came with the world's worst-ever influenza epidemic in 1918. Thomas fell ill with the 'flu followed by pneumonia but according to his nephew from Penlan he continued ploughing and planting wheat despite the rain. He died three days later in November aged only 41. This must have been a bitter blow for Clara who was now left a widow with a 306-acre farm to manage and 11 children aged from one-year-old Wilfred to May, now 14, who had had to leave school when Wilfred was born. The eldest son Percy would have been just 12 and was allowed to leave school to help on the farm.

It would seem that Clara's plight evoked the support of her Powell and Watkins family relatives and also the sympathy of her elderly landlord Herbert Howarth Wood. Because of the unexpected nature of his death Thomas had left no will and his affairs were put in the hands of administrators with his estate valued at £3.000. Soon afterwards H.H. Wood put Dolward on the market.[29] Clara, already suffering from tuberculosis, realised that in order to keep the family home she must do her utmost to purchase it. It took her the best part of three years with May, still only in her teens, making frequent trips to the Hereford solicitors. Finally the farm was purchased for £4,000, of which £2,000 had to be borrowed, and in desperation she turned to H.H. Wood, who had been such good friend to the family and now agreed to make a loan. The farm too had to be managed as there were only two living-in farm workers but Clara managed to secure the help of Alfred Watkins, a farm bailiff who not only ran the farm but was influential in helping with the young family. Tragedy again struck the family when in April 1922 Clara died aged 46, to be buried alongside her husband at Turnastone.

Clara's eldest child May was only 17 but she must have shouldered much of the burden of looking after her ten siblings, from Margaret Ann, who at 16 would no doubt have helped in the house, to the youngest, Wilfred, a mere four and a half years old. Harriet Layton is remembered as the capable housekeeper who brought up the children. In her memoirs May speaks highly of her, describing her as a 'remarkable person with remarkable qualities'. As if these trials were not enough, in 1926 Margaret Ann, who had always been delicate, died of tuberculosis at the age of 20.

May had been courted since 1922 by Phil Powell of Middle Cwm – they met at a Jeffersites' meeting at Michaelchurch – and in 1928 she left home to marry him at Vowchurch Methodist chapel and live at Middle Cwm, leaving Harriet Layton

Fig. 48 The Powell family at David's wedding 1938.
Standing, left to right: Ernest, David, Percy, George, Wilfred
Seated: Maud, Philip, May, Mary, Bill (P. Powell)

in charge at Dolward. There is evidence of the family rallying round, as *Kelly's Directories* of the period record that it was in the hands of Clara's unnamed administrators. Although the younger boys, David, George and Ernest were probably still at school the older ones, Percy, Jack and William, would have worked on the farm with continuing help from neighbouring farming relatives. Like their father they began to take part in the activities of the Eskleyside Agricultural Society. In 1923 P. and J. Powell came first and second in the under-18 ploughing class and there were also successes in sheep shearing.[30]

In the 1930s the brothers George and Ernest Powell were listed as the occupiers of the farm and in 1936 the family prepared to put it up for sale. As Clara had left no will Percy, as the eldest, could have claimed his rights but, May records, when approached by the solicitor his answer was: 'If my father and mother had lived we should all have had the same'. Percy married in 1936. By then three of the family were also married, probably leaving six still at Dolward. The auctioneer, Montagu Harris of Abergavenny, failed to obtain a suitable bid at the sale, but subsequently sold the farm by private treaty as an investment to 'a Breconshire gentleman', who has been identified as the Revd William Arvon Davies of Llanfihangell Cwmdu near Crickhowell.[31] He evidently agreed that the Powell brothers should remain as tenants so the change of ownership had no obvious effect on the farm.[32] As their three sisters had left Dolward on marriage, they engaged a new housekeeper, Gwendoline Holder. Later in the 1930s they asked Mary Jones, brought up at Upper Slough but then living in Garway, to help them out.[33]

George and Ernest farmed Dolward throughout World War II, when their youngest brother, Wilfred, was in the army. By 1946 Wilfred was back at Dolward and running the farm with his brothers. They are all remembered as keen horsemen who enjoyed racing and hunting, often joining the hunt a couple of times a week. In 1947 Wilfred married Maisie Alice Powell from Wigmore and they had two children, Heather (1950) and Nigel (1952). As both his elder brothers George and Ernest had also married and left, he took over the tenancy of Dolward on his own in 1947-8. In those post-war years he was friendly with his cousin and neighbour George Watkins of Penlan and on a Sunday morning they would often walk over to meet up on the boundary between their two farms.

In 1948, in need of help on the farm, Wilfred learned through mutual acquaintances that a young stockman at Talgarth was looking for a change. They met and Wilfred offered David Jones employment for the usual six-month term. It was in this way that at the age of 17 David Jones, who was descended from generations of farmers at Huntington and had been working on farms at Talgarth and Glasbury, came to Dolward. He can have had no idea that he would stay there for the next fifty years. In 1954 he married Jean Francis from Maes Coed, from where he would motorcycle and walk over to work at Dolward.[34] Jean Jones had connections with Whitewall. Her great aunt had married Luke Layton junior, Harriet's brother, and Harriet herself was a friend of Jean's mother. Wilfred and Maisie's plans were overturned by the news early in 1955 that the Revd Arvon Davies intended to put the

PARTICULARS

DOLWARD FARM, VOWCHURCH

The freehold farm known as Dolward, and situate at Vowchurch, which was offered for sale by auction at Peterchurch in September, has now been sold by Mr. Montague Harris by private treaty to a Breconshire gentleman. It is understood that the farm has been purchased as an investment, and Messrs. Powell Bros., who have farmed the farm for so many years, will remain on as tenants.

ALL THAT

VERY VALUABLE

FREEHOLD FARM

CALLED AND KNOWN AS

DOLWARD

Situate in the Parishes of ST. MARGARET'S and TURNASTONE, in the County of Hereford, and near Vowchurch Station on the G.W.R., the whole containing an

Area of 306 Acres (or thereabouts)

THE HOMESTEAD, which is very soundly constructed and is situate in the centre of the property, consists of Large and Convenient Farmhouse, affording the following accommodation : Dining Room, Drawing Room, Kitchen, and usual Offices, 6 Bedrooms and Attics.

THE OUTBUILDINGS are : Cider Mill, Granaries, Tool House, Nag Stable, Cart Stable, Spacious Cow Houses and Yards, Double-bay Barn, Engine House, Four Couple French Barns, Implement Shed, Bull House, Calves' Cot, Two Loose Boxes and Calves' Cot.

At White Wall there is a Double-bay Barn, and Cattle Shed and Barn.

At Little Dolward, Stone-built Cottage with small Outhouses, the whole being in the occupation of Mr. J. Blyth at a rental of £7, landlord paying rates.

There is a never-failing Water Supply laid on to the Homestead and all Buildings.

The Very Valuable Growing Timber, almost exclusively Oak and Ash, is included in the Sale, and a considerable portion is ripe for falling.

THE OUTGOINGS are : Tithes £28 (about), Land Tax, £4 7s. 10d.

The Auctioneer, having sold the whole of the draft Stock from this Farm for a period of nearly twenty years, has every confidence in recommending this Farm as one of the soundest and best, from a stock-raising point of view, in South Herefordshire.

Fig. 49 Sale particulars 1936 (HRO)

farm up for sale. Wilfred would have liked to buy it but it went to auction in May and the successful bidder was Milwyn Price, a farmer from Tre Maen near Builth Wells. Wilfred moved out with his family to buy Hartpury Court in Gloucestershire, so ending the tenancy-ownership-tenancy of Dolward by the Watkins-Powell family after seventy-five years.

Milwyn Thomas Price (1906-94) and his wife Hilda Annie came to Dolward with their four children, Barbara, Pamela, June and Clifford (Cliff). Like previous generations of Welsh farmers, Milwyn Price had wanted to find somewhere that was less hilly and steep than his farm at Builth and after looking at several farms in the area he settled on Dolward. His cousin Ivor Davies was living at Lower House, the adjoining farm. In 1955 the house at Dolward had changed little over the previous century, except for the installation of a bathroom and closet before 1911. However, since 1911 the census classification of 'scullery, warehouse and office or shop' had become the auctioneer's more precisely described kitchen, dairy with salting stones, pantry, boot-room, wash-house and fuel store.[35] Indoors in the 1930s there were a dining room, drawing room and kitchen downstairs and up the solid oak staircase six bedrooms and attics.[36] Nowadays a porch, added in 1970, leads into a hallway with a new staircase going up to five bedrooms and a bathroom. On the ground floor to the right of the hall the sitting room has exposed beams and a large open fireplace with the former bread oven alongside; the timber framing of the back wall is hidden behind plaster but the dado panelling on the front wall was removed fifty years ago. To the left of the hall in the cross-wing is another sitting room with a dining room behind converted in the 1960s from the old dairies. At the rear of the building a modern kitchen replaced the former one also in the 1960s, making the plan of the house T-shaped. The boundary wall outside just beyond the kitchen still has the hearth of the former kitchen built in it. About twenty years ago the two-storeyed granary was converted to create four service rooms and a large games room. The house was re-roofed in 1970 and has been rendered.

Like his predecessors Milwyn Price took a keen interest in the Eskleyside Agricultural Society. Both he and Ivor Davies were expert hedgers and judged hedging matches. In 1959 and in the early 1960s hedging classes were held at Dolward and, perhaps unsurprisingly, Cliff won the under-25s competition at Peterchurch in 1963. Together father and son won prizes for their sheep and root crops in the 1980s and Cliff was the Society's chairman, a position he held again in 1994, when a barbecue was held at Dolward.[37] When Milwyn Price came to Dolward four men worked the farm, himself and Cliff, David Jones and one other man. After a year or two Tony Pritchard came for some time, living in the farm-house, and David continued working at Dolward until eventually fully retiring in 2006.

Between 1957 and 1964 Milwyn's three daughters married locally and left home. Cliff, who worked on the farm with his father, married Hazel (née Evans) from Moccas in 1964, and they moved into Fairlands, a new bungalow built for them close to the farmstead above the old farmhouse, where they brought up their three

Fig. 50 Milwyn and Hilda Price at their diamond wedding 1994
(Mr and Mrs C. Price)

children, Caroline (1966), Michael (1969) and Alun (1971). In the early 1970s Milwyn and his wife went to live at Fairlands whilst Cliff, Hazel and family moved into the farmhouse. Hazel remembers with affection the kindness of her mother-in-law Hilda. Together they kept chickens and would sell their eggs in Hay. Hilda also had a sow and would give Hazel a piglet to rear. Hazel is well known for her talented and imaginative flower arrangements. Her hospitality has been enjoyed at numerous church fundraising functions and harvest suppers and she has been churchwarden for Turnastone from 1991 to 2009.

Further family changes may be recorded briefly. Milwyn died in 1994 and Hilda in 2004, both being buried at Turnastone. Cliff and Hazel's daughter Caroline married David Gwillim at Turnastone in 1987 and went to live in Longtown. Both their sons spent time away but have now returned. Michael now works on the farm with his father. He, his wife and two children went to live first at Brynanwen (which had been built in the late 1960s for David and Jean) and then in 2004 at Fairlands. Alun their younger son, with his wife and three children came in 2005 to live at Brynanwen.

THE FARM AND ITS LANDS
Peter Gunn-Wilkinson

The farm buildings
The changing function of the cluster of buildings that make up the modern Dolward Farm reflects three major factors: (i) the reduction in numbers employed on the farm over the past 200 years which has resulted in the demolition or conversion of

the smaller domestic farm buildings to agricultural uses, (ii) increased mechanisation since World War II which has required new buildings to store the range of new large machinery and (iii) the more recent conversion from mixed farming to predominantly livestock rearing which has required substantial new animal housings. Of the three farms that made up Dolward Farm – Dolward, Whitewall Grange and Little Dolward – only Dolward Farm retains its domestic function. Whitewall Grange farmhouse was demolished early in the 20th century, while Little Dolward became surplus to requirements in the mid 1950s and the buildings have since been used for agricultural purposes and storage.

The main Dolward Farm buildings were substantially larger than the outliers at Little Dolward and Whitewall Grange. The original buildings probably date from before 1800 and are identified on the 1842/1844 tithe maps as consisting of the open stone barn and threshing floor with L-shaped granary and cattle stores, and additional cow byres and pig sties.[38] Subsequent changes and additions may reflect the period of intensive building to meet the needs of the new agricultural practices in the 1850-60s.[39] The extensive range of buildings developed in the 19th century consist of a linked farmhouse and granary and, higher up the slope, a separate range of stone farm buildings and barns. The size and layout of the original buildings can be clearly identified on the map attached to the 1856 conveyance [40]

The layout of buildings in the *1911 Land Valuation plan* confirms that there had not been any substantial new building between the 1870s and 1950s. Many of the original farm buildings had low ceiling heights and access problems, which were ill-adapted to meeting the needs of intensive farming in the later 20th century. When the need arose, additional buildings such as a grain storage bin, a machinery store, new cowsheds, silage storage pits and cattle and sheep sheds were added in the 1960s and 1970s. These additions can be identified in the photograph which shows the original buildings and later additions. The new buildings now integrate the open stone cow byres forming the western boundary of the courtyard; the open stone

Fig. 51 The main farm buildings 2009

Fig. 52 Little Dolward Barn 2008

barn and granary/cow byre on the southern boundary. The other smaller buildings to the north, and the cart store east of the courtyard, have now been demolished or form part of larger modern buildings.

The main cluster of modern farm buildings is next to the home farm and now occupies an area some ten times larger than the buildings of the mid-19th century. They include a large barrel-vaulted 'Romney Hut', which was used in World War II at Wem airfield in Shropshire. It was bought from Hereford Market when that was redeveloped in 1962 and erected on the site by Cliff Price and David Jones. This workshop and implement store has been used to accommodate and service the machines developed since the war.

In 2008 a further sheep holding pen was developed at Little Dolward Barn to provide additional winter housing and lambing pens. The photograph shows that this significant outlier at Little Dolward Barn has seen extensive sheep pen development. The decline in the number of farm workers in the post-war period was matched by a demand for greater skills and flexibility in handling stock, cultivating the land and using machinery to increase productivity. In addition to these skills, Cliff and David used their engineering know-how to adapt the farm buildings to new demands. In contrast to the restricted spans of the stone buildings, the new buildings were able to support large open sheds by using fabricated metal structural frameworks to create large clad buildings during the 1970s and 80s.

The farm was supplied with electricity in 1947, when the Traffords of Michaelchurch Court paid for a line from Kingstone. Few farmers connected their farms, but Wilfred Powell did. Elsewhere locally, electricity was not installed until 1961-2. The whole farm had a good source of water for domestic use and to meet the needs of the livestock which was formerly supplied from springs on the north and east slopes of the ridge. Water supply for the house and farm was improved by sinking a 38-foot borehole just north-east of the house in an apparently dry meadow. It provides a consistent supply, which did not fail even in the summer drought of 1976. There is some evidence that the water table had fallen as a result of the growth in livestock and the increase in extraction during the drier periods in the 1990s, but the wetter winters and summers in recent years have refilled the aquifers.

A quarry, just west of the house, yielded slab stone suitable only for roofing and was last used in the 1800s. A limekiln below and to the east of the farm buildings was filled and levelled in 1955. Another kiln remains a little east-south-east of the disused kiln and others may be found in Whitehouse woods. The limestone belt is only about 40 yards wide and outcropped along the present drive to the farm, providing an easy source of lime which was widely used as fertilizer on the fields. The lime 'dressing' has several beneficial effects on the soil. It breaks down heavy clay soils, making it more workable and easily drained; it encourages bacterial nitrification processes; and it neutralises soil acidity. In the 19th century the 'lump lime' was transported to the fields by horse and wagon and either laid on the head-lands in small heaps or covered with soil and slaked with rain or moisture in the soil. When slaked or broken down it would be spread evenly over the fields. The lime dressings were applied at the rate of 5-6 tons per acre. [41]

A profile of David Jones' working life at Dolward Farm demonstrates the range of skills acquired in a farming career:

A Working Life at Dolward Farm

In 1948 David Jones, 17 years old, was hired by Wilfred Powell to work at Dolward for six months. He continued to work at the farm for the next fifty-eight years, a remarkably long time. David came from a farming family and began his own farming career at 15, working on his uncle's farm in Walton near Kington. He subsequently moved to a farm in Talgarth, and then to Glasbury, a position he found at the Hay Hiring Fair, as many young farm workers did at that time when a farmer might call out – 'Any of you boys interested in a job?'

Dolward in 1948 could be described as a typical west Herefordshire upland fringe farm, a mixed farm which combined livestock of mainly sheep and cattle, with arable production growing cereals, roots, hay for both feedstuff and the market. As a general labourer, David was expected to be involved in all aspects of the farm. An already experienced young farmer, he nevertheless had to learn some new skills, such as arable cultivation, grassland maintenance, and the use of new machinery, skills he learned not through special training but by simply watching and picking it up as he went along.

As was not uncommon on family-run farms such as Dolward, David lived at the farm until his marriage to Jean in 1954. One of the reasons David gives for remaining at Dolward after the six-month trial was the kindness of Wilfred and especially his wife Maisie. On their marriage, David and Jean went to live at St Margaret's. Jean at this time was working in Hereford, employed to look after a family of three children.

In 1955 their son Chris was born. In the same year Dolward was bought by Milwyn Price. David by this time had become an experienced and invaluable part of the group of people who ran the holding, and when he was asked if he would continue to work on the farm, he agreed without hesitation. As the decade progressed, land on the farm given over to cereals gradually increased, but there was still roughly the same mix of cattle and sheep, though the horses were reduced in number as the tractor, which first appeared on the farm during

---

World War II, was used more widely. With the arrival in the mid 50s of the combine harvester some of the often gruelling work associated with arable farming eased. While David himself did not drive the harvester in those earliest years, the ploughing skills he demonstrated from the start meant that in time he became the chief ploughman. They were skills that led to his winning many cups for ploughing – 30 prizes at the Eskleyside Ploughing Matches, the first one in 1949, the last in 2007. It was a job he loved all his working life.

As widespread modernisation changed farming practices in the 50s and 60s, the need for new housing for both livestock and produce became increasingly pressing. A family farm such as Dolward couldn't always afford the expense involved and so another of David's special skills led to his making farm gates and the gates for the sheep pens as well as for the cattle shed, all of which are in use today. He was also largely responsible for the welding and fabrication of the new lambing shed and the machine workshop which he and Cliff together constructed. These are also very much in use today.

In the late 60s David and Jean moved into one of two new bungalows that had been built especially for them by Milwyn on farmland not far from the farm-house. Cliff and his wife Hazel lived in the other one, next door to the farmhouse itself. By this time Jean was working for Mrs Wood at The Whitehouse nearby where she was to remain for the next eighteen years or so.

Fig. 53 David Jones's long-service medal 1991 (D. Jones)

Over time, Cliff, with the retirement of his father, took over the running of the farm. Nevertheless the close working partnership that had grown up between David and Cliff remained unchanged, and continued until David's retirement in 2006. Their practice of going to sales and auctions together to buy farm machinery, and to pick up implements which could be deftly modified by David, continued through David's working life. They had, in addition, of course, divisions of labour, as each had their areas of expertise and special interests.

Though the work of the farm could at times be extremely demanding and involve longer hours, for example at harvesting time, than the dawn to dusk rhythm normally to be found on a farm of this kind, it is for so many a very satisfying life. And so it was for David. In 1991, he was awarded a long service medal at the Three Counties Agricultural Show for his service to farming. After receiving the award he continued to work at Dolward for another fifteen years.

Changes in land use

Over the last 200 years of relatively stable ownerships and tenancies for Dolward, the practices and priorities of farming have changed a great deal. Whilst we have no specific evidence for the land-use changes for Dolward in the late 19th and early 20th centuries, the leading long term trends can be identified. The main sources for comparison are found in the tithe awards for Turnastone and St Margaret's in 1842 and 1844.[42] The 1936 and 1955 sale particulars for Dolward also provide schedules of land uses.[43]

Table 1. Main land-uses in 1842/44

• Arable   120 acres (41%)
• Grassland   127 acres (44%)
• Woodland   26 acres (9%)
• Orchards   14 acres (5%)

The main land uses identified in the 1842/44 tithe maps for Dolward Farm show a rich mixture of arable, grassland, woodland and orchard management which

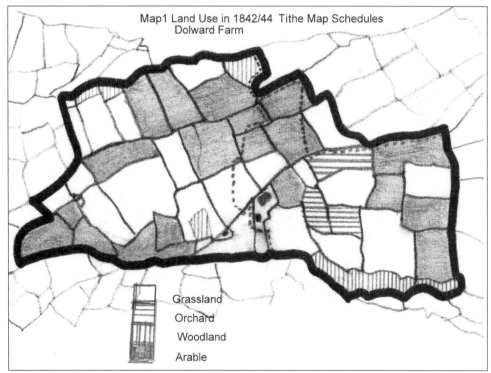

Map1 Land Use in 1842/44 Tithe Map Schedules
Dolward Farm

Grassland

Orchard

Woodland

Arable

Fig. 54 Land use 1842/44

offered a degree of resilience to fluctuations in both market and growing conditions. The distribution of arable fields at this time was substantially more extensive than the pattern in the mid 20th century (Fig. 54), when the smaller steeper fields in the south-west of the farm were returned to grassland. The areas of enclosed woodland and orchards were also substantially reduced and converted to grassland.

Table 2. Main land uses in 1936
- Arable   29 acres (10%)
- Grassland   251 acres (82%)
- Woodland   26 acres (8%)

The 1936 sale particulars demonstrate that the farm was going through a very lean time with most of the land devoted to grassland. Arable production had declined from 120 acres to 29 acres over the previous century (Fig. 55). Some of the grassland had also reverted to rough grazing. The farm was operating on a maintenance basis at this time because low prices could support a bare minimum of input costs. Only four fields were retained in arable production compared to the nineteen fields under arable crops in the 1840s. The field boundaries show the first evidence of adaptation to more mechanised production since the 1850s with two large fields formed from four smaller fields on the south-east corner of the farm.

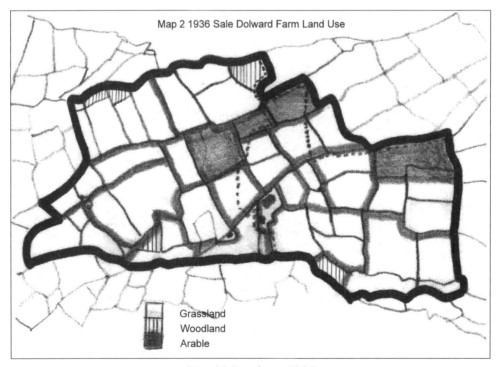

Fig. 55 Land use 1936

Table 3. Main cropping areas in 1955
- Cereal crops   54 acres (17%)
- Root crops   14 acres (5%)

  Total arable   68 acres (22%)

- Reseeded grassland   22 acres (7%)
- Grass ley fields   41 acres (13%)
- Grassland pasture   155 acres (51%)

  Total grassland   218 acres (71%)

- Woodland   20 acres (7%)

The more diversified farming pattern was restored in 1955 with the proportion of grassland similar to the sub-region, and arable production (22%) was significantly higher than in 1936 and over twice the average for the sub-region in 1936 (Fig. 56).

The 1955 sale particulars described the farm as being one of the 'foremost Stock Rearing and Corn Growing Farms in the Golden Valley and South Herefordshire'.

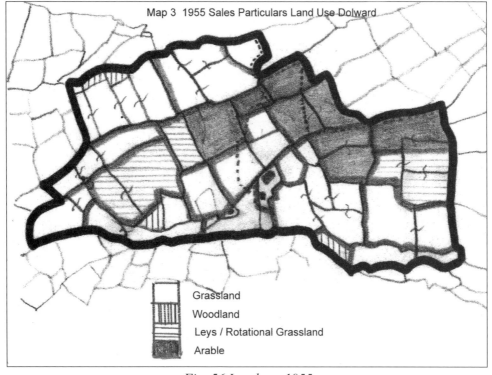

Fig. 56 Land use 1955

The total acreage at this time was 306 acres and the land use pattern reflected a mix of arable and pasture land, with significant stocking levels of 125 Hereford cattle and 200 breeding ewes. During this period, the reseeded grassland was used for red clover seed for the market and over 50% of the cereals were also sold. The diversity of grassland grazing, grass leys, and seed clover provided a well managed mix of grazing, hay, silage - complemented by grain feed stocks.

Table 4. Main cropping areas in 2008/09.
-       Roots /Corn / Leys   32 acres (11%)
-       Grassland   259 acres (85%)
-       Woodland   15 acres (5%)

The most significant feature of the modern land use pattern is the dominance of grassland pasture and the relative decline of any significant arable production for feedstock or the market. A comparison of the land use maps confirms the decline in arable land. In 1955 one-sixth of the acreage (53 acres) was arable but during the war an additional 17 acres had been ploughed. Now only 10 acres out of 320 are cropped (see Fig. 57).

More recent developments in farming patterns have seen further shifts which have transformed the mixed arable and livestock diversity of the 19th-century farming practices to one increasingly focused on grass management and sheep rearing. Cliff explained the reasons behind this transition since the 1950s. The changes in

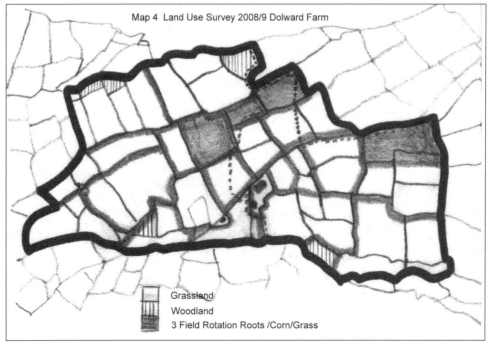

Fig. 57 Land use 2008-09

farming practices encouraged by the government since the war supported intensi-fication of farming and increased mechanisation, which resulted in higher yields and greater carrying capacities for stock. Because of market conditions there was also increased specialisation of land use, with the main cereal-producing areas in Herefordshire concentrated in the drier, lowland soils and in the eastern counties of England where the easier use of larger machinery, lighter soils and drier climate produced higher yields. It became uncompetitive for Dolward Farm to grow its own arable crops for feedstock and bedding because of the close proximity of corn growing areas within the county. The farm now concentrates on grass clovers, silage/hay and managed strip grazing of grass and root crops. The field pattern is now characterised by large grazing paddocks to support a flock of over 800 breeding ewes. Three fields are used as part of a short rotation for roots/corn /grass leys to provide some supplementary feed.

Field boundaries and hedges

The field boundaries found today at Dolward reflect for the most part the changes that have taken place in agricultural practices in the 20th century. The tithe maps of Turnastone in 1842 and St Margaret's in 1844 define the field boundaries at that time, and from this data we are able to identify the fields which had subsequently been joined to form the larger fields found today on the farm.

Since the 1840s many fields have been amalgamated, leading to a reduction of the 55 different fields identified in the tithe maps to 19 on the current farm. Larger

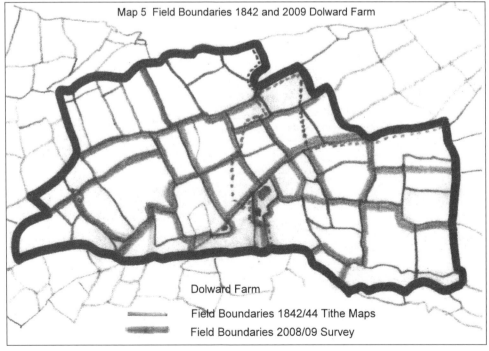

Map 5 Field Boundaries 1842 and 2009 Dolward Farm

Dolward Farm

Field Boundaries 1842/44 Tithe Maps

Field Boundaries 2008/09 Survey

Fig. 58 Field boundaries in 1842 and 2009

fields were created to meet the needs of post-war mechanisation and the changes in the methods of managing grazing that have taken place. The original smaller fields allowed for the movement of stock between fields to encourage the growth of new grass in a managed system of small paddocks. The current field boundaries and those in the tithe maps are shown in Fig. 58.

A survey of Dolward Farm in 2008-9 found several distinctive characteristics in the tree and shrub species found in the hedgerows.[44] The first type, which is adjacent to streams, tracks, woodland edges and in a number of upper fields is quite species-rich and has residual woodland trees. This kind of hedgerow may indicate hedges once forming part of woodland clearance, such as the trees at Cothill Tump. However, the majority of the hedges associated with the relatively level fields along the central upland ridge of the farm have been planted with hawthorn and hazel to provide good stock-proof hedges and are less species-rich and have few woodland type species. The hedges that form boundaries to the farm have much higher frequencies of field maple, dogwood, wych elm, ash and oak than the field hedges across the more level fields of the central uplands of the farm, where hawthorn, hazel, elder and blackthorn predominate. The old approach trackway known as Turnastone Lane runs from Turnastone to Dolward and Cothill along the parish boundary with Vowchurch. Here the hedgerows are earthed up and have a variety of species before the track continues as City Lane towards Coed Poeth.

The enlargement of fields previously enclosed by hedges has significantly reduced the length of hedgerows and the associated intensive maintenance costs, but the remaining hedges are valued for winter shelter for ewes and lambs. In the past, before wire netting and with additional labour on the farm, 1 to 1½ miles of hedge would be pleached every winter to regenerate growth from the base. All the hedges have probably been pleached three or four times since 1955. Both Milwyn Price and his son Cliff have taken great pride in their hedges and have won prizes for their hedge cutting and pleaching skills. Cliff has also been assisted by Tony Pritchard, and together they would pleach up to 30 yards of hedgerow per day. The introduction of pig wire to secure the bottom of hedges

*Fig. 59 Ivor Davies and Milwyn Price hedge-laying
(Mr and Mrs C. Price)*

against stock grazing was introduced over thirty years ago and has reduced the need for layering.

The hedges are now managed to a high standard with a programme of layering every twelve years to encourage their stock-proofing abilities. Some hedges have been closely flailed and most require fencing to be reliably stock-proof and to prevent sheep grazing the base of the hedge. The general heights (5-6 feet) and strong growth from the base demonstrates that the farm recognizes the importance of good, healthy hedgerows and considerable resources have been devoted to their maintenance. The tall hedgerows with field trees also provide additional habitats and good green corridors across the farmland for the movement of wildlife.

However, Cliff explained that in recent years many hedgerow trees have been removed because they compete with and reduce the vigorous growth of the hedgerow planting. For up to twenty feet either side of the tree the loss of vigour creates gaps and reduces the effectiveness of the hedge for stock proofing. The removal of the trees left gaps which were replaced with new hedgerow planting and these were able to be pleached. The loss of natural shade for the stock was made up by the use of areas of open woodland which are no longer fenced off.

A notable feature of the farm is the remains of hedgerow trees forming evenly spaced rows of very mature, oak and ash where old hedgerows have now been grubbed out. These hedgerow trees are particularly evident in the series of what would have been narrow fields in the north-west of the farm where the fields fall steeply away to the wooded valley of the Wallstone stream. The 1814-15 drawings for the first Ordnance Survey maps show that the woodland clusters on the farm were more extensive than today. By the mid 19th century, the 1840s tithe maps

Fig. 60 Old hedge line

show that parts had been converted to arable and some of the rest was given over to grassland.

The 1910 Land Valuation map shows that the woodland areas had not substantially changed, but in more recent times the woodland areas south-west of the farmstead have been felled. The cider apple orchards, which at one time were quite extensive in the fields adjacent to Dolward farmhouse, have also been cleared for grazing land. The woodland areas on the farm were formerly enclosed but they are now left open to livestock and provide shelter and a certain amount of woodland grazing for sheep. They are predominantly planted with oak, ash and some cherry where they have been coppiced and show evidence of natural regeneration along the brook forming the southern boundary of the property. Here the oak, ash, maple and hawthorn are mixed with willow and alder.

Recent Developments

Since the 1950s, the farm has increasingly concentrated on rearing stock. However, the stock levels have changed significantly since 1955, when the average head of stock carried was 125 Hereford cattle, 5 horses and 200 breeding ewes. Now there are no cattle, since the last went in 2002 after the 2001 foot-and-mouth outbreak in the district. Cliff, and his son Michael Price, now manage a farm which runs around 800 breeding ewes, which are retained for five to six years, and produce on average 1,000 to 1,200 lambs per year.

Michael and Cliff have introduced several innovations to enable the two of them to cope with the demands of the lambing season. The breeding ewes are scanned to see how many lambs they are carrying so that their diets can be adjusted to meet the additional demands of more than one lamb. Five large sheds are used for lambing and are divided up into pens of varying sizes, large enough to accommodate 20-40 ewes waiting to lamb, a single ewe and lamb(s) immediately after birth, and three

Fig. 61 Cliff and Michael Price (Mr and Mrs C. Price)

Fig. 62 Ewes in the lambing pens 2009

or four for the first day or two before they are let out into a field. Shortly after the birth the lambs are treated with iodine. Ewes with single lambs are separated in the fields from those with twins for some days, and given different feed supplements. Television in the lambing sheds is checked for weather forecasts of changes in wind direction and closed circuit TV is used to monitor the sheds when no one is on hand between shifts. The management of sheep movements has been assisted by the use of additional small gates linking the fields. Otherwise, ewes tend to take their lambs up to the exposed tops where the lambs suffer hypothermia. In early spring, small groups of twenty ewes and lambs are released at a time and moved according to the wind direction to more sheltered fields.

The farm is currently managed as a predominantly grazing farm with grass pastures reseeded on a rotation of grass/clover mix (no rye grass, which becomes dominant), roots, cereals, grass leys. Almost all the fields on the farm have been part of this rotation and ploughed in the last fifty years except those where the under-lying limestone rocks are near the surface, such as the field below the Tump on the boundary with Cothill. In addition, the narrow fields sloping steeply to Wallstone Wood in the north-west corner of the farm have not been ploughed since the early 1950s. The grassland is 'top-dressed' with fertilizers, rolled in early spring and 'topped' with a light cut in summer to encourage new grazing.

In reviewing the period since they have been at the farm, Cliff considers that govern-ment incentives and European Union subsidies have restricted the farmer's ability to manage the farm to maximise its output and maintain sustainability. Government requirements to monitor livestock movements and stocking levels became very prescriptive and resulted in marginal returns. Cliff and Michael moved out of store cattle rearing after 2002 because of the increased insecurity from the risks of tuberculosis and other livestock diseases. The effect of EU subsidies has been to increase the breeding stock rather than support increased production of lamb for the market. This resulted in over-stocking and the depletion of hillside grazing.

In the light of current market support mechanism Cliff and Michael see the future of the farm as relatively secure because they own the farm and intend to farm in a way which lowers outgoings and maximises grant provisions where eligible. They want to be as self-sufficient as possible with use of family labour, the managed use of grazing land and growing supplementary feed stocks and by developing their breeding ewes and lamb livestock farm to meet new demands.

That Dolward survived the challenges of the 19th century and continued into the 20th century and beyond was undoubtedly because throughout its existence it has been a mixed farm. Mixed farms were common in the west of Herefordshire and could, when necessary, adjust their mix of arable and livestock with relative ease according to market conditions. But another key reason for the survival of a farm like Dolward is that it was, and is today, essentially a family farm set among other farms run along very similar lines and as such has been able to rely on the ties of kinship and traditions of mutual help when times got very tough. When financial hardship or shortage of labour threatened, wage bills could be reduced as the family took on more of the jobs around the farm. There were periods when farming had a very uncertain future and decisions had to be taken without the certain knowledge that they were the correct ones. For many farmers the challenges proved too great.

10   CHURCH AND CHAPEL

Cynthia Comyn

In 1797, when after 30 years as rector the Revd James Roberts resigned the living of Turnastone, the church had been little altered since the early 17th century (see page 13). The much-travelled ecclesiastical antiquary Sir Stephen Glynne described it in 1864 as 'somewhat neglected' with a picturesque south porch but the east window 'destroyed and replaced by a very mean one'. He concluded his brief survey with the final remark, 'The interior is dreary, containing a few old pues'.[1]

The new rector was to contribute to this neglect. Appointed by the patron of the living, Eliza Boughton of Poston, the Revd Richard Sandilands was her guardian – a man of about 39, who had attended both Balliol College, Oxford and Sidney Sussex College, Cambridge (from which he graduated LLB in 1787). Whilst rector here, if not before, Richard Sandilands obtained the position of chaplain of St George's Proprietary Chapel, Ebury[2] and was soon petitioning the bishop for leave of absence to attend his parishioners in London. Even today with cars and trains, it is difficult to imagine how a clergyman could possibly perform his duty in two parishes in different dioceses over 150 miles apart but in the late 18th and early 19th century this did not seem to trouble many bishops unduly. George Isaac Huntingford, the bishop of Hereford from 1815 until his death in 1832, was regarded as an efficient organiser of his diocese but only left his home in Winchester College to come to Hereford during the summer months, entrusting his day-to-day episcopal duties to a much younger clerical nephew.[3]

From *c*.1810 to 1820 Sandilands was permitted to be absent from Turnastone but there is little evidence that he was ever here much at any other time of his incumbency. He only signed the parish registers once between 1800 and 1834 – on 25 May 1819.[4] After 1820 he continued to be absent, with or without permission, and was openly Minister to the English congregation at St Omer in France.[5] However, in 1832 there was a change in the hierarchy at Hereford and the new bishop (Dr Edward Grey, youngest son of the 1st Earl Grey) acted fairly swiftly. By May 1834 he had granted John Fretwell of Poston (who was probably acting on behalf of the patron) an Order of Sequestration which effectively removed Sandilands from Turnastone and, more importantly, from the income he derived from it.[6] Sandilands died bankrupt in 1836 in France aged 77 and left no will.[7] He did however leave at least three sons (born between 1791 and 1803) who followed him into the church.

During his incumbency, Sandilands carried out little or no maintenance to either the church or the rectory, and allowed the latter to become almost derelict. The next incumbent, Thomas Powell, was obliged to oversee the rebuilding of the house after his institution here in November 1836. He was newly and, from a career point of view, advantageously married, having secured the hand of Clera (*sic*), the youngest daughter of the Revd Thomas Prosser, whose family owned the benefice of Dorstone. The Powells were probably living here as soon as the new rectory was completed in May 1838 and two of their daughters, Louisa Boughton (no doubt named to honour his patron) and Clera Ann were baptised here in 1841 and 1842. However, in 1843, Thomas Prosser died and his son-in-law was appointed to Dorstone, so another long period of absentee incumbency began as Powell retained his living here until his death in 1886 but resided in Dorstone. However, despite living some eight miles away, he did continue to take services and sign the registers on a fairly regular basis and also engaged various curates to do duty in his absence. Sometimes the vicar of Vowchurch, which for much of the first half of the 19th century had no vicarage house, lived in the rectory here and he probably took services as part of the arrangement. Where the curates lived is not known.

In the 18th century, the clergy of the Church of England was still very much divided between the rich and the poor. Those fortunate enough to have powerful friends and connections could be certain of enjoying a comfortable life without the necessity of earning their positions by hard work and diligent care of their parishioners. Their less fortunate brethren could expect a lifetime of ill-paid work and spartan living. But in the new Age of Reform in the mid 19th century many began to believe that everyone should actually perform the tasks for which they were paid – even extending this belief to their parish priests. Between 1836 and 1840 Parliament managed to reform the unequal distribution of clerical wealth, plurality (the holding of several livings at once) was restricted by law and several new dioceses created to minister to the new industrial regions. The Whig Government of 1836 also passed the Tithe Commutation Act which in the countryside introduced a rental charge on property in place of the one-tenth of farm produce due to the parish clergy – a practice which had long been resented in farming communities. In the same year, Nonconformist Dissenters were at last enabled legally to marry in their own churches and chapels in the presence of new officials named registrars instead of being obliged to marry in an Anglican church regardless of their religious persuasion.

The Revd Beresford Lowther became vicar of Vowchurch in 1836 and served as curate at Turnastone until he resigned his living in 1874. He came from a family with aristocratic connections and much of his career was shaped by his relations. He succeeded the Revd Harry Lee at Vowchurch, who was also patron of the living and almost certainly the instrument by which Lowther, his brother-in-law, obtained

Vowchurch. His mother Julia-Tahourdin Lowther was one of the favoured nieces of George Isaac Huntingford, bishop of Hereford, who was keen to advance them (and their husbands) when he could. Beresford Lowther and his wife were recorded at the rectory in the census of 1851 but thereafter were never at home on census night, though judging by the registers, Beresford was not entirely absent from the parishes in his care. He appointed one fairly well connected curate in Claude Stephen Magnay (son of a former lord mayor of London), who was living at the rectory in 1861 while the Lowthers were away in Hampshire. Another curate was William Wilson Todd from county Durham who died and was buried at Turnastone in 1869 aged 66, never apparently having held a living of his own. He was an example of those amongst the poorer clergy with neither influence nor connections who eked out a living as curates hoping perhaps to catch the eye of a wealthy patron with a benefice to spare.

During Thomas Powell's incumbency and the curacy of Beresford Lowther, there were few baptisms or burials here but the numbers peaked during the period 1860-79 despite the decline in population from 1841 (see the tables on page 5). In 1851, on the same day as the national census organised by the Registrar General, the Home Office made a survey of every church and chapel in the country enquiring *inter alia* about the numbers of those regularly attending divine service over the previous twelve months and, in particular, how many had attended on Sunday 30 March that year.[8] Beresford Lowther declared that an average of 28 parishioners (or 40% of the inhabitants) came to Turnastone's Sunday service at 3 pm, that there were fourteen free sittings and a further twenty places for those who paid for them and that the incumbent received tithes amounting to £100 a year.[9] Today, weekly services here attract approximately 25% of adult villagers but, whilst this might seem high compared with the country as a whole, in this parish it really represents a congregation of about four.

Turnastone lay also within the Primitive Methodist Circuit of the Cwm (now the Cwm and Kingstone) which embraced Vowchurch, Peterchurch and a congregation from as far afield as Michaelchurch Escley, Abbey Dore and Much Dewchurch.[10] Separate establishments for Baptists (with a Free School attached) and Wesleyan Methodists existed in Peterchurch. In the short period from 1829 for which the Cwm Circuit registers survive, nine ministers are named. Many of them were expected to move from one circuit to another, often some distance away, and sometimes after only a year or so in each. One such, Joseph Grieves (baptising in Vowchurch in 1835) was born in about 1800 in Durham and had two daughters born in Peterchurch in 1832 and 1833, one in Cornwall in 1836 and another in Staffordshire in 1841. After the death of his first wife, he re-married in 1842 in Dilwyn and had a daughter in 1847 in Vowchurch, another in 1849 in Staffordshire and a son in 1851 in Shropshire. In 1861 he and his surviving family had been moved to Birmingham.

There was no nonconformist chapel in Turnastone but in 1842, William Pugh, Mary Powell and Jeremiah Smith (a shopkeeper at both Commerce House, standing

Fig. 63 Commerce House

behind the churchyard in Vowchurch village, and at Bryn Farm on Vowchurch Common, where he lived) were issued with a certificate enabling them to set apart a dwelling house in Vowchurch for use as a Primitive Methodists' place of worship. This was Commerce House itself, which used to have the date '1842' above the front door. In 1851 Thomas Hall, the Primitive Methodist minister, who was lodging at Rose Cottage in Turnastone, filled in the Ecclesiastical Census for the villages in his care in which he claimed that his meeting house in Vowchurch was built in about 1842 and that it could (and did) seat twenty people at the morning service and a staggering 120 in the afternoon. It seems impossible that Commerce House could have accommodated quite so many, but changes in the brickwork and windows suggest that the original cottage was enlarged in the 19th century. It was certainly found unsuitable as the congregations grew, for in 1863 the brick-built chapel behind Commerce House, now used as a garage workshop, was built in its place.[11] Some of Mr Hall's flock may have come from Turnastone but apart from the farm labourers and servants (about whom not so much is known) farming families like the Proberts of Turnastone Farm and the Burnetts of Cothill appear to have been Anglicans. The intermarried families of Watkins, Herring and Gwilliam at Dolward had all come from the Llowes area of Radnorshire, mostly with teenage children; they seem to have returned there for burial so do not figure much in the Turnastone parish registers and might have been nonconformists. It is, of course, possible that some parishioners and nonconformists in Turnastone, as elsewhere, attended both church and their own chapel at different hours on

Sunday. The popularity of Old Testament forenames among people recorded in the parish registers and census returns suggests the presence of parishioners with nonconformist leanings.

Beresford Lowther resigned his living in 1874 and was succeeded at Vowchurch by Charles Longfield, who in 1879 was living at Turnastone rectory but had moved into the newly built vicarage in Vowchurch by 1881. He was the first incumbent not to have been educated at either Oxford or Cambridge, having taken his degree at Durham. During his time at Vowchurch, considerable improvements were made to the church. In the restoration in 1884 the south porch was rebuilt, the chancel and nave re-floored and re-seated, bringing about the end of the 20 individually owned seating places, and a stained glass window inserted at the east end. All this work cost about £450 but it is not known whether this money was raised by local subscription or was a gift.

Thomas Powell died in 1886 and was succeeded at Turnastone by the Revd Frederick Richard Green, son of the vicar of Leintwardine. After graduating from Oxford, he had begun his local career by serving several years as a curate in Peterchurch before his induction in 1887 at Turnastone. Like his predecessor, Green had made an advantageous marriage, to Anne Caroline Trafford of Michaelchurch Court. He was very much a gentleman parson, riding to hounds as often as his duties allowed (and judging by the registers, he performed these effectively until old age or infirmity prevented him). His congregations must have been fairly large as the parish had a choir during his tenure. It was reported in the parish magazine that "Early in December the [Turnastone] Choir had their annual supper after which they all went to the Theatricals at Dorstone where a most enjoyable evening was spent. The service on Christmas Day was at 3 o'clock and at the close, the Carols were sung. They all went exceedingly well and reflect great credit on the performers. After the service, the Choir had tea at The Rectory.'[12] On his death in 1918, and for a little while before, services were taken by a number of clergymen until a new rector could be found. Frederick Green was the last incumbent of the parish to live in the rectory and is commemorated by a stained glass window by his seat in the chancel, dedicated in 1924 by the Archdeacon of Hereford, the Revd R.T.A. Money Kyrle.

After a period of over three years during which the services held were very few and far between, Edward Allen Whitfield was instituted at Turnastone in June 1922.[13] He had been the vicar of Vowchurch since 1910 and it is possible that most of Turnastone's parishioners had been encouraged to worship there until his new position was made clear. In 1934 his health had become so bad that he resigned the livings, which had been joined together in 1927, and there was another interval of about two years before Thomas Lawrence was appointed in 1936. Four months later, the parish celebrated the accession of King George VI and in 1938 he dedicated a new set of hymn books. Lawrence seems to have been a hard-working man who took regular services, kept neat service books, registers and vestry minutes but whose health was poor. From the beginning of Advent in 1937, most services were taken by S.G. Farrar and the next year Thomas Lawrence accepted the offer of a living in Worcestershire from Sir Reginald Coventry and resigned. The air of that county obviously agreed with him rather better than that of Herefordshire, as he only disappears from *Crockford's Directory* in about 1965.

Lawrence was followed by another short-lived incumbency – that of Joseph Harold Gorst, who lasted only about a year before giving way to William Russell Hancock, who was appointed in 1940. He spent nearly four years on active service as a chaplain to the Forces, not returning until July 1946. That winter the service book is full of cancelled services and references to snow, deep snow and floods until the end of March 1947. In 1948 Mr Hancock resigned, to be replaced by Reginald Griffiths Hayden, who was an ardent monarchist. He rang the church bell with the assistance of Miss Nancy Watkins of Turnastone Farm, secretary of the Parochial Church Council, on 15 November 1948 'in honour of the little Prince [HRH the Prince Charles] born to HRH Princess Elizabeth at 9.14 pm on 14 November' and was pleased to note that on 15 August 1950 it was rung again to celebrate the birth of HRH the Princess Anne.[14] On this occasion, his assistant was Miss Pamela Pritchard. Between these two royal births, the parish had celebrated the 400th anniversary of *The Book of Common Prayer* which is still in almost exclusive use in the church today. Mr Hayden marked the occasion of the silver jubilee of his ordination in September 1950 and in January 1951 dedicated the new electric lighting.[15] In February 1952 George VI died and Hayden tolled the church bell. Six months later he resigned his livings, spent about six years in Abbey Hey, Manchester and then emigrated to Australia with his wife and family. His daughter Sally visited Turnastone and signed the visitors' book in 2008.

Our next rector was the Revd James Sowerby de Carl Bensted, who had been born in Derbyshire in 1911 and read history at Exeter College, Oxford. He was appointed vicar of Peterchurch from 1949 and of Vowchurch with Turnastone from 1953. During this time, Turnastone was closed from Easter to September 1955 while repairs were carried out. In November 1956 Bensted resigned and the Revd Dilwyn Pugh nobly took most of the services until June 1957.[16]

In July that year, the Revd John Conway de la Tour Davies was inducted into the joint benefices of Peterchurch, Vowchurch and Turnastone and the following week, he duly read the Thirty Nine Articles here. He was born in 1916, the eldest child of the Revd Conway Davies and his wife Mabel Ruth Hensman, graduated from Jesus College, Cambridge with a degree in natural sciences in 1938 and was ordained in 1941.[17] He came to Herefordshire from Chipping Norton with Heythrop in Oxfordshire as a married man with three daughters. Although John Davies is remembered as eccentric, particularly in later life, he introduced a long period of stability and regular services here, which had not been the case since the death of Frederick Green forty years earlier. In Turnastone he held evensong at 6 pm rather than the long-accustomed 3 pm, he invited other congregations (once from as far away as Swansea) to visit for harvest festival, and in his first year held a carol service in which the church was apparently overfull.[18] He oversaw the re-roofing

128

of the church in 1958-59 when the building was closed for 14 months and services were held at Vowchurch. In the course of the building work the workmen caused considerable damage to the Parry monument beneath the altar. In 1964 sixteen candidates (eight from this parish) were confirmed in Turnastone by the bishop of Hereford in what may have been the first service of this kind here.

John Davies was accustomed to noting details of the weather in the service book, from which we learn that for several winters in succession up to 1964 quite a few services were poorly attended or had to be cancelled due to snow or floods. In 1967, he counted the parishioners and found there to be 39 all told. During his time several trees were planted in the churchyard – the standard cherry in the hedge adjoining the field between the church and Turnastone Court marks the occasion of the 75th Jubilee of the Women's Institute in England whilst two limes were planted by the front gates.[19] Another planting was of a red hawthorn bush, also near the gates, in memory of Thomas Pendino, grandson of Mrs Hardwick of St Margaret's, who died in Norway as a young man.[20]

In 1966, new heaters were put in and, after a considerable amount of trouble over the next two years when they repeatedly filled the church with smoke and fumes, finally began to work properly in November 1968. They were an enormous asset and were extremely efficient, gaining Turnastone the reputation of being the

Fig. 64 Strawberry teas 2009 (D. Core)

129

warmest church in the Golden Valley. Sadly after over thirty years, they began to fail and the firm which had supplied them could no longer provide an engineer familiar with their internal workings. To our great regret, they had to be taken out and have since been replaced with a collection of small electric heaters sponsored by individual parishioners. While the heaters provide welcome heat and are not so difficult to manage as the old ones, they are not nearly as warming.

Mr Davies was a great advocate of the new service books known as Series A and Series B but Turnastone has remained a Book of Common Prayer church thanks to the determination of the churchwardens. Nowadays, we have three services each month here: we share a service of holy communion at Vowchurch on the first Sunday, then have an early communion service on the second Sunday, evensong on the third Sunday and on the fourth invite Vowchurch to share morning prayer with us. This has worked well for many years but from June 2009 evensong has been replaced by a family service at 9.30 am in an attempt to draw in the many children and their parents at present living in the village.

In addition to the regular services, there is a special service at harvest-time (followed by a harvest supper, held for many years at the Old Rectory but for the last few years at Dolward) and a carol service lit partly by candlelight near Christmas (with mince pies and mulled wine afterwards). Sadly, numbers at both of these have much declined since Mr Davies observed in 1957 that the church was 'overfull'. Even as late as 1995, we could expect to set out extra chairs for harvest and the carol services but recently this has not been necessary.

Fig. 65 Martin Kibblewhite 1995, founder of the GVSG (Mrs C.J.F. Comyn)

The financial arrangements for the provision of clergy pensions, a welcome and necessary purpose, have had a devastating affect on parish funds. When the writer first came into the parish in 1974, Turnastone was able to pay its parish quota to the diocese and still have some money left over to reserve for future repairs and expenses. Occasionally, a flower festival or other fund-raising activity was organised, usually for a specific project like resurfacing the tarmac path or buying new hymn-books, but of late it has become essential for the parish to hold at least four fund-raising events every year just to pay the quota. It has been becoming apparent that should a large repair

130

become necessary, Turnastone will not be able to afford it and, should there be no means of obtaining grants, the church will have to close.

Most social activities emanate from the church though all are, of course, open to all. We no longer cut the churchyard grass by hand but as late as the 1990s, parishioners would meet in the churchyard one evening some six weeks after the daffodils had died back and the grass would be cut. Martin Kibblewhite from Slough Cottage and Cecil Thomas from Slough Forge would appear with their scythes like two Father Times whilst others would use strimmers and rakes round the gravestones; at intervals, cider and squash would be dispensed in the porch and fruit cake distributed. The cut grass would be left to make hay and Mr and Mrs Green (who kept goats on a small-holding in St Margaret's) would bring down a small cart to collect it. The daffodils (mostly of the wild type) are a special pleasure to parishioners and visitors in the spring. Mr and Mrs John Comyn were married in 1974 and spent their honeymoon in India where John Comyn had previously been a tea-planter in North Bengal. While at the Coimbatore Club, they were astonished (and delighted) to find a picture of the churchyard, resplendent with daffodils, on the front cover of *Country Life*. This picture was used for many years as the church postcard.

After Mr Davies's retirement,[21] Turnastone with its fellow parishes of Vowchurch and Peterchurch had another period of short-stay clergy including Phillip Alan Williams (who was here for about three years) and Philip Clarke (who was here for under two years and resigned for family reasons). When it became apparent that the incumbent at Abbey Dore (whose cure included more than ten parishes in all) was considering retirement, there was much discussion about the possible re-arrangement of the deanery and even of our parishes being serviced by a 'flying cleric' sent out from Hereford. We were thus thankful when the Revd T.R.N. Jones, who was already installed in Madley, Tibberton and Preston-on-Wye, agreed to take on Peterchurch,

Fig. 66 Cecil Thomas 1995 (Mrs C.J.F. Comyn)

131

Vowchurch and Turnastone although to his regret, he was obliged to give up Preston. He remained our rector for nine years before moving to Taunton, when his place was taken by our current parson, the Revd Simon Lockett, who lives with his wife in Madley.

Clergy and Patrons

Incumbent	Instituted	Patron	Reason for leaving	Curates
Richard Sandilands	1798	Eliza Boughton	Sequestration, 1834; death 1836	Many, as rector non-resident
Thomas Powell	1836	Newton Dickinson and his wife Dame Eliza Braithwaite Boughton	Inherited living at Dorstone but retained Turnastone until his death in 1886	Beresford Lowther, Claude Stephen Magnay, William Wilson Todd, Charles Longfield
Frederick Richard Green	1887	Higford Higford of Aldermaston co Berks	Death in 1918	
Edward Allan Whitfield	1922	Mrs Thresher	1934, ill health	
Thomas Lawrence	1936	Bishop of Hereford	1938, ill health	
Joseph Harold Gorst	1939		1940 to go to Easton Mauduit	
William Russell Hancock	1940		1948 to go to Ashton under Lyme	Rector absent on war service as an army chaplain
Reginald Griffiths Hayden	1948		1952 to go to Abbey Hey	
James Sowerby de Carl Bensted	1953		1956 to go to Ewhurst	
John Conway de la Tour Davies	1957		c. 1992 on retirement	
Phillip Allan Williams	1993		1996 to go to Holmer	
Philip John Clarke	1996		1997 for family reasons	
Timothy Richard Nigel Jones	1998		2006 to go to St James's, Taunton	
Simon Lockett	2006			

11   THE SCHOOL AND MEMORIAL HALL

These two buildings, central to the life of Turnastone in the 20th century, stand across the river Dore, a few yards within Vowchurch. Both were built to be shared by the two parishes and at times the facilities of both were used together.

THE SCHOOL
Sheila Harvey

On May 11 1874 a purpose-built small school with a school house opened in Vowchurch to provide compulsory free schooling for the children of Turnastone, Vowchurch and St Margaret's. Children from other parishes were allowed to attend at a charge of two pennies a week for each child. It had been built following the Education Act 1870 as a Church of England school, aided financially with an annual government grant.

Fig. 67 The school c.1910 (Mrs S. Major)

It opened with Miss Marianne Thomas as its first head teacher and was managed by a formal committee that included both church and local representatives under the chairmanship of Mr H.H. Wood of Whitehouse. Major decisions about the running and development of the school were made by the committee, which had financial control. Members made frequent casual visits and appear to have had a very active role in the life of the school. Mr Wood himself had statutory responsibilities, including a weekly check of the school register.[1] He and his family provided financial support, especially in the early years, by supplying sets of books, materials and equipment for the children. Mrs Wood often visited the school with buns and cakes for the children and, with the help of Mrs Longfield, wife of the rector, gave end-of-term tea parties. Sometimes she included the parents on these occasions 'so that they could all get to know each other'. Then in December 1875 the ladies donated prizes at the end of term for good attendance, which seems to have been the beginning of general prize-giving at the school. The vicar of Vowchurch, the Revd Charles Longfield, was the school correspondent. In the early 20th century E.L.G. Robinson of Poston Lodge and Arthur Wood were prominent in the school's management but, by the last years of the school in the 1960s, the social shift was evident. The chairman was the incumbent, the Revd John Davies and the correspondent was county councillor Eric Lewis of Vowchurch.

At the opening there were twelve pupils, three of whom were from Turnastone. The first Turnastone boy to attend was John Williams, aged 12, from Ladywell Cottage, and the first girl was his sister Ann, aged nine. The third Turnastone pupil was Joyce Davis, aged 11, from The Slough.[2] By 1880 six more boys and two more girls from Turnastone had joined the school, and the numbers steadily increased through the 1880s and 1890s. By 1910 about 40 boys and 26 girls from Turnastone had attended for various periods of time.

To begin with the children were all taught together in one classroom, but as numbers increased, they were separated into infant and junior groups in different parts of the classroom. Eventually, the junior group was divided into lower and higher standards. With rising numbers the committee decided in March 1875 to appoint an assistant teacher, Miss Mary Pritchard, who was newly qualified and called 'a paid monitress'. Pupil numbers continued to rise so in 1876 a pupil teacher was added to the staff, and this remained the complement right through to the 1900s, when pupil numbers declined a little and the school managed with the headteacher and one assistant. From 1947 student teachers from the Hereford Teacher Training College often spent two or three weeks helping with classes as part of their practical training. By 1962, with numbers reduced to only 23 or so, and from then on until its closure in 1968, the school was run just by the headteacher and the children were again taught together in one class.

Headteachers

Name	From	To	Age on appointment and other details
Mrs Marianne Thomas	May 1874	Dec 1889	Aged 33, from Madley. Qualified teacher. Salary of £50 pa, rent-free, 5 tons of coal and half the government grant. Resigned because of ill-health
Albert Addis	Jan 1890	Dec 1892	Aged 21. Qualified teacher. Married assistant Mary Featherstone in Jan 1890. Appointed headmaster at Wellington Board School 1892
Richard and Ann Orton	Jan 1893	Apr 1898	He was aged 26, born Nuneaton; she was 20 born Birkenhead. Appointed headmaster of board school at Desford, Leics.

Gomer and Emily Lloyd	May 1898	July 1936	He was aged 26, born in Glamorgan, she about the same age from Bedwellty, Mon. Four sons born in Vowchurch and two buried there
Miss Elsie Brown	Sept 1936	July 1939	No further details traced
(G.R. Jones	Sept 1939	Oct 1939	Temporary supply teacher
Mrs Rita L. Morgan	Oct 1939	Mar 1961	Aged 35, born in Ledbury. Resigned because of ill-health, d.1964
Mrs Margaret Price	Mar 1961	July 1961	Assistant teacher from Jan 1957. Took up appointment at Michaelchurch Escley school 1961. Retired and living in Peterchurch
Mrs Gwen C. Brazier	Sept 1961	July 1968	Aged 44, married to Harry Brazier, cabinet-maker. Two daughters and son married local people

The changing age at which children left school affected pupil numbers. At first many children were only three or four years old when they joined but few stayed on until they were 14. Boys could apply for an Agricultural Labour Certificate which allowed them to leave school at 12 or 13 and girls often left at 13 'to go into service'. May Powell from Dolward , for instance, left school at 13 to help look after her ten brothers and sisters in 1917. She had not enjoyed herding her younger siblings to school over the fields from Dolward and being responsible for their good behaviour, but in her old age she had only praise for her schooling:

> What a debt we eleven children owed to the headmaster, Gomer Lloyd and his wife. Seventy children on the roll and when you hear in this day and age of the 1980s that children of sixteen can't read or write, what's gone wrong? In those days I don't think one child left the day school who couldn't read and write.[3]

These village schools in the 19th century were all-age schools; children did not move on to a secondary school at the age of 11 until early in the 20th century. Even then it was not always possible to find sufficient places in an accessible secondary school so in rural schools like Vowchurch & Turnastone School, children had to remain in their primary school and be taught along with the younger pupils.

However, the Education Act 1944 brought changes. On September 24 1945 the school managers (as they were then called) organised a meeting of all the parents with the Herefordshire Director of Education present to explain these changes. The length of the school holidays and of the school day (9 am to 12 noon and 1 to 3 pm) would be fixed. School leaving age at secondary schools would be 15 and at grammar schools 16. As a further consequence of the Act, in January 1952 Vowchurch & Turnastone Primary School was awarded Voluntary Aided Status with more money coming from the local education authority.

Already, though, pupil numbers were declining – to 38 in 1955, 22 in 1961 and 17 in 1963, all taught in one class. In May 1966 the headmistress received notice of a proposal by the County Council to close the school and transfer its pupils to Peterchurch Primary School. In June she and the school managers met representatives of the Herefordshire Education Committee to discuss the issue, after which the managers appealed to the Ministry of Education, but without success. Pupil numbers were now down to 11. In December 1967 it was decided to close the school at the end of the summer term.

On July 19 1968 a party was held for pupils, past pupils, parents and school managers to mark the school's closure. Mrs Brazier, the headteacher, was presented with a bouquet and a gift of £19 by Mrs McMichael, a school manager, on behalf of the managers, parents and friends.

The school buildings
The school was built of red brick to a design typical of Church of England schools at that period. The school house was built at the same time for use as a headteacher's residence, rent-free, right up to 1961. From then until the closure of the school in 1968 it was let to private tenants and was finally sold as a private dwelling.

It consisted originally of one large schoolroom for 60 children, even after 1875 when the junior and infant classes were taught separately. Toilet facilities seem to have been almost non-existent, but in 1894 the school committee agreed that Mr Pritchard, a local builder, should construct cloakrooms for the junior girls and all the infants; there was no mention of facilities for the junior boys!

By 1900 there were two classrooms, one about 450 square feet, the other of 276 square feet. Coal-burning stoves were fitted in each room two years later. The regular visits to the school by HM Inspectors (HMIs) included reports of all the school buildings and facilities. The school managers were expected to act on any recommendations for improvements and general maintenance. The children's safety appears to have been taken into consideration especially with respect to the playground surface which initially was of gravel and not covered with tarmac until well into the 1900s. Its condition was important because it was not only a playground but also where the children had their drill lessons, later known as P.T. (physical training).

The last change to the buildings appears to have been in 1953 when the local education authority extended the small cloakroom to fit in three wash hand-basins with running water.

Attendance
One of the school's earliest problems was the irregular attendance of the pupils. Until the visits of the school attendance officers in the late 1890s parents often kept their children away from school to help in the house or, more often, to work on the land. The attendance officers, however, had the authority to visit parents and issue

threats of fines for non-attendance. In 1894, for example, it was recorded that one Turnastone family was fined one shilling for a son's continuous absence.

There were, however, many unavoidable absences caused by severe weather conditions or outbreaks of illness. Each winter brought a spell of bad weather, usually heavy falls of snow or prolonged periods of rain with severe flooding. Some Turnastone children, for example those from Dolward and Cothill farms, who had to walk two miles without coats in all weathers over the fields, had difficulties in getting to school in such conditions. Even in later years, as in 1967, when children were transported to school, the roads might be impassable in bad weather.

Some bad winters were immediately followed by outbreaks of serious infectious illness. Outbreaks of mumps, measles, whooping cough, diphtheria or scarlet fever were common. To control their spread the school was often closed completely on the advice of the local doctor, the local sanitary inspector, or in later years, the appointed medical officer of health. In January 1895 only five children out of 60 were attending because of an epidemic of measles and on the advice of Dr McMichael the school was closed completely for two weeks. Thus, in the years before transport and health improvements, children's schooling could be badly disrupted from September through to March or April.

However, one of the recurrent reasons for absence from the earliest days to long after World War II was that the children were needed to help with the harvest, including blackberry-picking. This absence was sometimes official; in June 1941, in the depths of wartime, the local education authority issued a directive for rural

Fig. 68 School class c.1910, including two girls from Dolward
(with bows in their hair) (Mrs M. Powell)

schools to close for one and a half weeks during the potato harvest so that children were available to help.

Happily, there were some authorised days of holiday to allow the children to attend or participate in local functions, such as the Peterchurch May Fair and also, from 1905, the Vowchurch May Fair. The school was used as a polling station from 1906, giving the pupils another occasional day off school, while a funeral at Vowchurch Church often meant that the school would be closed for at least half a day. Well into the 1900s harvest thanksgiving services were held on weekday afternoons in the churches of Vowchurch and Turnastone, and the school would be closed to allow the children to take part in the services. Country-wide extra holidays were also given for important national events, such as a week's holiday for the coronation of King Edward VII in 1902 and three days' holiday in June 1953 to celebrate the coronation of Queen Elizabeth II.

The school curriculum

Throughout, every effort was made to give the children a well balanced all-round education. Lack of sufficient funding, especially in the early years, sometimes slowed down these efforts. There was little equipment to begin with but more was gradually added by the generosity of the Wood family and other local landowners. As the school developed and parents became more involved, fund-raising events were held in order to buy more expensive pieces of equipment. For example, as early as 1891 a concert had been held and the proceeds of £1 11s 6d were used to begin a fund towards the purchase of a harmonium. This was followed by a general fund, the last purchase from which was a microscope in July 1964.

Apart from English, reading, writing and arithmetic Miss Thomas was anxious for the children to be taught other things as well. She introduced needlework for the girls and art for both boys and girls, and she taught them to sing hymns and songs by heart. The vicar came to the school to teach religion and it was also his responsibility to test the children before the regular visits from the diocesan inspectors, an arrangement that continued into the 1960s. History and geography were gradually introduced and by 1893 elementary science was also being taught. About the same time 'exercise' classes were held during recreational breaks, consisting of musical drill, with the 'music' provided by the children ringing pairs of bells. However, an HMI report in 1904 criticised the lack of proper P.T. so more formal physical education lessons were introduced. The girls were taught darning and sewing, embroidery and button-holing by Mrs Lloyd and during World War I Gomer Lloyd taught all the older children the elements of first aid.

Arrangements were sometimes made for a few pupils to take lessons in other schools. In the early 1930s groups of juniors went to Clifford for instruction in woodwork and housecraft and that arrangement still seems to have been in place during the 1940s. In the 1960s children were taken to Kingstone for swimming lessons and about 1965 these lessons were either at Peterchurch Primary School or Fairfield Secondary School. From the 1950s until the closure in 1968 many visiting speakers from abroad, especially from Commonwealth countries, were invited to talk to the children about their own countries, their geography and wildlife and as a result some pupils corresponded with schoolchildren in those countries.

In later years outings were organised by the head teacher, helped by parents. The earliest were to the Christmas pantomimes in Hereford, but from 1953 there was an annual summer coach outing for a day's visit to a place of interest, such as Clifton Zoo, or the coast, perhaps to Aberystwyth or Porthcawl.

Standards and achievements

Soon after the school opened in 1874 the headmistress recorded that the children were exceedingly ignorant and untrained! However, after the HMI's first inspection, in 1875, the inspector's report stated 'considering how little the children knew to start with, Miss Thomas has done well to improve the standard since the school opened'. These inspections, which included assessments of the buildings, equipment and management as well as the pupils' attainments, were annual events during the early years but less frequent later. As pupil numbers increased, together with more regular attendance, there was a gradual improvement in standards, achievements and discipline. By 1910 HMI reports described the school as 'a creditable specimen of a rural school'.

The children's religious education was always monitored by an inspector from Hereford diocese. Inspections were carried out annually throughout the life of the school, with both oral and written tests. The reports were always full of praise for the high standards maintained in religious education (R.E.) and shortly before the closure the report included a comment on the excellence of the pupils' R.E. examination results. The general school atmosphere seems to have been positive, happy and well ordered. There was even, reported the diocesan inspector in 1943, a tone of reverence within the school!

At the age of 10 or 11 pupils sat for the 11-Plus examinations at the school under the invigilation of the headmaster of Kingstone County Secondary School. In the 1960s when the numbers were declining the exams were held at Fairfield County Secondary School in Peterchurch. Some, but by no means all, of the results were recorded in the headteacher's log book, and they were above average for a small rural school. In 1955, for example, a boy was awarded a scholarship to Lady Hawkins Grammar School in Kington and in 1963, with only 22 pupils, two grammar school scholarships were awarded; in 1967, with only 12 pupils, two girls won scholarships.

Herefordshire Education Authority organised competitive events, mainly for art, drama and music. In 1944 a first prize for a still life painting was achieved by the school and other pupils were 'highly commended'. In 1949 the school entered a three-act play in the Hereford Schools Drama Festival, winning the first local round held in the Memorial Hall and a certificate in the finals held in Hereford. They participated also in the County Music Festivals and when for the first time they entered for the Diocesan Bible and Prayer Book examination in 1963, of the 14 children who took part, 11 gained awards, four being 'First Class'. The children were encouraged to take part in other national tests and competitions from at least the late 1940s, such as Junior First Aid for a Red Cross Certificate, and the National Brooke Bond Art and Handwriting Competition in which in 1962 Christine Lloyd from Cothill won a first prize for handwriting.

The school during World War II
School life seems to have carried on as normal until May 1941, when four evacuees were added to the register, boys from Bootle who had been billeted in the area. In June thirty more evacuees arrived, also from Bootle, with one teacher, Miss M.B. Butterfield. Hazel Williams, now living in Peterchurch, remembers two girls being billeted with her family at The Forge, just across the Slough brook in St Margaret's. The evacuees were merged with the local pupils to form three groups, of which one was taught in the Memorial Hall next door to the school. HMIs visited to check the arrangements as well as the new arrivals. By November 1943 all the evacuees had returned to Bootle, but the annual 'Christmas' party must have taken place considerably before Christmas that year, as it was held in the Memorial Hall rather than the school as, with the evacuees, there were 73 pupils altogether, and extra room was needed.

From March 1942 until the end of the war the children's gas masks were inspected and, if faulty, replaced; in December 1946 they were eventually collected in at the school. The school was also given the responsibility of supplying supplementary clothing coupon certificates to families with children growing fast to an adult size.[4] Perhaps the greatest change at school was the provision of school dinners. The first were served in January 1943 – hot healthy meals cooked, served and eaten at proper

Fig. 69 The school building today

dining tables in the Memorial Hall. At first the cost was 4*d* per meal. On that first day 36 pupils sat down to dinner. The meals became so popular that, in 1947, a cook-supervisor was appointed to help the cook and relieve the teaching staff from supervising the children at dinnertime. After the war, the government decided to continue school dinners and they were provided at Turnastone and Vowchurch until November 1964. By then, so few children were having dinners that to save expense it was decided that from January 1966 meals would be brought from Fairfield Secondary School in Peterchurch and so Mrs Ruth Seaborne of Vowchurch left, having cooked school dinners in the Memorial Hall for ten years. Her meals are still happily remembered by past pupils!

The Memorial Hall
Sylvia Teakle

Vowchurch schoolroom being quite small, the need for a village hall had been felt for some years, and on 2 March 1912 a fund for the erection of a suitable building was started by the doctor's wife, Mrs M. McMichael of The Croft, Vowchurch, who organised the first whist drive and dance to take place in the parish and with the proceeds started a bank account with the deposit of £6.[5]

By means of whist drives, dances, concerts, tennis tournaments and garden sales, the fund steadily increased, and had reached £112 10*s* when the outbreak of war in 1914 rendered further progress very difficult. However, by the end of the war in 1918 a sum of £216 had been collected, a suitable site next to the school had been bought from T. Pearce of Vowchurch Court, and a number of chairs and other items of furniture had been acquired.

A public meeting was held in 1919 to decide how the inhabitants of Vowchurch and Turnastone would commemorate those who had served in the war. It was suggested that Mrs McMichael might amalgamate her fund with whatever sum could be raised by subscription, and that by the united efforts of the parishes a Memorial Hall should be built and brass memorial tablets placed in the two village churches. This was agreed, and Gerald McMichael ARIBA of Colmore Row, Birmingham was asked to submit a plan.

The building work was carried out by local men using local materials. A barn at Lower Wellbrook, Peterchurch containing some fine old oak timbers was purchased and the construction was placed in the hands of James Bowyer of Peterchurch. In the autumn of 1919 the foundations were laid out but the building did not begin until the summer of 1920. The greater part of the stone was bought from the barns being demolished at Wellbrook, and a considerable amount from the quarries at Whitehouse, as the gift of H.H. Wood. The price of labour and material in the years immediately following the end of the war was very high, and in 1921 the financial position became rather strained even though money was being steadily raised by public entertainments. A fete and draw took place with great success in June and resulted in an addition of £186 to the fund. The secretaries to the Fete Committee were G. Jackson, F.J. Parker, and A.S. Wood, chairman and treasurer. After this, sums of money were lent free of interest by the Trustees and others, and finally the Trustees guaranteed an overdraft at the bank.

At a public meeting held in 1921 the broad lines upon which the Hall should be managed were laid down and afterwards embodied in the trust deed drawn up by Stephen W. Walters, a solicitor from Pontrilas. Trustees elected at that meeting were as follows: Dr A.W. McMichael of The Croft, W.E. Parker of Chanstone Court., J. Pearce of Vowchurch Court, W. Watkins of Turnastone Court Farm and A.S. Wood of Whitehouse, all of whom, except William Watkins, were magistrates. The stone-slated roof of the Hall was completed on Christmas Eve 1921 and ten months later the Hall was opened on 25 October 1922 by S. Roberts MP. Major L. Beaumont Thomas also consented to speak. The opening ceremony in the afternoon was followed by refreshments, and a whist drive and dance were held the same evening.

Fund-raising had to continue. In February 1923 the debit balance at the bank amounted to £438 8s 7d but by December 1925 it had been reduced to £38 0s 11d. With a committee of management formed in 1932, with Mrs McMichael as manager, further improvements could be put in hand. In 1932 one of the windows was replaced by a fireplace at a cost of £35 5s and the ladies' cloakroom was enlarged. A new use for the hall came about in the spring of 1942 when the Herefordshire Education Committee applied to rent it for the purpose of providing school dinners. The kitchen was needed daily in term-time from 8.45 am to 3 pm each weekday, an arrangement that continued until 1966. The small but steady income allowed the committee to consider providing a men's toilet in 1948 (though they postponed it). Electricity was put into the hall but the two electric heaters installed in 1950 were found to be unsatisfactory, so in 1959 the committee applied successfully to the Carnegie Trust for a grant to update the heating.

In the following years a shortage of funds prevented the hall committee from purchasing land for a car park in 1978 and providing a new toilet block in 1984. These setbacks brought about a reform of the dual arrangement of trustees and management committee, with the immediate result that the new single combined committee obtained a new trust deed approved by the Charity Commission. The committee began a series of monthly events – coffee evenings, bingo, fancy dress dances, whist drives, duck races – anything which would raise money. A VAT 50 Club (standing for Vowchurch & Turnastone 50 members club) was formed to hold a monthly prize draw scheme, very successfully organised by Mrs J. Powell and over the years making a lot of money. An architect, Duncan Horne of Dorstone, drew up the plans for the extension, and a grant was obtained from the County Council.

In July 1986 the Country Market was started and every Saturday sold produce, plants, vegetables and anything that was marketable. It was run on a cash and carry basis, with the hall taking a percentage of the income for its funds. It was well attended and a very popular meeting place. The following year the Hall came second in the 'Small Village Halls' section of the Best Kept Hall Competition and overall best in the South Herefordshire District Council area.

The hall continued to function successfully although in 2004 the markets had to be curtailed to four a year as David Price of Vowchurch, our main supplier for many years, ran down his contributions. By 2000 it was evident that the roof of the hall seriously needed attention and that a very considerable amount of money would be required to put matters right. In 2003 Dr Ellie Parker of Chanstone offered to apply for a grant to repair the roof and other matters that needed updating. A grant of £3,982.50 was awarded for a Feasibility Study, architects were interviewed and Trevor Hewett of Hereford selected. In November 2003 a public meeting discussed the various options for the work which was to include re-roofing the hall, provision of double-glazing, access for the disabled, a new kitchen and toilets and new heating system. The estimate was £282,500 plus VAT (Value Added Tax); the credit balance at the bank was £13,566.

A fundraising committee was formed and applications for funding made to the National Lottery and DEFRA (Department for the Environment, Food and Rural Affairs). Both applications were successful, the Lottery contributing £172,092 for all the inside work and DEFRA £107,545 for the external work. All goods and chattels were moved to a barn at Vowchurch Court where monthly markets continued to be held, the builders started work in November 2005, and the refurbishment was completed and the hall handed back in May 2006. A further windfall followed. National Grid, the body which laid the gas pipeline from Milford Haven to Gloucestershire, offered support to local communities through which the pipeline passed in recognition of the disturbance caused by the works. Vowchurch and Turnastone suggested new furnishings for the Memorial Hall, which National Grid generously provided.

Fig. 70 Country market 2009

143

Since then the Hall, well equipped and freshly decorated, has resumed its traditional functions. It is once again the place for social meetings and lectures, birthday parties and gatherings after christenings, weddings and funerals. The monthly Saturday market was restored, with a range of stalls for locally produced breads and meat, jams and sweets, craftwork and presents. New activities include a 'keep-fit' Latin-American dancing class for ladies and a weekly drama session for children.

12   TRAVEL AND TRANSPORT

Maurice Church

Roads and drovers

This chapter explores how people in Turnastone have moved about the parish and journeyed outside it. We have to keep in mind that the roads and railway through the valley have followed the ancient course of the Roman road between Abergavenny and Hay and that the one minor side road through Turnastone and most of the 12 footpaths within the parish existed long before 1800. This road and some tracks are marked on maps in 1754 and 1812-13, leading to the villages to the west and the local mills, smithies and fords. The lack of good communication within this region was a major reason why towns failed to flourish in the 18th and 19th centuries. Although a small market was held at Peterchurch this is the one part of the county without a prosperous market town. Hereford, therefore, was the favoured nearest market, a two-day journey to walk cattle or sheep if they were to arrive in good condition, four hours by horse and cart, and three hours for W.S. Wood of Whitehouse, an energetic long-distance walker who in 1820 walked all the way to the Scottish Highlands with his friend, the artist-traveller James Wathen of Hereford.[1]

At that time Herefordshire roads were still notorious for their atrocious condition, especially in winter. An Act of Parliament in 1555 had placed responsibility for roads on each parish, and householders had to give four days free labour every year to their maintenance, usually consisting of little more than clearing ditches, cutting hedges to allow the sun to dry the mud and filling the worst holes with adjacent stones. With the 18th-century increase in wheeled traffic, coaches, carts and waggons struggled through the mud and cut up the roads further. In these parts deep ruts in ever-deepening hollow lanes were formed by the movement of Welsh drovers with hundreds of cattle on the march from mid-Wales to the south-east England and London markets and the haulage of timber of local landowners from the woods on the hills flanking the valley. Possible drovers' routes into the Golden Valley at Peterchurch include the 'road to Brecon' from Wilmaston, marked on Isaac Taylor's map of Herefordshire in 1754, and Long Lane, from where they may then have continued eastwards over Stockley Hill or run south down the valley past Turnastone. The hauliers had difficulties in taking their timber on carts with six-inch wide wheels from the Whitehouse and Poston estates and through Turnastone, Vowchurch and Madley to the wharf on the river Wye at Canon Bridge. William Downes, the solicitor transporting timber from the Whitehouse woods between 1798 and 1800, tried to get an agreement with the Poston estate to restrain purchasers at timber sales from hauling during winter months and appealed to Madley to repair their part of the route, 'knowing how very unwilling the husbandmen of the County are to repair the roads at their own door'.[2] The river Wye also presented major problems for navigation above Hereford as in summer the flow was too shallow and in winter too often in flood.

The magistrates were responsible for ensuring the upkeep of the county roads and in 1794 had ordered Vowchurch and Turnastone to improve the state of the road to Michaelchurch and in 1796 to repair Vowchurch bridge. Though the 1835 Highways Act replaced statute labour by allowing groups of parishes to be joined as Highway Boards funded by local rates, there are no records of the Dore Highways Board until a further Act in 1862 which empowered the local justices to compulsorily unite parishes into highway authorities where they thought it necessary. The highway surveyor for our area in 1863 was John Probert, who had just succeeded to the tenancy of Turnastone Court. Ironically, some thirty years later in 1896 legal proceedings were taken by the new Dore Rural District Council against him, ordering him to trim all the hedges alongside the roads in Turnastone. Residing at the farm was a carrier employed to deliver stone for road improvements, as the creation of the Board meant that, instead of each parish having to make its own arrangements for collecting stone from its fields, there was a communal yard at Abbey Dore workhouse for breaking up stone brought in from the local quarries and for sorting and grading it for transport to the required road. During the Board's period of control there is no record of any major improvements, just minor repairs.

Turnpikes
The main roads were maintained by trusts set up individually by Acts of Parliament from the late 17th century with powers to levy tolls for their upkeep. The tolls were collected at locked gates or 'turnpikes' with toll houses where the turnpike keepers would take the fees and issue a ticket to pass the traveller through a series of gates. Charges varied and there were usually some exemptions, such as foot passengers, churchgoers, post horses and horses going to be shod. The Hereford Trust, created in 1730, had a gate at the bottom of Batchy Hill (known locally as the Batcho) where the side road to Kerry Gate branches off. All these gates were designed to catch traffic from Turnastone and the Golden Valley on their way to the local markets at Hay and Hereford. Evasion was challenged: a Dorstone farmer appeared in Hay Petty Sessions in 1850 for taking his sheep to market through Cusop Dingle to avoid the toll on the main road. The greatest improvement to the local main road never came about. In 1832 a local surveyor proposed a new marvellously straight turnpike road from Skenfrith via Abbey Dore and Vowchurch to Hay but bypassing

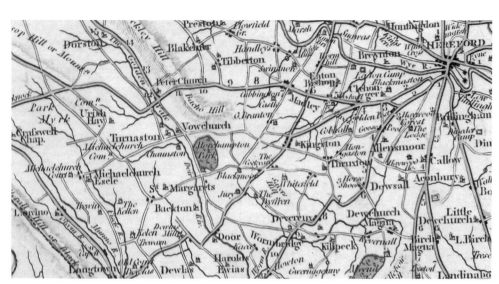

Fig. 71 Turnpike and other roads 1787 (HRO)

Bacton. It would have linked the main roads at Hay and Ewyas Harold, connected with the 1829 tramway from Abergavenny to Hereford and have straightened the roads around Vowchurch.

Coaches and carriers
Only the gentry would have run their own carriage. The farmers, doctors and clergy would have had a pony and trap as well as riding horses for local journeys whilst for longer travel they could turn to the coach services. Poorer people might have a nag; otherwise, they walked or, if they were lucky, got a lift with one of the local carriers. The heyday of the mail coaches was from the mid 18th to mid 19th century. Hay had mail coaches from London from 1811 and by 1830 there were up to 40 coaches a day running from Hereford to many destinations including a network of daily services to South Wales, Builth and Carmarthen. The *Lily of the Valley* ran from Cheltenham to Builth via the Golden Valley and Hay on alternate days. A service from Hay to Ross called the *Prince of Wales* started on 8 December 1841 subsidised with £70 by major landowners for six months as agreed in a meeting called by the Revd Thomas Powell at the Boughton Arms Hotel in Peterchurch.[3] Fares from Hay via the Golden Valley to Ross were: 6*s* outside, 10*s* inside, and to London 32*s* outside and 50*s* inside. The gentry of Hay were delighted to have a direct service to London avoiding delays in Hereford and taking only 12 hours, cut to 10 hours in 1849. In 1859 W. & J. Bosley ran a mail coach to Turnastone from the King's Head in Hereford at 5.30 pm every Wednesday and Saturday. It was called the *Mazeppa*, the name of the hero of a poem by Byron which had been given earlier to the express coach from London to Hereford.

Another essential network was that of an often changing variety of carriers, going regularly between the villages and the nearest market towns. In 1851,

William Garrett, farmer and landlord of the Red Cross Inn at Turnastone, had a licence to transport goods to Hereford on Saturdays and Wednesdays and to Hay on Thursdays, returning from Hereford at 4 pm with his horse-drawn goods van. James Garrett ran a similar service between Hereford and Peterchurch. Additionally by 1871 there were butchers who drove to the large estates and bakers delivering bread on horses with side panniers.

Tramways and railways

The coming of the railways, which were to replace transport by road for half a century, was heralded by the earlier construction of horse-drawn tramways, running on rails, developed from those used in mining areas and primarily designed for the cheaper passage of coal to the towns. In our countryside there were two. One, from Abergavenny to Hereford, was built in 1800 to transport coal, lime and freight to or from South Wales, and passed through Pontrilas; the other ran from the Newport-Brecon canal at Brecon to Hay and Eardisley. Although not directly affecting the Golden Valley villages, vast quantities of freight were moved on these tracks by wooden carts or 'drams' pulled by horses. On the first day of the Abergavenny-Hereford tramway 33 train loads of coal arrived. Coal was charged at 4*d* per ton per mile, a cow at 2*d* per mile; passengers might also travel – at the same price as a cow. A tramway was similar to a railway line but had more curves and height variation, allowing for a team of horses to pull in line. It must be remembered that coal, however delivered from the Forest of Dean and South Wales, was expensive, and farming communities were poor. These tramways were strengthened and straightened to suit steam locomotives between Hay station in the west and Pontrilas station in the east, at each end of the Golden Valley.

The railway from Abergavenny to Hereford was opened in 1853, followed by lines to Shrewsbury in 1854, and Worcester and London in 1861. Branch lines advanced into mid Wales, to Knighton in 1861, Hay and Brecon in 1863-4, and Builth Wells in 1866, taking livestock at a price and speed that the drovers could not compete with. Some drovers are recorded as still conducting business in 1869 but their trade, like that of the turnpike roads, was killed by the rapid spread of the railways, even in places like the Golden Valley where the population was declining. On a Sunday in September 1864 the Midland Railway company sent a train from Hereford to Hay and Glasbury, demonstrating to the locals the power and speed of a steam train in action. In the Golden Valley this new form of transport was seen as a means of bringing goods and business into the area and carrying out timber and livestock. Agents for the landowners agreed that trade such as timber sales suffered because of the valley's isolation. Hauling timber from the woods along stony tracks and poor roads to either tramway or river was very costly. Much other heavy farm equipment was frequently on the move. A threshing machine required 12 horses to draw it to its next location. Mobile cider presses assisted small farmers. Tenant farmers in the valley wanting Radnor lime from Kington to fertilise the clay soil were faced with similar transport problems.

In a letter to the *Hereford Times* in August, 1875 C.E. Lane, the shop and store-keeper of Peterchurch, proposed a railway line from Pontrilas to the junction at Eardisley. He also wrote to the Great Western Railway who showed no interest. However, some major landowners supported the proposal vigorously and offered to finance it, notably E.L. Gavin Robinson, newly married to the heiress of the Poston estate of 3,334 acres. With the support of Sir Robert Green-Price of Shrewsbury, who had influence in central government, an Act of Parliament allowing construction and compulsory purchase of land was obtained. The Act gave them power to alter roads, tracks and rivers (including the diversion of a quarter-mile stretch of the river Dore in Turnastone) within a corridor similar to the one 40 metres wide which was allowed for the national grid gas pipeline between Milford Haven and Tirley (Glos.) laid through Turnastone in 2007. In anticipation of the benefits of the railway, Gavin Robinson also developed Turnastone Farm and put it up for sale in 1878, the year in which the line was completed from Pontrilas to Peterchurch. In the event the farm did not sell but progress on building the railway continued, to Dorstone in 1881 when it was opened with Edmund Taunton as manager, based at Vowchurch on a salary of £130 per year, and eventually in 1889 to Hay to connect with the Midland line.

The local station was named 'Vowchurch' but actually stood on the Robinsons' land mostly in Turnastone where Birch Cottages were built and initially used for the railway staff.[4] The station's facilities consisted of lamp room, office, waiting room, ladies' waiting room and toilets in the main wooden station building. A store stood at the end of the platform and in the yard were the weigh house with weighbridge, plate workers' hut and coal store. There was a loading gauge and ground frame to check overloading of waggons and a large advertisement for Sutton's seeds.

Fig. 72 Vowchurch station and stationmaster c.1910 (Mrs S. Major)

The three gas lamps on the platform were at head height, allowing operation from ground level. The level crossing gates over the road between Vowchurch bridge and Turnastone Farm were manually opened and shut by the station master. Passengers from Vowchurch could travel by first or third class compartments.

From the start the railway did not pay its way. Most passenger trains carried on average only 22 passengers in each direction. Season tickets were only sold in 1883 and 1884. The annual rent of £125 for using Pontrilas station took four months of third class passengers to recover. Goods and freight locally was sparse and no freight passed through, as hoped, from Chepstow to Liverpool. The rejection of the Monmouth link had the effect of routing traffic from Newport to Liverpool via the Hereford line. Locally no livestock was taken to market from 1887 to save driving the cattle to Hereford as there were no cattle pens at Vowchurch station. At one stage the desks and other articles were seized from Vowchurch station for outstanding debts. But the Royal Mail did start using the railway, which explained the good postal service in Turnastone. The morning post was delivered at 8 am from Hereford via Pontrilas and the afternoon post came via Hay on the last train of the day.

Nevertheless the railway was in a poor state. E.L. Gavin Robinson lost heavily and resigned as chairman, being replaced by Sir Richard Green-Price until 1891. Seven years later the line closed. In 1899 the Great Western Railway purchased the defunct Golden Valley Railway and re-opened the line in 1901.[5]

Transport choices from 1900[6]
The railway made travel to Hay and Abergavenny and South Wales more convenient, but the valley still looked to the county town of Hereford for many purposes. It was the nearest large market and shopping centre, the place where the assizes and quarter sessions were held and where the recently created (1889) county council was based. Direct contacts with Hereford remained essential. About the time of World War I Thomas, Clara and May Powell of Dolward used to go fortnightly into Hereford by pony and trap, and May recalled how they often passed an elderly lady from Dorstone who still regularly walked to and from Hereford. As a teenager in the early 1920s May drove the trap alone the 13 miles to attend her butter-making classes at the Shire Hall and (presumably) when she had to visit the family solicitors during the time her widowed and ailing mother was buying the farm in 1920.

In the same year that the railway line was opened Tom Maddox was running a 12-seater passenger carrier's cart from Dorstone to Hereford via Vowchurch and Turnastone at 7 am and returning at 9 pm every Wednesday market day and Saturday. He also distributed local deliveries from the station and was still operating to Hereford through Vowchurch in 1900. William Prosser, a carrier from Michaelchurch, passed through the village, and others went along the main valley road from Dorstone and Vowchurch Common. In the opposite direction throughout the 1890s Mrs Powell of Edgar Street, Hereford had a horse carrier service out to Vowchurch, while Mrs Fleet, a farmer from St. Margaret's, had a cart going through Turnastone to Hereford.

For daily needs, however, everything could be bought without leaving the valley and indeed it is said that some people never went beyond the Bacho pass. Most food was produced locally and sold loose (so there was little wasteful packaging). The Golden Valley was noted for its milk and poultry and a weekly poultry market was held in Peterchurch. There was a larger monthly market as well as the fairs for horses in February or March and hiring fairs in midsummer and autumn. Clothes might be obtained at the markets in Peterchurch or made at home from material obtained by mail-order and fetched from the station or by the carrier. A master tailor could be found at C.E. Lane's stores in Peterchurch, the largest shop in the valley, and other shops supplied a vast range of goods. The farmers' wives from Dolward and nearby were in the habit of walking down to Peterchurch on a Saturday afternoon to buy groceries which their husbands would collect at the end of the working day after a glass of beer at one of the village pubs. Flour could be bought straight from the corn-mills. A bootmaker, the postmaster, stonemason and chimney sweep were available in the village and, most importantly, publicans. Wood for the fire came from local woods not controlled by the big estates interested only in timber sold to distant dealers but coal would be delivered from the railway stations. Carpenters and wheelwrights were in great demand to keep the carts running on all the unmade roads and blacksmiths for shoeing the horses and repairing agricultural machinery, the two nearest to Turnastone being opposite The Croft in Vowchurch and at the Slough.

Right through to living memory cattle were herded to Hereford market, either left overnight at Arkstone or Clehonger or leaving the valley by the light of lanterns at 3 am. According to elderly farm workers they never used the railway for taking stock to Hereford but presumably those who sometimes went to Hay or Talgarth did so. When Peterchurch market closed in 1936 many of the farmers' traps would take produce to Hay on a Thursday.

The state of the roads slowly improved. Responsibility for the main roads was transferred to the county council on its creation in 1889. After the Dore Highway Board had widened the road up the Slough, and repaired and metalled it between Vowchurch station and Michaelchurch in 1890-92, the county council agreed to take it over as 'a main road'.[7] Soon afterwards the council persuaded the Board to carry out the maintenance in 1897, encouraging them to buy an Aveling & Porter steam roller, with water cart and van, to crush the stones into the road surface and seal it with tarmacadam. It was still at work in the 1920s, long after the Highway Board's functions had passed to the Dore Rural District Council in 1905. Their monthly minutes were also much taken up with repairing footpath bridges to the schools in the valley; in 1929 the surveyor was ordered to repair, if necessary, the footbridge in the meadows between Vowchurch station and Whitehouse.

Meanwhile the railway recovered with the resources of the Great Western railway behind it. In 1899 John Lewis Smith, the draper, grocer and beer dealer of Commerce House, Vowchurch, was put in charge of Vowchurch station during its closure. On 1 May 1901 the first train under the new ownership travelled empty to

Dorstone. The return journey to the Wednesday market in Hereford made the running of this train a paying proposition with passengers in first, second and third classes. By 1902 the railway was in full operation from Pontrilas to Hay with W. Parton as the Vowchurch station master. (Among the other station masters at Vowchurch were William Arrowsmith 1883, Dan Davies, 1913, John W.J. Bowes 1917 and J. Williams 1927.) By 1912 the service was reduced to two trains in each direction showing the continued isolation of the Golden Valley. World War I brought further reductions resulting in the trains only going between Pontrilas and Dorstone.

After the war the timetable returned to three mixed trains up and down to Hay on weekdays. From 1920 to 1940, a market was held at Ewyas Harold to serve the farming community. Wool, still a major farming product, was still being sent out of Vowchurch station in the passenger brake van. But large passenger numbers were rarely achieved; an excursion taking 103 passengers to the Royal Show at Newport in 1927 was exceptional. Tales are often told of the rural railways. It was said of this line that there was a driver who would stop the train to pick mushrooms, a story that cannot be corroborated, but there is also a first-hand report of the passenger who 'returning from Hay one day could not understand the long wait. On looking out he saw the driver coming up the track with a bunch of water cress in his hand'.[8] One unexpected effect of the coming of the railways was the standardisation of time. Every station in the country had to show the same Greenwich mean time with the result that in Turnastone 12 minutes were 'lost' when the clock at 11.48 am was reset to 12 noon.

Coal, lime and goods continued to come in by train and be delivered by horse and cart from the station yard. The milk, corn, timber and livestock leaving the valley were despatched likewise. Timber trains from Vowchurch or Maentwlch

Fig. 73 Goods train at Vowchurch 1953 (Mrs C.J.F. Comyn)

were special Sunday workings employing large gangs of men. Timber was still being loaded at Vowchurch station in 1946.

Horses remained the mainstay of transport in the valley till 1939. The first motor car had been paraded in Hereford in 1904, but in 1906 there were only seven lorries registered in the whole of Herefordshire. The first car owners in the Golden Valley were Randolph Trafford of Michaelchurch Court, with a Lagonda, and his mother Mrs Capper. In 1921 Charles Wilding at Glendore obtained a licence to store petrol and since 1922 his 'West End Cycle Depot' has been selling petrol in Turnastone.[9] In 1925 the price of petrol was 8½*d* a gallon. The garage developed by stocking motorcycle spares and offering car repairs.

The first motor bus operated in Edinburgh in 1898. Country people used to say that the biggest change in their lives was the arrival of the country bus. Here in Turnastone it was probably the train, but in 1920 Reg Hallard of Poston Mill established the first motor coach service with a large ex-army van running to Hereford. It was still a rough ride on appalling road surfaces and almost impossible hills as the roads were not surface sprayed with tarmac until 1932. Another bus service started in Longtown via Turnastone to Hereford and another from Hay via Vowchurch to Michaelchurch as 'Hereford Transport' had an outstation in Michaelchurch Escley. The General Strike of 1926 gave them an unexpected boost, driving goods traffic, milk and farm produce off the railway and on to private lorries and the public on to buses. Two years later a bus service was started in 1928 from Bob's Shop, Michaelchurch at 8 am. Coinciding with market days it went to Abergavenny on Tuesdays, Hereford on Wednesdays and Hay on Thursdays, each time passing through Turnastone and Vowchurch to pick up passengers.[10]

In the 1930s the valley was still quite isolated, except for the increase in motorised transport. The 'Red and White' bus company ran a service from Hay to Hereford through the Golden Valley, but withdrew two other services in the area. Wilfred J. Pritchard of Crossway House, Vowchurch applied for a licence to run buses to fill the gap and in 1932 a 20-seater Bedford, initially operated from Michaelchurch but later moving to Longtown, was still passing through Turnastone to replace the 'Red and White' bus.

Post-war change

The railway and Vowchurch station came alive during World War II as timber was collected for transport to Elm Bridge, the ammunition stores down the line at Ewyas Harold. Most of the hardcore for building Madley aerodrome was brought into Vowchurch, where there was large storage space and a steam crane. The war affected transport in the valley, increasing goods traffic on the railway but discontinuing passenger services (to allow uninterrupted working of the branch line to Elm Bridge ammunition dump) and reducing motoring by road to essential journeys by strict petrol rationing.

After the war, when the nationalised British Rail took over the GWR in 1948 the goods traffic increased through the valley, especially deliveries to Hay. Livestock

Fig. 74 The last train from Vowchurch 1953 (Mrs C.J.F. Comyn)

and poultry, a mainstay of the local farms, was still being transported by rail with a
train going straight to the large station at Abergavenny on market day. At Vowchurch
there was usually one goods waggon in and one out every day, with timber loading
made easier by a mobile crane on the railway track.

The last passenger train out of Hay steamed sadly down the Golden Valley on 31
December 1949 and the last truck of sugar beet was hauled away on 9 January 1950.
A special rail excursion to Porthcawl ran on 17 April 1950 taking five coaches from
Dorstone via all stops in the valley. From that year the branch line was for goods
only and, although in November 1952 building materials were brought up to repair
Vowchurch station, British Rail closed the line at Abbey Dore a few weeks later
on Saturday 31 January 1953. The stage was set for photographs of the mayor of
Hereford going on the last train from Dorstone to Pontrilas. Vowchurch station did
echo to the sound of a steam train during August 1954 when goods were delivered
and demolition materials from Dorstone and Peterchurch were removed by contrac-
tors but in 1956 the track and station buildings had been removed, leaving the bus
and car our saviour.

The bus, however, was soon also in decline. A daily service from Vowchurch to
Abergavenny via Turnastone and Longtown was tried but quickly died due to lack
of passengers. In 1971 the 'Red and White' bus company was operating a double-
decker bus service from Hay via Vowchurch to Hereford and the 'Midland Red' a
double-decker from Hereford; at the end of the working day three double-deckers

set out from Hereford, one destined for Clehonger, another for Peterchurch and the third going all the way to Hay. One Friday in 1992 a single-decker was introduced for the 5 pm out of Hereford to Brecon, and I counted 22 people standing in the aisle. Today the buses, for which Turnastone passengers have to walk up to the stop at Vowchurch crossroads, are run by 'Stagecoach in South Wales' and 'Yeomans Canyon Travel'; on Wednesdays, market day in Hereford, Bowyers of Peterchurch run a popular bus for the morning only. Nowadays it would be impossible for many to get about at all without our own cars or a taxi.

Fortunately and unusually there is still a filling station in Turnastone village, the only place to buy petrol before Hereford to the east (10 miles), Clyro, beyond Hay, to the north (11½ miles) and Allensmore or Ewyas Harold (both about 6½ miles southward); to the west there is none this side of the Black Mountains. In 1948 Hedley Wilding bought out the garage business at Glendore, naming it West End Garage and trading under the name P. & H. Wilding, Automotive and Agricultural Engineers. Keeping Dr Boraston McMichael on the road with his two vehicles was itself a major occupation. In 1949 the doctor, who owned two cars, a Vauxhall and a Wolseley, was using six gallons of fuel in three days at *2s 1d* per gallon, having the car serviced every month and on average paying for body repairs every three months. The records show the doctor to have been accident prone and for a month he tried the garage's taxi

Fig. 75 Hedley and Percy Wilding c.*1960*
(Hereford Evening News courtesy of Hereford Times)

155

service. The garage also repaired many lorries – a Dodge, a Ford, a Bedford, brands no longer built in Europe – and sold paraffin, which was still widely used in the 1950s for household heating and lighting before the arrival of electricity from 1951.

Another important survival is the network of footpaths criss-crossing the parish. The large-scale Ordnance Survey map of 1904 marks many more footpaths than exist nowadays, but some were for private access not public rights of way. The latter, defined as a highway over which the public has a right of way on foot only, were registered under the Town & Country Planning Act 1949 and are now mostly used purely for recreational purposes. But think as you walk them. The registered public footpath TU1 joins Turnastone Church and the school with Cothill and Dolward farms and in 1900 this was the shortest way for 25 workers and schoolchildren to get to the centre of the village. Footpath TU2 joins Turnastone village with Poston Mill bakery and Poston Court by a pleasant walk alongside the river Dore and is a short cut to Peterchurch. Bridleway TU3 from the village was in 1900 the direct route for the rector and Dr McMichael to ride to Peterchurch. In the opposite direction the bridleway, here listed as VO1, takes you from the village to Chanstone Court and on to Bacton and St Margaret's villages. Footpath VO50 runs from the railway station to St. Margaret's by a direct route through Chanstone Wood. On the way it meets the Slough brook at a point with two footbridges and six radiating paths where there are relics of sluice gates in the brook to form a sheep dip or divert water on to the fields.

13 THE WIDER WORLD

Brian Smith

The links created by the road and rail were the ways by which Turnastone people ventured into the outside world. But increasingly the outside world invades even the smallest rural communities, most notably in the form of local and central government. This incoming flow has, of course, existed for centuries. The parish registers, census enumerators' returns and electoral registers providing the facts about people and households, and the tax assessments, tithe awards and maps revealing the field-names and husbandry of the farms, were created to implement Acts of Parliament for other purposes but demonstrate how all our lives become unavoidably tied into the wider world.

Before 1800 the impact of officialdom was intermittent and largely restricted to national taxation and keeping the peace, delegated respectively to county commissioners and magistrates. The parish chose churchwardens and vestry to care for the church; under legislation for the care of the poor from 1597 and 1601 they elected two overseers to relieve the aged poor and ensure that paupers from elsewhere were moved on before they became a burden; from 1555 they appointed one or two surveyors of the highways to maintain the roads through the parish. These parochial officers could levy local rates and inevitably in a small community these responsibilities would have fallen on the same few farmers. For Turnastone none of their records has survived. We know, though, that the lord of the manor of Snodhill still called together the jurymen of his manor court to confirm the boundaries of the manor in 1824 and that rents for copyhold property (administered under the manor courts) still lingered on in the 19th century in the neighbouring manors of Ewyas Lacy and Jenkin ap Richard *alias* Whitehouse. In Turnastone copyhold tenure had been replaced by leaseholds long before 1800. Also long before then Acts of Parliament from Tudor times had loaded more and more administrative work upon the county magistrates, from the licensing of alehouses to the examination of vagrants, the registration of enclosure awards and the recording of land tax assessments. Their attention had been drawn, for example, to the poor state of the road through Turnastone in 1794 and 1796.

Then in 1801 the compilation of the first census of the nation's population introduced a more obtrusive example of central government's thirst for information about its citizens. Every ten years afterwards the parish overseers of the poor and from 1841 the Registrar General were required to supply information on the numbers of houses and people in each parish. The enquiry steadily became both more searching and better organised though, judging from the inconsistencies recorded, it was apparently answered with a measure of ignorance or suspicion.

The surge in population after the Napoleonic War in 1815, the development of industry and the large migration from the countryside to rapidly growing towns strengthened demand for reforms. The Parliamentary Reform Act 1832 and the Municipal Reform Act 1835 did not directly affect Turnastone, but the Poor Law Amendment Act 1834 most certainly did. The responsibility for the care of the poor was transferred under the direction of a national Poor Law Commission from individual parishes to unions of a group of parishes administered by a local Board of Guardians and funded by rates raised collectively from the parishes within each union. Parishes had previously had their own small workhouses. Vowchurch in the 1790s used Piccadilly on Vowchurch Common and later is said to have used the Old House by the church as its parish workhouse but there is no evidence that Turnastone had its own workhouse, and indeed it is unlikely that such a small place would have required one.

The new Dore Union embraced 27 parishes in west Herefordshire and nearby Monmouthshire. Ten of these parishes failed to provide a member to serve on the Board, which was dominated by the local landed gentry. Although sceptical about the suitability of poor law unions in rural areas where the local poor and their circumstances were already well known personally, the Board from their first meeting in 1837 set about appointing relieving and medical officers and building a Union workhouse at Abbey Dore (now Riverdale).

Fig. 76 Dore Union workhouse

Their policy continued earlier practices – providing support at home if possible, finding employment for those fit for work, and taking the aged, sick and single mothers into the workhouse. They met the same intractable problems that occur today but they were motivated by a genuine sense of responsibility. In line with the spirit of reform the unions appointed teachers well before there were schools in rural areas, though it must be said that the turnover of teachers at the Dore Union workhouse was frequent and their standards of teaching woefully low.[1]

The Poor Law reform of 1834 cannot have been much welcomed in Turnastone. The parish contained few cottages, many farm workers lived-in on the farms and others probably came in from Vowchurch Common and Maescoed. Only rarely can anyone have needed poor relief that could not have been provided in their own or a relative's home. Now, all the houses in the parish had to pay the poor rate knowing that few people from Turnastone would benefit. Indeed, the records of the Dore Board of Guardians contain few references to Turnastone. For several months in 1848 Mary Price was living in the workhouse. She was possibly the Mary Price, a maltster's widow who from 1841 lodged with Samuel, a labourer, and Ann Jenkins in one of the cottages on the site of Yew Tree House. If so, her stay in the workhouse did not last long, for she was back in their household by 1851 where she died the following year at the age of 80.[2] Two other elderly Turnastone people were admitted to the workhouse later but again neither apparently ended their days there, for only one person from the parish is recorded in the Union's register of burials between 1839 and 1914. Many of those taken into the workhouse were discharged quickly either at their own request or because they themselves or the workhouse master had found them employment, like Anne Matthew, a 35-year-old servant who only spent ten days there in 1860. No one would claim that the Dore Union workhouse was lavish in its comforts, but at least it was relatively small. In 1841 the four staff – master, his wife, a cook and the school teacher – had care of 21 adult paupers over the age of 20 and 20 children between 6 months and 14 years old. The numbers crept up. In 1863 there were 62 people there, but none from Turnastone, and two years later it was enlarged to take up to 90.[3]

Like care of the poor, the inability of parishes to cope with the growth of traffic on the roads led to the formation of area Highway Boards in 1862. The Wood family of Whitehouse had long agitated for road improvements in the Golden Valley, so it was appropriate that H.H. Wood should have been the chairman of the Dore Highway Board until its powers were handed over to the Dore Rural District Council

Fig. 77 H.H. Wood, his wife Alice and an unidentified friend (T.J.R. Wood)

in 1905. He was active in local affairs, also being a magistrate and a deputy lord lieutenant of the county, a royal appointment that indicates his social and political standing. From 1888 he was also chairman of the Dore Rural Sanitary Authority, created under further legislation in 1872, arising less from troubles in the countryside than cholera epidemics in the towns. There are no specific references to Turnastone in its minute books from 1872 to 1895.

Slowly, almost imperceptibly and always with the best of intentions, central government was extending its interest, oversight and control of matters that had previously been considered private or local, a process that has gained momentum to the present day. Under the Local Government Act 1888 county councils were formed to take over the administrative responsibilities of the county magistrates and turnpike trusts and in due course the school boards and boards of guardians. A few years later, by the further Local Government Act 1894, urban and rural district councils (UDCs and RDCs) were created to succeed the rural sanitary authorities. H.H. Wood of Whitehouse continued as a councillor on the Dore RDC but, as earlier, the minutes contain few references to Turnastone, one being the unsuccessful request of the rector for the repair of the bridle road from the village to Poston Court in 1896. The Great War brought an unprecedented barrage of instructions from the government on national economies, agricultural wages, housing and public health, coalmining, 'Government timber', and other matters affecting life in general but not peculiar to Turnastone.

By that time people had more important personal concerns. Among the population of 63 men, women and children in 1911, seven men served in the armed forces, including Arthur Charles Croft, the groom at the Rectory, who was in the Royal Field Artillery, George Powell from Cothill in the Herefordshire Regiment, William Smith in the Machine Gun Corps and Rowland Charles Wilding in the King's Shropshire Light Infantry.[4] One soldier did not return.

Fig. 78 Lance Corporal William Jones (M. Jones)

160

Fig. 79 Mark Skyrme with Dr McMichael's trap and pony Gloria 1907
(Miss M. McMichael)

23-year-old Lance Corporal William Jones, Royal Engineers, the son of John Jones, the labourer and roadman who lived with his wife Harriet at Brook Cottage, was killed in action on 10 June 1918 and is commemorated in the war cemetery at Sains-en-Gohelle, near Béthune in north-east France. Turnastone was lucky that the other six men came back safely, for everyone must also have known the thirty other men in the neighbourhood whose names are read out annually by the British Legion at Peterchurch on Remembrance Sunday.[5] And not only the men. Horses too were sent to war, including Dr McMichael's pony, Gloria, who did not return home.[6]

After the war the Dore RDC, amalgamated in 1930 with the Bredwardine RDC, concentrated on condemning houses unfit for habitation and providing new housing but rarely touched Turnastone directly except for occasional road repairs and the regular renewal of J.C. Wilding's petrol licence. The threat of a second European war produced a renewed flow of instructions from the government. The experience of the Spanish civil war led many to expect that an outbreak of war would be accompanied immediately by devastating air raids on major cities. From early in 1939 the government disseminated plans for the evacuation of the cities and nationwide air raid precautions. The Dore area was selected to receive 760 children and their mothers from Liverpool, and soon after the beginning of the war on 3 September 1939 the first trains of evacuees arrived at Pontrilas station. But the bombers did not come. By October the evacuees had returned home and new arrangements were made in the spring of 1940 for evacuees to come from Liverpool and more specifically from Bootle. The children would come alone, unaccompanied by their mothers, and 'only when serious air attack appears certain'. It was 1941 before that happened. In that second evacuation children were billeted throughout the Golden

Valley, in houses along the Slough road, at Maescoed, and in Turnastone at Little Dolward, Cothill, Ladywell House and Turnastone Farm. Local people and children became familiar with the sudden influx of the young northerners unfamiliar with country living and filling the school at Vowchurch. Whitehouse was occupied by the Redgate School for Girls, evacuated from London, whose pupils still occasionally revisit – most recently two coachloads of sprightly but now elderly ladies in October 2009, signing themselves in Vowchurch visitors' book as the 'Chalet House Girls'.[7]

Meanwhile the Dore RDC was deluged with government exhortations about collecting salvage, wearing protective clothing when dealing with casualties, the repair of war-damaged water mains and buildings, National Savings, fund-raising flag days for War Weapons Week, War-Ships Week and other such causes, the disposal of surplus vegetables and fruit, ambulance and fire services and the supply of sand bags. It sensibly and modestly occupied itself with only the more relevant and familiar matters of local water supplies, setting up an ARP (Air Raid Protection) post at Bob's Shop in 1941, opposing the closure of a public footpath adjacent to Madley aerodrome (but, by contrast, approving the closure of another footpath across a ploughed field), the control of bulls and the damage to houses by a heavy snowfall in February 1941. Evocative though these RDC minutes are to elderly people today, they do not reveal any special evidence of the effects of the war on Turnastone. As in other country areas remote from the big cities, the chance of stray bombing or an aircraft crash was small (though one such accident occurred at St Margaret's) and even the constraints of petrol and food rationing were ameliorated by the recognised need for the farmers to travel to market and the ready availability of home-grown produce.

Once again the young men not classed as essential for work on the farms left for military service, including Wilfred Powell and Hedley Wilding. The nature of World War II resulted in fewer casualties than the horrendous losses in the trenches of the Great War and the Turnastone men all returned safely. On the other hand the military combat and civilian displacement was more widespread. George Disley at Cothill (see pp.91-3) was an evacuee from Bootle who chose not to go home after the war. German and Italian prisoners-of war were housed at Peterchurch and Hay and employed on local farms and treated hospitably; one of them stayed in England after hostilities ended and later lived in Brook Cottage (see p.51).

In post-war years both the County Council and Dore RDC, though increasingly constrained by the demands of central government and legislation, returned to their traditional activities – the provision of schooling, upkeep of the roads and housing. The County Council widened the road between the village and Ladywell and planning permission was given for building the two bungalows at Dolward Farm. In 1961-2 the Dore RDC, pressed by councillor Eric Lewis of Vowchurch Common and aware of the shortcomings of some existing property, proposed building council houses in Vowchurch or Turnastone, or both. The Ministry of Housing approved the building of twelve, of which ten were for the elderly or to replace houses unfit

Fig. 80 Flooding at Turnastone Farm c.1960 (Mrs C.J.F. Comyn)

for habitation and two for general purposes. Roadside fields at Vowchurch Turn, Chesshyre's Turn and in Turnastone between the Old Rectory and Yew Tree House were identified as potential sites but none was found suitable. The Turnastone site, perhaps predictably, aroused local opposition and was rejected when the District Valuer reported that the owners, the Misses Watkins, not merely disapproved but were unmoved by the threat of compulsory purchase and flatly refused to enter into negotiation.

Under the Local Government Act 1972 the county councils of Herefordshire and Worcestershire were merged to form the short-lived Hereford & Worcester County Council. As a consequence the old district councils were also amalgamated into larger local authorities, for this area into the South Herefordshire District Council. The next step lower in the hierarchy, the parish councils established under the Local Government Act 1894, were also merged. Small places might have no more than occasional 'parish meetings' but no minutes or other records of a Turnastone parish council or meeting have been traced. The creation in 1973 of the Vowchurch Group Parish Council, covering the parishes of Michaelchurch Escley, Newton, St Margaret's, Turnastone and Vowchurch did therefore introduce a genuine voice of local government. Local people such as Eric Lewis of Vowchurch, Verdi Lloyd and Sylvia Teakle of Turnastone have over many years taken an active part in executing its business. The council was largely concerned with passing local complaints or problems up to the county council and receiving from the county council notice of planning applications for which local approval was sought. The complaints embraced such recurrent matters as the daily dangers of the crossroads at Vowchurch Turn and seasonal flooding of the road near Whitehouse and Turnastone Farm, resulting in some alleviation of both problems. On the other hand it appears to an outsider that local influence on planning matters has been eroded.[8] Current (2009) discussions within the civil parish signal the continuing desire of people to be involved in the future of their own communities.

14 CONCLUSION

A first impression of Turnastone is its changeless appearance – the absence of modern houses, the roadside pumps measuring petrol by the gallon, the eye-catching Raleigh bicycle advertisement on the village shop, the Book of Common Prayer and King James Bible still contentedly used in the little parish church, the bulky Hereford cattle grazing languidly by the river Dore and the acres of sheep dotted distantly on the hill pastures. There are few people to be seen – an early morning dog-walker collecting the newspaper, a worker at Turnastone Court moving about the farmyard, the horses exercising from the nearby stables. Lying off the spinal road running through the Golden Valley and with the Black Mountains of Wales closing the westward view, the parish seems to lie undisturbed despite the passing vehicles negotiating the right-angled bends as they head to or from the scattered hill farms and villages. A casual conversation will reveal that many of those farms have been held for generations by the same families with a preponderance of Welsh surnames.

Archival evidence initially confirmed these early impressions. For much of the last two centuries the parish was divided between two landed estates of relatively moderate size. The low-lying land was mostly in the Poston estate, which descended to the Robinson family in the 19th century until its division and sale in 1912. The higher ground was owned by the Wood family of Whitehouse, on the western boundary of the parish, until sales in 1922 and 1986. The heads of both families had been prominent as landlords and magistrates, promoting new ventures to benefit the community and serving on the boards and councils of local government. Until late in the 19th century the parson was a lone incomer among the landed gentry, farmers and farm-workers, and even then the only rector to reside for any length of time was the Revd F.R. Green from 1887 to 1918. For some of that same period, from 1889 to 1901, his next door neighbours in The Cross House (then Turnastone Cottage) were a succession of doctors.

Farming and forestry have always been the dominant occupations in the parish and throughout both centuries the farms were held by dynasties of inter-related farmers, of whom a notable number had indeed migrated from the adjacent Welsh counties. Throughout the 19th and well into the 20th century Turnastone, despite its small size, was largely self-sufficient. Stone for building and roofing, bricks, timber and lime were all available close at hand. The blacksmiths by the Slough bridge and in Vowchurch provided ironwork, repaired tools and shoed horses. The farms were suited to stock rearing, until quite recently growing the feed for their own animals, which were bought from and sold to neighbours privately or driven to the nearby market and fairs in Peterchurch, Hay and Hereford. It was a two-day journey to walk them to Hereford but, just as the local timber trade was boosted by the opening of the Golden Valley Railway in the 1880s, so motor transport a generation later made it easier to attend the larger markets in Hereford, Hay and Talgarth. A house-cow was kept for milk, an orchard grown for cider apples and corn threshed on the farms and sent to one of the nearby flour watermills at Poston and Chanstone. In Peterchurch, a walk of only two miles, there were shops which delivered goods, tradesmen and public houses, and nearer at hand there was an inn in Turnastone itself until the 1860s and later small village shops in both Turnastone and neighbouring Vowchurch. The local carrier, the railway and eventually the country bus provided links to more distant shopping.

This apparently idyllic, unchanging scene is misleading, even if the physical grind of farm work before the introduction of farm machinery was borne with the vigorous equanimity expressed by Mrs Edie Turner, caretaker of the village hall. When asked in the late 1950s if her weekly routine on the farm was not all a terrible lot of work she responded:

'Work? Yes, it was a lot of work. But no one had ever told us, you see.'

'Told you what?'

'Told us there was anything wrong with work! We didn't think there was anything wrong with work. We liked work!'[1]

By subjecting the three farms and ten other dwellings in Turnastone, now occupied by fewer than thirty inhabitants, to a detailed historical and genealogical examination it has been possible to trace the astonishingly large number of over 1,100 residents during the last two centuries and to study their homes and livelihood. The outcome of this deeper research has been a revelation, hugely broadening our knowledge and sweeping away disappointingly meagre or misleading evidence to expose myths and explain mysteries.

First, living conditions were harsh even in those households with indoor servants. By modern standards both farmhouses and cottages were crowded. Tuberculosis was still present well into the 20th century. Babies were brought into the world by the local midwife and even after the doctors set up their practice at the end of the 19th century care for the sick was largely a matter for self-help, for to call out the doctor was to incur a fee which many could not afford. Life expectancy was consequently less than today, especially among the men working out-of-doors in all weathers. Widowhood led to the threat of the loss of home as well as livelihood. As for the animals, they had to be treated without the aid of a vet.

Second, some changes were universal and unavoidable. Like other country parishes the increasing population of the early 19th century peaked in 1841 at 76 before steadily falling to its lowest level of 21 in 1991. The formation of new statutory boards and councils for local government led to the decline of the landed gentry's influence, already weakened by overspending, the agricultural slump in the later 19th century and sales of land. The mechanisation of agriculture had a consequential effect on rural employment. The improvement of communications by rail, road, telegraph, telephone and information technology, together with the spread of electricity into the countryside, revolutionised both business and home life.

Further research not only supplied the evidence for the effects of these universal changes upon Turnastone but also uncovered the less obvious changes and individual successes and tragedies that contribute to the overall picture. In the course of the 19th century the owners of the Whitehouse and Poston estates enlarged their mansion houses and invested in improving their estates, most obviously by rebuilding their farmsteads. The Woods of Whitehouse were prominent in county affairs, E.L. Gavin Robinson of Poston in promoting the ill-fated Golden Valley railway. The subsequent sales of their farms in the early 20th century brought in new owner-farmers lacking the capital to maintain the inconvenient older farm buildings to the same standard. The wartime demands and controls, extending to those of post-1945 governments and the European Commission, are commonly credited or blamed with encouraging or enforcing changes in husbandry but these had long been preceded by the demands of landlords and practices of farmers. From at least 1812 Turnastone Court had been converting woodland and arable land to pasture; short-lived experiments in growing hops were attempted; tenants' leases contained prescriptive husbandry clauses. In the late 20th century the Watkins family at Turnastone Court resisted changing their ways but the farmers at Cothill and Dolward took advantage of subsidies to build new stock sheds and concentrate increasingly on sheep-rearing.

The ebb and flow of the Welsh population in west Herefordshire is a neglected matter for research. In Turnastone the influx of young Welsh farmers was prevalent throughout the 19th and first half of the 20th centuries and to this day the farming community in the Golden Valley is linked by a ramification of family ties. Their labourers and house-servants, as recorded in the database of *Who's Who in Turnastone,* were recruited more widely not only from nearby Wales but also locally and from central Herefordshire.[2] A few are known to have been engaged in the customary way at annual mop fairs, but in other cases employers relied upon personal recommendations and contacts. The occupancy of the few village houses became rather different. In the mid 19th century many were occupied by two households but a century later, with the decline in the number of farm workers, the landlords had to find new tenants for their tied cottages. Thus the community attracted a wider variety of sometimes rapidly changing newcomers, who looked to improve the living conditions of the countryside. House by house they were sold and modernised. Similarly, as the traditional farm buildings fell out of use they have been, or are destined to be, converted into dwellings or used for other purposes. However, at present there are still only the three farms and ten houses in the parish, of which only two houses have been built since 1925. The occupants of six are engaged in farming, five are self-employed (three within Turnastone). Two are retired but work part-time in voluntary activities.

Inevitably, therefore, changes have come about through these two centuries, but as an almost imperceptible evolution. The isolated farming network dominated by the two local country houses in 1800 has developed into a community with broad experience and wide knowledge, but nevertheless still sharing a deep, sense of continuity in a genuinely rural environment.

Appendix   WHO'S WHO IN TURNASTONE

Who's Who in Turnastone is a detailed database of more than 1,100 inhabitants of the parish since 1800, which has been of central importance in the research for this book. It is a private venture compiled over many years by an experienced professional genealogist, and greatly expanded in the course of this project.

The unusually extensive coverage of the database, only made feasible by the small size of Turnastone's population, comes from sources already in the public domain. Most are accessible in the Herefordshire Record Office. They include the civil registration of births, marriages and deaths from 1837, the parish registers of baptisms, marriages and burials, monumental inscriptions on tombstones and memorials, and wills. The tithe commutation award and map of 1842 gives both names and places of residence of owners and occupiers of property as also, among the civil records, do the census enumerators' returns of the decennial censuses from 1841 to 2011, land tax returns (used as a qualification for election purposes) from about 1800 and electoral registers. In addition, the licences for the clergy and alehouse keepers, the registers, records and rates of the poor law union from 1834 and later local authorities are available for research from various dates in the 19th century up to the last 100 or 30 years depending on the rules for their public access.

Unfortunately it is impractical to publish the *Who's Who in Turnastone* here, not only on account of its size, which might be overcome by publication in a digital format, but also on other grounds. Some of its content may be accessible for research but is inappropriate for a wider publication. Data protection laws have in some instances now restricted access to material which formerly was freely available for research without hindrance. Other material of recent date or general local knowledge may well technically fall within the data protection law. Perhaps, most importantly, the database is not static. No end-date for its content can be sensibly (or sensitively) suggested. Moreover, it continues to grow as further sources of evidence are trawled.

However, any reader who wishes to trace a specific forebear from Turnastone may in the first instance write to Mrs John Comyn at The Cross House, Turnastone, Hereford HR2 0RD, giving her their e-mail address for her reply.

Endnotes

Abbreviations used

GVSG   Golden Valley Studies Group
HRO   Herefordshire Record Office, Hereford
TNA   The National Archives (Public Record Office), Kew
TWNFC   *Transactions of the Woolhope Naturalists' Field Club*

Chapter 1
1. HR0, O5/1.
2. R.E. Rewel and J.T. Smith, 'The Old House, Vowchurch', *Trans. WNFC*, vol.47, pt.1 (1991), p.48.
3. Turnastone Court was named Turnastone Farm until the 20th century: see chapter 4.
4. All figures are based on the printed summary census statistics and Mrs C.J.F. Comyn's transcripts of Turnastone parish registers, both original sources being in the HRO.

Chapter 2
1. C. Saxton, *Herefordshire* 1577, reproduced in B.S. Smith, *Herefordshire maps*, Almeley 2004, plate 1; W. Camden, *Britannia*, edition in English with additions by E. Gibson, London 1695, col. 575.
2. F. & C. Thorn, *Domesday Book, Herefordshire*, Chichester 1983, p. 187b.
3. B. Coplestone-Crow, *Herefordshire place-names*, BAR British series 214, Oxford 1989; p. 192; 2nd edn, Almeley, 2010. Tournai-sur-Dives is in Normandy south-east of Caen.
4. HRO, Turnastone tithe map 1842.
5. D. Lovelace, 'Turnastone Court Farm historic landscape conservation plan', Draft final report, September 2004, pp. 7, 16; HRO, Turnastone tithe map 1842; F37/8.
6. M.P. Siddons ed., *The visitation of Herefordshire1634*, Harleian Society, new series vol. 15 (2003), pp. 178-9; C.J. Robinson, *Mansions and manors of Herefordshire*, 1872 reprinted with indexes, Almeley 2001, pp. 310, 312-3; T.J.R. Wood, *A short history of Whitehouse, Vowchurch, Hereford-shire, and its owners*, privately 2000, pp. 6-9.
7. Pedigree by C.J.F..Comyn.
8. W. Dugdale, *Monasticon Anglicanum*, 1825, vol. 5, pp. 555-6.
9. HRO, F37/3-6.
10. HRO, F37/7; F37/11.
11. M.A. Faraday ed., *Herefordshire taxes in the reign of Henry VIII*, WNFC 2005, pp. 323-4, 381.
12. Wood, *op. cit.* in note 6, pp. 7, 8. The suggestion on p. 6 that this may be the place *More in Stradel* recorded in the Domesday Book is not borne out by the tenurial evidence, which identifies that as Allensmore: Coplestone-Crow, *op. cit.* in note 3, pp. 24, 194.
13. Wood, *op. cit.* in note 6, p. 28. See also Royal Commission on Historical Monuments (England), *Herefordshire*, vol. 1 (1931), p. 226. (But note that N. Pevsner, *Herefordshire*, Harmondsworth 1963, p. 301 dates it to the 17th century).
14. G. Charnock, 'South-west Herefordshire: post-ice age landscape and settlement features, *TWNFC*, vol 56 (2008), p. 26 and *ex inf.* R. Richardson, though not mentioned in R. Shoesmith and R. Rich-ardson, *A definitive history of Dore Abbey*, Almeley 1997.
15. J. Thirsk ed., *The agrarian history of England and Wales, vol.IV, 1500-1640*, 1967, pp. 180-182.
16. HRO, F37/139; O5/1.
17. Despite extensive research Dr Katherine Stearn, herself a manager of flood meadows in Wiltshire, has not been able to unravel how Rowland Vaughan's scheme could have operated successfully in practice. Her lecture at Vowchurch on water-meadows is summarised in the *GVSG Newsletter*, vol.1, no. 5 (2004), pp. 4-16. Scholars have in general been cautious in not attributing more to Rowland Vaughan than publicity for the innovation of 'drowning'.
18. HRO, F37/8; Lovelace, *op. cit.* in note 5, pp. 16-17. Some existing hedges were re-aligned in the mid 19th century.

19. Survey of Whitehouse estate 1796, HRO, F37/147; HRO, BB2/277; will of Philip Davis, 1798; abstract of title to Firs Farm and other property in Michaelchurch Escley 1733-1863 (Private, *ex inf.* Longtown Historical Society). See also p.96.
20. Robinson, *op. cit.* in note 6, pp. 312-13.
21. HRO, Will of Nicholas Philpott of Hereford, proved 1681; HRO, O49/2; .C.J.F. Comyn, Philpott pedigree.
22. H. Colvin, *A biographical dictionary of British architects*, 3rd edn., Newhaven USA & London, 1995, p.239, correcting Pevsner, *op. cit.* in note 13.

Chapter 3
1. J.P. Dodd, 'Herefordshire agriculture in the mid-nineteenth century', *TWNFC*, vol.43, Pt.2, 1980, pp.203-22.
2. J. Clark, *A general view of the agriculture of the county of Herefordshire*, 1794, pp.10-14.
3. HRO, Land Utilization Survey 1936 / British Geological Survey Map Sheet 214 Talgarth.
4. Figure calculated from the tithe maps *c*.1840-46.
5. D. Lovelace, *Historic Landscape Conservation Plan for Turnastone Court*, Draft Plan, 2004, p.9.
6. Schedule of land uses, *op.cit* as in note 3.
7. HRO, F37/153, Survey of the Whitehouse estate, n.d., probably *c*.1833.
8. G.E. Mingay, *Rural Life in Victorian England*, 1976, p.27.
9. HRO, BH74, 'A Century of Agriculture in Hereford', *Hereford Times Supplement* 1832-1932.
10. HRO E.L.Jones. 'The Evolution of High Farming 1815-65 Part II Herefordshire', D.Phil. thesis 1962.
11. Dodd, *op. cit.* in note 1.
12. M. Robinson, *West Midland Farming 1847-1970*, p. 79.
13. W.A. Armstrong, 'The Workfolk' in G.E.Mingay, ed., *The Vanishing Countryman*; 1989, p.36.
14. G.E. Mingay, ibid, p.68.
15. 'Herefordshire Parish Registers', Hereford Library.
16. *Herefordshire Planning Survey*, 1946.
17. *Agriculture in Post War Britain*, Reading University Museum of English Rural Life (MERL) website.

Chapter 4
1. HRO, BB2/296, 297.
2. HRO, M5/31/6, sale particulars of the Poston Estate, with a newscutting reporting that some lots had been sold privately before the auction.
3. Eva Morgan of Peterchurch (née Watkins of Penlan) has generously allowed us to quote from her family history, 'The Watkins Family of Newton, Bacton, Marden, Turnastone, Vowchurch and Peterchurch', (2009, in progress) and much of this section relies upon her knowledge. The Watkins family of Turnastone Farm were her cousins, her grandfather Arthur Watkins and Lizzie Watkins, the wife of William Rogers Watkins of Turnastone, being brother and sister. She always knew Rene and Nancy Watkins as 'Auntie'. Her younger sister, Mary Layton (née Watkins) of Pontypinna, Vowchurch, a goddaughter of Rene Watkins, has contributed further information.
4. In the west midlands 'Court' is the name given to the residence of the lord of the manor where the manorial courts were held. As there is no evidence that the farm ever had this status its traditional name of 'Turnastone Farm' would be more correct.
5. William and Lizzie Watkins were cremated at Cheltenham.
6. A faint inscription on a concrete lintel of one of the farm buildings, apparently by Verdi Lloyd and a German presumably dates from Verdi Lloyd's short time working on the farm in 1941-2 but does not refer to Marschall.
7. Rene Watkins believed that the timber-framed stable in the yard was part of the old farmhouse, but this is some distance from the site marked on the tithe map.
8. Eva Morgan records the family's belief that the present house was built away from the farmyard following a fire at an unknown date.

9. *Ex inf.* Eva Morgan and David Watkins, Lower Park, Abbey Dore.
10. Historical information about the buildings are taken from Joan Grundy's notes 2004 and her report for the *Historic Farm Buildings Group, Herefordshire Conference 2005 Programme*, pp.14-15.
11. *Ex inf.* David Watkins; HRO, Turnastone tithe map.
12. TNA, MAF 32/24/61.
13. Ibid., plot nos. 16, 17 and 19 on the Ordnance Survey map of 1904, sheet 38.5.
14. Tithe map; RAF aerial photograph 11 July1946; aerial photograph of ploughing match 1947 in possession of Watkins family; *ex inf* David Watkins.
15. Countryside Restoration Trust publications.

Chapter 5
1. Sources used for this article include information from Margaret Disley; parish registers; census returns 1841-1911; school registers and log book; electoral rolls; local *Directories*.
2. Photograph presented to Vowchurch church by the late Penelope (Wood) Bletchly. George Disley suggests that the portrait hanging on the wall may be of Lord Baden-Powell (1857-1941), founder of the Boy Scouts movement in 1907.
3. Royal Commission on Historical Monuments, *Herefordshire*, vol. 1, 1933, p.242; the RCHM's files held by English Heritage at Swindon contain notes, plan and photograph of Rose Cottage, 1929. Listed Building description, 2006.
4. *Cassey's Directory of Herefordshire,* 1858.
5. She does not appear to have been a daughter of the previous Lewis tenants of Rose Cottage.
6. See pp.90-91.
7. Sale particulars of Turnastone Court 2001 from an unknown source and not corroborated in J. Eisel and F. Bennett, *The pubs of Hay-on-Wye and the Golden Valley,* Almeley 2005, pp.132-33.
8. The deed was found with one of Turnastone Court after the sale in 2003 and will be deposited on loan in the Herefordshire Record Office for safekeeping.
9. http://ewyaslacy.org.uk/-/-Randolph-Trafford-The-Flying-Years-by-James-Baxendale;A. Eames, 'Parish pumps', *Daily Telegraph*, 27 December 2003. Randolph Trafford, a flamboyant socialite, private flyer and local landowner was killed on active service in a flying accident in World War II.
10. Sources are local knowledge; the parish registers, information and family photographs kindly supplied by Michael Jones of Newport, Gwent, a descendant of John and Harriet Jones; electoral rolls; the school log book; census returns 1841-1911. Although in the distant past a branch of the Slough brook appears to have run down towards the cottages, the name more probably comes from the Brookes family who lived in the larger cottage from about 1932 to 1967.
11. The illustrations of the Jones and Brookes family were kindly provided by Michael Jones.
12. Frances Brookes married Cyril Jones in 1950, Marjorie Brookes married Stanley Woolhouse in 1953, both in Turnastone. They return at intervals to tend their family graves and visit the church.
13. *Ex inf.* Erwin F.W. Marschall of Ledbury, where his mother also lives, 28 November 2009.

Chapter 6
Sources:
Turnastone parish registers, electoral rolls, tithe map and sale particulars.
Alehouse recognisances in the HRO.
Medical registers and *Medical Directories* for the doctors; Kelly's and other Herefordshire *Directories*.
Lucton School admissions book at HRO; Vowchurch & Turnastone school log books; Vowchurch Sunday school register.
Information and recollections from the late Mr Hedley Wilding; the late Mrs R.A. Comyn, Mrs S.D. Teakle (parish clerk and churchwarden) and the late Mrs F.J. Parker of Chanstone.
Research by Mrs John Comyn and also by Mrs Reason Challoner regarding the Aulton family.
A bible or prayer book belonging to either Emma Chambers or her mother which was once exhibited at Vowchurch during an exhibition of local farm tools and from which much information was gleaned.
Census returns 1841-1911 for Turnastone and other places relating to residents.

Nonconformist records at TNA and PCC Wills for the McMichael family.
Family papers relating to the purchase by Mrs RA Comyn of The Cross House in 1950.
Army Lists and the births, marriages and deaths columns of *The Times* for Colonel Thompson.

1. Royal Commission on Historical Monuments, *Herefordshire*, 1933, pp. 241-2.
2. HRO, F37//142.
3. J. Eisel and F. Bennett, *The Pubs of Hay-on-Wye and the Golden Valley,* Almeley 2005, pp.131-2.
4. HRO, Q/SM/24.
5. Further biographical details of the doctors and other owners are available from the *Who's Who in Turnastone*. See the Appendix.
6. S. Exton, M.D. is recorded as foreman of the Snodhill (Peterchurch) manorial court jury in 1824 (HRO, O 5/2).
7. The census for 1901 suggests that Mrs McMichael, Boraston and Helen were staying with her mother-in-law in Great Malvern.
8. Another contender is Timothy Wood's elder sister Joan and her parents (Thomas Geoffrey and Norah Wood of the family from Whitehouse, who lived here about 1932-34 when she was young.
9. Percy Jones Henry, gent., occurs in 1902.
10. *Ex inf.* George Disley, who recalls walking stock down from Cothill through this field on their way either to market or to other grazing.
11. The date of the change may have been nearer to 1867 – there were 10 houses in the village in 1861 but only 8 in 1867 according to one of the local *Directories*.
12. James Cornelius Morgan was the head of a household (which included his parents Samuel and Mary as well as a sister Sarah aged 19) in Much Dewchurch in 1851. Sarah was born in Ross as were her parents. A Cornelius Morgan (son of Samuel and Mary) was baptised 12 July 1829 at Grosmont and may be the one mentioned at Much Dewchurch in 1852.
13. HRO, BB2/70, Clive of Whitfield papers: lease and release dated 29 and 30 November 1852. Their Minister was Samuel Tillotson.
14. A common place-name in Wales and not identified but most probably Llanfihangel Crucorny between Turnastone and Abergavenny.

Chapter 7
1. T.J.R. Wood, *A short history of Whitehouse, Vowchurch, Herefordshire and its owners,* privately 2000, for which we are indebted throughout this chapter.
2. Ibid., pp.15-21.
3. *The agricultural state of the kingdom in February, March and April, 1816,* London 1816, pp.101-107.
4. HRO, F37/140. This copy of the lease was not sealed and signed.
5. Much of this family history, additional to that published in *A short history of Whitehouse* (see note 1) has been provided by Mr T.J.R. Wood of Littleham, Devon.
6. *Ex inf.* Fred Reece of Bracknell, Bucks. (son of William John Reece) after a visit to Turnastone in 2008, and his sister, Mrs Rosalind Morgan.

Chapter 8
1. J.E. Grundy, 'Herefordshire farmsteads in their agrarian context, *TWNFC.*, vol. 54, (2006), pp. 71-100, more particularly pp. 86-87. We are also indebted to Joan Grundy for visiting Cothill and pointing out features which we would otherwise have overlooked.
2. W. Marshall, *The rural economy of Glocestershire...together with the management of orchards and fruit liquor, in Herefordshire*, vol. 2, Gloucester 1789, p. 237.
3. HRO, F37/136.
4. HRO, F37/139.
5. HRO, F37/139. The wording of the lease is unclear and may be referring to the repair and re-building only of Whitehouse.

6. HRO, F37/147.
7. Marshall, *op. cit.* in note 2, pp. 233-6; J. Duncumb, *General view of the agriculture of the county of Hereford*, London 1805, pp. 120-7.
8. HRO, F37/140.
9. *Ex inf.* Robert and Alison Lloyd in 2007-08.
10. HRO, F37/153.
11. *Ex inf.* Elizabeth (Poppy) Lloyd in 2007.
12. From 1795 to the abolition of the tax in 1851 the windows of dairies and cheese-rooms were exempted from the Window Tax provided they were properly identified: N. Harvey, *A history of farm buildings in England and Wales*, 2nd edn 1984, p.105.
13. The iron straps around tie beam and kingpost at the west end are similar to a barn and stable block near Bromyard dated 1831: *ex inf.* Joan Grundy
14. HRO, F37/152. The document is undated but written on paper with an 1844 watermark.
15. HRO, Turnastone tithe map, 1842; census enumerators' returns. 1841. In this census the ages of adults were rounded down to the nearest 5 years; the baby's name of Jeremiah is probably a copying error for Isaiah.
16. HRO, electoral registers 1910-25; Land Valuation register, *c.*1911; *Kelly's Directories*, 1913. Bessie (Herring) Watkins lived later at The Villa.
17. *Ex inf.* Robert Lloyd of Cothill, George Disley of Peterchurch, Cliff Price of Dolward.; Crofts pedigree by C.J.F. Comyn.
18. TNA, MAF 32?24/61 Cothill.
19. We are grateful to Elizabeth (Poppy) Lloyd for information in this paragraph.
20. We are grateful to George Disley of Peterchurch for all the information in this panel.

Chapter 9
1. The sources give the acreage variously as 306 (1856 conveyance and 1955 sale particulars) and 295 (1935 sale particulars); the figure of 340 acres in the 1861 census may be incorrect.
2. R.W. Brunskill, *Illustrated handbook of vernacular architecture*, 1970, pp. 210-211.
3. Photograph lent by Mrs Maisie Powell.
4. Will proved 1799.
5. HRO, BB2/275-277.
6. C.J.F. Comyn, 'Who's Who in Turnastone', notes on parish registers, graveyard memorials, wills, family pedigrees, land tax returns, electoral rolls and other genealogical sources.
7. Comyn, as in note 6.
8. HRO, F37/128, will of W.S. Wood, proved 1862.
9. HRO, F37/129. See Plates 25 and 27.
10. Gwent RO, D.1583.367.
11. Comyn, as in note 6; will of Philip Davies, proved 4 April 1799.
12. Comyn, as in note 6.
13. Gwent RO, D.1583.367.
14. Comyn, as in note 6.
15. *Ex inf.* David Jones.
16. Comyn, as in note 6.
17. HRO, M5/30A/24 sale particulars.
18. Comyn, as in note 6: Price and Davies pedigree and notes; death certificate.
19. Comyn, as in note 6: Watkins and Herring pedigree.
20. Ibid.
21. *Ex inf.* Eva Morgan of Peterchurch.
22. Comyn, as in note 6: Watkins and Herring pedigree.
23. Ibid. David and Martha Gwillim both died in 1938 and were buried at Dorstone.
24. Ibid. Watkins pedigree. Arthur and Jane Watkins later moved to Penlan, another nearby farm in Peterchurch, where she died in 1935 (*Ex inf.* Mrs Eva Morgan of Peterchurch, her granddaughter.
25. C. Pritchard and G. Davies, *Escleyside Agricultural Society Reflections 1897-2002,*[2003].

26. Ibid.
27. Comyn, as in note 6: Powell of Dolward pedigree.
28. May Powell, 'Life on a farm in the uplands, 1904-1986', typescript (private, *c*.1986).
29. Ibid.
30. Pritchard and Davie*s, op. cit.* in note 25.
31. TNA, MAF32/24/61, Farm returns 1941, in which he is named as the owner. Land Tax returns of the 1940s give the Dolward taxpayer's name as Miss E.M. Davies of Lower House, the adjoining farm,apparently no relation. Local information that the investment was for the benefit of his family of eleven children appears to be a confusion with Clara Powell's family; the Revd Arvon Davies (*c*.1875-1960) had only two sons, (*Crockford's Directories* and *ex inf.*, a former churchwarden of Llanfihangell Cwmdu, 2009.
32. HRO, M5/30A/24.
33. She later married Hedley Wilding. *Ex inf.* Robert Wilding, her son.
34. *Ex inf.* David and Jean Jones of Peterchurch.
35. Comyn as in note 6: census 1911.
36. HRO, M5/30A/24 and AN55, Sale particulars, 1935 and 1955.
37. Pritchard and Davies *op. cit.* in note 25.
38. HRO, Tithe maps for Turnastone 1842 and St Margaret's 1844.
39. N. Harvey, *A history of farm buildings in England & Wales*, David & Charles, new edn. 1980, pp.123-5.
40. HRO, F37/129.
41. Virginia Morgan, *The limekilns and associated quarries in Walford,* Ross on Wye and District CivicSociety, 1993.
42. Schedule of land uses *op.cit* as in note 38.
43. Schedule of land uses *op.cit* as in note 36.
44. Field survey by the authors and David Jones of land-use and field boundaries in 2008-09.

Chapter 10
Sources

Oxford Dictionary of National Biography; Crockford's Clergy Lists; *Alumni Oxoniensis* and *Alumni Cantabrigensis,* Kelly's and other Herefordshire *Directories*
GE Cokayne's *The Complete Baronetage; Burke's Commoners* (a forerunner of Burke's *Landed Gentry*)
Parish registers of Turnastone, Vowchurch, Peterchurch and Dorstone
Turnastone service register 1919-c 1970
Methodist Cwm Circuit registers, typescript at HRO
Census returns 1841-1911
HRO, Poston Estate papers.

1. J. Leonard ed., *Herefordshire churches through Victorian eyes. Sir Stephen Glynnes's church notes for Herefordshire,* Almeley 2006, p.99.
2. Otherwise known as St George's, Hanover Square, London.
3. See his entry in the *Oxford Dictionary of National Biography*.
4. HRO, HD6/3/14 and 66 licences for non-residence.
5. He incurred large debts and was therefore eager to remain abroad to avoid his creditors and where the cost of living was considerably lower than in England. He was not the only absentee incumbent: 1814 was a bad year for the Golden Valley – not only was Richard Sandilands absent (still then ministering to his flock at the proprietary chapel of St George's) but James Bullock of Vowchurch (apparently held in plurality with Grendon Bishop, Sutton St Michael and Long Staunton in Shropshire) was appointed Prebendary of Ewithington and needed leave of absence as did Henry Davis of Peterchurch.
6. HRO, F 94/IV/25b. Order of Sequestration 21 May 1834.
7. Mrs S.D. Teakle, deeds of Old Rectory.

8. The survey included the name and address of every place of religious worship, the date it was founded and the numbers who attended on average during the previous 12 months. The records are at TNA, HO 129) and at the HRO. Many ministers were reluctant to fill in the forms.
9. In contrast, Vowchurch [population 323] had an average congregation of some 80 persons plus 24 children attending Sunday School; there were 76 free sittings and 30 others; the tithes here brought in £200 a year.
10. TNA, RG4 for the years 1829-1837. A transcript by M.A. Faraday is in the HRO.
11. The 1863 date of the building is given in *Kelly's directories of Herefordshire.*
12. Abbey Dore Deanery Notices: January 1931; I am grateful to Mrs Sheila Harvey for drawing my attention to these.
13. The earliest Service Book held in the parish records begins in 1919 and records only 2 services (in September); in 1920, four services were recorded (between September and December) during the *inter regnum* between the death of Mr Green in 1918 and the institution of Mr Whitfield. Edward Whitfield generally appears to have held no service in Turnastone between Christmas and Easter, none at all in August and often only three between September and Christmas. In 1926, only 12 services seem to have been held in the entire year. Later clergy appeared to try to hold at least two services a month here.
14. There are in fact two bells: one cast *c.*1520 and the other in 1774 by Thomas Rudhall of the Rudhall family of Gloucester bellfounders *c.*1684-1835.
15. Electric lighting was installed in 1950 by the gift of William Watkins of Turnastone Court; electricity came initially from the generator owned by Trevor Wilding at The Old Rectory and it was not until some years later that the church was connected to the mains supply.
16. Dilwyn Pugh was educated at Lampeter and ordained 1937 (Swansea); he was Vicar of Hardwicke and Rector of Dorstone from 1953.
17. Curiously, a Conway Davies – perhaps our incumbent's father – signed the Turnastone Service Book on 26 February 1936 when 13 people took Holy Communion at 6pm.
18. In the summer months, when Evensong was still at 3pm and the congregation often consisted of only Mrs R.A. Comyn and Mrs Naylor, it was not uncommon for both of them to fall asleep during the sermon leaving Mr Davies's words to fall on deaf ears.
19. One of these was replaced *c.*1979 by Mr John Comyn of The Cross House in memory of his late mother Mrs R.A. Comyn who died in 1976 and is buried at Kenchester.
20. His parents, Maurice and Esther Pendino (of Paris in 1994) had at some time been tenants of The Villa.
21. He had been appointed at a time when clergymen were expected to die in harness rather than retire so was not obliged to resign his living even when long past the new retirement age of 70.

Chapter 11
1. HRO, J15/2 and 4, Vowchurch School registers and log books. The recent records remain closed to the public. I am grateful to the staff of the HRO for identifying accessible material for me to examine. In order to conform to the Data Protection Act the names of the Turnastone schoolchildren have, with a few exceptions, not been revealed. I am also grateful to former pupils Margaret Disley, Elizabeth Lloyd, Margaret Price, Robert Wilding and Hazel Williams for sharing their memories with me.
2. As recorded in the register. But all the houses beyond Slough bridge are in St Margaret's parish.
3. May Powell, 'Life on a farm in the uplands, 1904-1986', typescript (private), 1986.
4. Clothing, like food, was in short supply and rationed by an allocation of coupons.
5. The story of the Vowchurch & Turnastone Memorial Hall is drawn from the minute books of the Trustees and of the Management Committee of the Hall, supplemented by information known to the author, who has served on the Committee.

Chapter 12
1. HRO, F37/193; T.J.R. Wood, *A walk through Britain*, (privately, 2001).

2. HRO, F37/113, 14.
3. HRO, F37/194-196.
4. *Ex inf.* David Parker of Chanstone.
5. C.L. Mowat, *The Golden Valley Railway,* Cardiff, 1964; W.H. Smith, *The Golden Valley Railway,* Didcot, 1993.
6. Late 19th to early 20th-century Kelly's and other *Directories of Herefordshire* have been used extensively.
7. HRO, T23/M/4.
8. May Powell of Dolward relating her husband's experience.
9. HRO, TM23/?/19, Rural District Council minutes 1919-23, 27 October 1921.
10. J.E. Dunabin, *The Hereford Bus,* St. Albans, 1986.

Chapter 13
Sources
Minute books of the Dore Union, Rural Sanitary Authority and Rural District Council.

1. HRO, K42/88, p.134.
2. HRO, K42/88. Her age is variously given in the census returns.
3. HRO, K42/91, pp. 110, 328.
4. War memorial in the church.
5. The local branch of the Royal British Legion covers the area from Dorstone to Michaelchurch Escley.
6. *Ex inf.* Miss Mary Mc Michael, 2009.
7. Named from the girls' story books by E.M. Brent-Dyer.
8. Vowchurch Group Parish Council minutes from 1973 (exercising the 30-year access rule for public records) and personal knowledge.

Chapter 14
1. Quoted in J. Seymour, *England revisited*, 1988, p. 118, from a conversation *c.*1960 with an elderly 'Miss Turner' living in the Dore valley below Vowchurch Common. Local residents in 2009 identify her as Mrs Edie Turner of the Stall House.
2. For the scope of and access to the *Who's Who in Turnastone,* see the Appendix on p.168.

Index of Personal Names

Index of Place-names and Subjects

Places of origin and former or later residence of people living in Turnastone have not been included